Higher Education in the World Community is set in today's context of the social, political, and environmental interdependence of nations. The United States is seeking, as a national purpose, to achieve better understanding and fuller cooperation among nations. To this end, the higher education enterprise is called upon to participate in important ways through its missions in teaching, research, and service.

This volume, drawn from papers presented at the fifty-eighth Annual Meeting of the American Council on Education, benefits in breadth from the several contributions by educators from other countries and from national and international organizations, both public and private.

Among the topics:

● **Support for emerging universities:** Explores goals for support, evaluation of purpose of both sending and recipient institutions, interpretation of needs as seen by the recipient institutions themselves.

● **Higher education and the food crisis:** Looks at the critical problems of stockpiles in terms of the increasing world population and environmental factors. Points up needs beyond direct transfer of research, technology, and teaching that may be unsuited or inadequate for the developing institution and the nation which the institution serves.

● **Public and private international organizations** and **the international intellectual community:** Compare and contrast their differing roles in education, data gathering, meeting grounds, assistance, and communication. Discussions of mission

HIGHER EDUCATION
IN THE
WORLD

choice by private organizations, constrictions on public organizations from their national constituencies, the unity-disunity among disciplines — all illuminate the possibilities for future international interchange and service.

- **Academic exchanges** and **the changing employment market:** Highlight characteristics of, and possibilities for, benefits to institutions and students. Particular attention is given to employment beyond the academic marketplace and to the increased need for language and cultural studies.

Throughout their papers, distinguished American and foreign educators illuminate domestic realities within the higher education community.

AMERICAN COUNCIL ON EDUCATION
Roger W. Heyns, *President*

The American Council on Education, founded in 1918 and composed of institutions of higher education and national and regional education associations, is the nation's major coordinating body for postsecondary education. Through voluntary and cooperative action, the Council provides comprehensive leadership for improving educational standards, policies, and procedures.

HIGHER EDUCATION
IN THE
WORLD COMMUNITY

EDITED BY STEPHEN K. BAILEY

AMERICAN COUNCIL ON EDUCATION
WASHINGTON, D. C.

Library of Congress Cataloging in Publication Data

American Council on Education.
  Higher education in the world community.

  Papers from the 58th annual meeting of the American
Council on Education held in Washington, D.C.,
Oct. 8–10, 1975.
    1. Education, Higher—Congresses.   2. International
education—Congresses.   I. Bailey, Stephen Kemp.
II. Title.
LB2301.A369   1975   378   77-674
ISBN 0-8268-1321-6

Printed in the United States of America

Contributors

Agnes Akosua Aidoo   Assistant Professor of African History, University of California, Los Angeles

Ishaya S. Audu   Vice-Chancellor, Ahmadu Bello University (Nigeria)

Duncan S. Ballantine   Director, Education Department, World Bank

Rivka W. Bar-Yosef   Director, Work and Welfare Research Institute, The Hebrew University of Jerusalem

Asa Briggs   Vice-Chancellor, University of Sussex

Barbara B. Burn   Director, International Programs, University of Massachusetts, Amherst

Remunda Cadoux   President, National Federation of Modern Language Teachers Associations

Melvin A. Eggers   Chancellor, Syracuse University

Luis Garibay G.   Rector, Universidad Autonóma de Guadalajara

Stephen R. Graubard   Editor, *Daedalus, The Journal of the American Academy of Arts and Sciences*

Dale E. Hathaway   Director, International Food Policy Research Institute

James M. Hester   Rector, The United Nations University (Japan)

Torsten Husén   Professor of International Education,. and Director, Institute of International Education, University of Stockholm

Ali Mohammed Khusro   Vice-Chancellor, Aligarh Muslim University (India)

Ramón Mancilla H.   General Coordinator, Gran Mariscal de Ayacucho

David Mathews   The Secretary of Health, Education, and Welfare

Dragoljub Najman   Assistant Director-General, Cooperation for Development and External Relations Sector, United Nations Educational, Scientific and Cultural Organization (France)

Robert M. O'Neil   Vice-President—Bloomington Campus, Indiana University

James A. Perkins   Chairman, International Council on Educational Development

Ralph H. Smuckler   Dean, International Studies and Programs, Michigan State University, and Board Member, Midwest Universities Consortium for International Activities

David Stager   Associate Professor of Economics, University of Toronto

Glen L. Taggart   President, Utah State University

Kenneth W. Thompson   Commonwealth Professor of Government and Foreign Affairs, University of Virginia

Tsunesaburo Tokoyama   President, Japan Private School Promotion Foundation

Betty M. Vetter   Executive Director, Scientific Manpower Commission

Aldo Visalberghi   Professor of Education, Institute of Philosophy, University of Rome

Hans N. Weiler   Director, International Institute for Educational Planning (France)

Contents

Foreword

THE UNITED STATES has become inextricably involved with the other nations of the world in the realities of economic, social, and political interdependence. Now, as never before, the citizens of our country must be disposed to deal effectively with the complex agenda of international affairs. For its part, our educational system—and especially the higher education sector—must contribute to that level of understanding which necessarily precedes the development of effective worldwide cooperation aimed at the improvement of life for all people.

In keeping with that spirit, the American Council on Education dedicated its fifty-eighth Annual Meeting to the national purpose of achieving better understanding and fuller cooperation among the nations of the world. The theme of the meeting, "Higher Education in the World Community," represented more than a gesture to the growing interdependence of peoples and nations. The rationale was that educational institutions throughout the world confront common issues and common dilemmas transcending parochial barriers of language and culture.

The American Council publishes this volume of papers from the meeting to help inform the deliberations and actions of the higher education community in this country and abroad and also of the national and international organizations and institutions whose missions are linked with higher education. By this means, the Council hopes to further the contributions that higher education can make to the world community.

The conception of this meeting originated with Stephen K. Bailey. We are grateful to him for his guidance throughout the planning period and for editing this volume. Meeting plans and programs were directed by John F. Hughes and coordinated by Donna C. Phillips. The Council is indebted to the contributors to this volume and to the staff members who helped prepare for and carry out this Annual Meeting of the American Council on Education.

ROGER W. HEYNS, *President*
American Council on Education

Preface

THE AMERICAN COUNCIL ON EDUCATION, in its fifty-eighth Annual Meeting, held in Washington, D.C., October 8–10, 1975, sought to encourage exchanges of views among representatives of higher education institutions and organizations in this country and from abroad. Panel members from developing institutions abroad described kinds of aid that would promote education and training appropriate to their institutions and to national needs in their countries. Throughout the meetings, speakers associated with the national and international agencies and governmental and nongovernmental organizations discussed the nature of aid as differing from direct transference of the educational concepts and technologies of the developed nations.

On specific levels, the panel members examined institutional exchanges, need to enlarge language and area studies, education and work, means of intellectual communication, and collection and dissemination of international education data.

The meeting owed much of its success to John F. Hughes, who directed the planning and arrangements. The Council is grateful for the travel grants from the Bureau of Educational and Cultural Affairs of the U.S. Department of State and the Ford Foundation, which gave the meeting its truly international dimension.

STEPHEN K. BAILEY

· 1 ·

To Illuminate Tomorrow: Higher Education in an Interdependent World

JAMES M. HESTER

THE LEADERS of American education are confronted now with the need to make a major decision, a decision that could affect the quality of education millions of Americans will receive and that could determine in large measure whether the people of this country now and for generations to come will be adequately prepared for world citizenship.

The world is in the midst of its greatest metamorphosis since the cataclysm of the Second World War. A concatenation of crises and events unmatched in history—energy, food, population, environment, inflation, recession, upheavals in the monetary system, the assertion of Third World rights, détente, the emergence of China, the Middle East, reappraisal of United States capabilities after Vietnam (the list is seemingly endless)—all, in one way or another, have contributed to the dissolution of the post-World War II international structure and the creation of a global condition in which new uncertainties, attitudes, and possibilities abound.

Each nation and group of nations is being impelled to reexamine its international perspectives, relationships, and obligations. And on no nation does this necessity fall with greater force than on the United States, whose wealth, power, and influence dominated the world order that emerged from World War II.

It is inevitable that any substantial change in America's international position should be profoundly felt in her colleges and universities. It is substantially the responsibility of America's academic leadership to determine how that reevaluation will affect the educational experience of American students. In considering higher education and the world community anew, the questions we must ask, then, are: What do emerging global circumstances require of the men and women who are in college classrooms today? Is the education they are receiving adequate for the

1

kind of world in which they and their nation will live? Will intelligent existence in the world ahead require a larger measure of international understanding than most students now acquire? If so, what must be done to increase and improve the internationalization of American education? Are American educators doing what is required to meet this need? These, it seems to me, are the fundamental questions that must be addressed.

The American academic community has been talking about the internationalization of education for some time—at least thirty years. Some educational spokesmen drew conclusions from the nature of the world at the close of World War II that larger numbers seem to be drawing today. After Hiroshima and Nagasaki, it was not unreasonable to conclude that warfare was no longer feasible and that a new set of international values had to be substituted for the precepts of traditional nationalism. The establishment of the United Nations in 1945 was celebrated by many in that spirit.

Throughout the intervening years, a continuing effort has been made by a relatively small but persistent group inside and outside academe to awaken the academic community and its patrons to the need to increase the internationalization of education. There has been much general sympathy for this ideal, but not enough sense of urgency to compel thoroughgoing, widespread change.

The weight of academic tradition, the intellectual and cultural inheritance focused on western Europe and the United States, the preoccupation of the social sciences with the Western and—particularly—the American experience, the obsession of Americans with the drama and problems of America and, in more recent years, the obsession of students with trying to understand themselves—all these have presented formidable barriers to fundamental change in the international dimensions of the curriculum and most subject matter. It is precisely these barriers—composed of tradition, preoccupations, inherited values, as well as the familiar limits of time available in class schedules—that must be penetrated if any real changes are to come about.

New Necessities for Internationalization

What will make such penetration possible? The only answer seems to be: a new sense of urgency. It takes a sense of urgency to arouse any establishment from its accustomed ways. As Dr. Johnson once remarked, "The prospect of imminent execution concentrates the mind exceedingly." Only if sufficient numbers of educational leaders acquire a profound sense if "imminent execution" concerning the international content of education will students experience a greater exposure to the realities of the present and emerging world.

What will create a new sense of urgency? What will take the place of Hiroshima and Sputnik in moving higher education closer to a genuinely international posture? Most recently, the lines in front of the gas stations helped many Americans suddenly realize that America is not a self-sufficient island. But then the lines went away, and that valuable reminder of international interdependence was denied us. Statistics like those of the Club of Rome arouse the reading public temporarily; then the statistics are challenged and contradicted, and all too many people throw up their hands and go back to their old habits of mind.

I assume agreement on the reasons that internationalism is an important subject now. Americans know, or at least have been told, that the world has been changed, that its constituent parts have become interdependent in ways entirely different from anything we recognized before, and that we must think globally and behave as citizens of the world if humanity is to survive. We have been hearing such assertions for several years. We know that in some sense, to some degree, they must be true. And if they are true, they are obviously very important. And if they are important, we should do something about them—particularly as educators. But what?

The task is, for many reasons, one of the most difficult we have ever faced. One matter is that of rationale. In part, the failure of higher education to keep pace with the reality of an increasingly interdependent world has been the inadequacy of the rationales that have motivated efforts to internationalize American thought and action.

There has always been a core of true believers who shared Wendell Willkie's vision of one world and gloried in the celebration of internationalism that accompanied the founding of the United Nations. Several of our greatest statesmen of that era and since have given profound evidence of that persuasion. And many of the American intelligentsia inside and outside academe have long been convinced that the inevitable world involvements of the United States demand a far less parochial frame of reference than we have been able to devise.

Harry Truman set the stage for an era of international generosity of revolutionary proportions with the Marshall plan and the Point Four program. But then American international altruism, or intelligent self-interest, became increasingly mixed with the effort to contain the spread

of communism, and the rationale for making Americans more international-minded became muddled and bogged down in the conflicts of the
cold war. The conversion of internationalism into a function of nationalism was completed with the response to Sputnik, when an outpouring
of support for the study of foreign cultures arrived under the title of the
National Defense Education Act. The failure to achieve funding of the
International Education Act of 1966 reflected, in part, a continuing inability to find a convincing rationale for a major alteration in America's
international outlook.

INTERNATIONALISM IN THE CURRICULUM

The key question now is whether we are capable of formulating, ex-
pressing, believing, and acting on a conception of interdependence appropriate to the reality of world conditions. Part of the difficulty must be
that too many people are not yet convinced—by which I mean sufficiently
disturbed—that conditions have actually changed all that much. Yes,
there were the gasoline lines, but then they went away.

The inadequacy of rationale is not the only difficulty. The task of
giving greater emphasis to international subject matter in the college
curriculum is made even more complicated by a lack of consensus on the
purposes of education. We had a kind of consensus thirty years ago: one
fixed firmly on Western civilization, the American experience, an introduction to the principal modes of intellectual inquiry, a major and some
minors. That structure still survives in some form in most institutions,
but it has been altered by several forces, including the introduction of
non-Western studies as legitimate options.

In many colleges, curricular requirements have been loosened, and
students have been given greater freedom of choice, including the freedom to choose a non-Western focus for their education. This liberalization
largely reflects faculty acquiescence to student pressures—particularly
resistance to required courses taught routinely by instructors who had
not shared in their conception. But this liberalization also reflects a lack
of consensus, a lack of shared conviction, an inability of the faculty to
reach agreement about what students should know. Students are being
encouraged to design their own programs, partly because some of them
are intelligently mature enough to do so, but also partly because the
faculty is unable to agree on a body of essential knowledge.

In these circumstances, the idea of introducing a new major emphasis
in the collegiate curriculum is extremely formidable. How can consensus

on such a complicated proposition be achieved, particularly when it would demand so much of so many? From some relatively coherent campuses under exceedingly able leadership, remarkable progress has been reported. But for most institutions, slow, painstaking, incremental results, as in most curricular matters, may be all that can be expected, particularly at a time of financial stress.

The task is not impossible, however. Despite the present inadequacies, we must derive considerable encouragement from the great progress that has been made in the internationalization of American higher education since World War II. American colleges and universities are now far better equipped than they were to prepare area specialists, to teach languages other than western European, and to provide courses in non-Western studies. And at most institutions, students wishing to do so can now learn in great depth about the world at large. Such opportunities were not the rule before the war.

American institutions can take pride in greatly enriched faculty expertise, course offerings, and library holdings. Moreover, the provincial climate of most American campuses has been significantly altered by the increase in the number of foreign students and faculty members, the growth of study abroad, and the influence of participation in assistance programs overseas. Although shortcomings in all these areas are well known, there is no denying that the total effect has been to familiarize thousands upon thousands of Americans with foreign societies, while at the same time helping to educate many students from other countries and, in the process, familiarizing them with the United States. What has been achieved is encouraging. Accomplishments are genuine.

There has been tangible gain in the pursuit of international expertise and understanding in American institutions of higher learning. But has this development gone far enough? Can we be satisfied with the present degree of international exposure of American students? As I have already indicated, I believe that the answer to both questions is a resounding *no*, that the effort is profoundly inadequate, that today, thirty years after the golden days of euphoria immediately following World War II, international education in the United States is in the midst of what has been correctly termed a crisis of enormous conceptual, organizational, and financial proportions. This problem may well be so complex, so large, so formidable that it is not subject to a frontal attack. It may be the kind of problem that can be solved only by inexorable events rather than by programmed action.

FACULTY ROLES

Increasing numbers of humanists and social scientists are becoming more international-minded and taking a new look at the values to be derived from studying experiences in other societies. This shift is occurring in literature, the arts, sociology, economics, administration, urban studies, and other fields. International interaction has been taking place for a long time in the basic and health sciences, but is now increasing.

Perhaps the revolution will only occur—as it must ultimately—through individual faculty professional conviction. But what is happening now is marginal and slow—too slow—for only the exceptional faculty member is revising subject matter to recognize the new nature of the world. Can this process be accelerated? Is there some frontal attack worth trying? The answers, I believe, are yes, but only if the leaders of higher education give form and substance to the movement. They can do so, however, only if they acknowledge the crisis, if they accept and admit the inadequacy of the current international exposure of American students, if they accept the implications of the logic that lies at the heart of the matter. Logic says we have only just begun a process toward which we have been groping, not simply since World War II, but since 1918 and earlier. It is a logic that requires reorienting our international intellectual prejudices just as we have had to reorient our domestic racial prejudices.

We have considered ourselves virtuous if we could direct education toward responsible national citizenship. Now we must consider the implications of world citizenship. Few of us have come to grips with the full implications of that logic. The logic has become familiar, almost to the point of boredom, but we cannot ignore it. The nature of human societies has been profoundly changed by applications of science and technology. On a planet of new economic, political, and environmental facts and relationships, the nation-state can no longer be the principal focus of thought and action for intelligent people. All major national problems now interlock and interrelate with conditions elsewhere in the world. Therefore, if the educated person is to be suitably prepared for a world of shifting power centers, growing environmental vulnerability, misused and depleted resources, uninhibited capital consumption in some countries and unchecked poverty in most of the others, he must possess knowledge, perspectives, and values that only a relatively few global-minded pioneers possess today.

But, our universities are staffed to a considerable extent by men and women whose mental furniture was put into place in another era, whose highly specialized disciplinary skills frequently exclude potential comparative international perspectives. These are the teachers of young men and women who will be in charge twenty or thirty years from now, students who are, fortunately, far more disposed to accept the whole world on equal terms than we were at their age.

I may be accused of stating the problem in a manner typical of a university president—by putting the blame on the faculty. And to be fair, some faculty members have been crying for years for increased institutional support for international studies. Part of the problem has been that much of what internationalists have had to offer has been of special interest to a relatively few students. Much of what has been offered as international studies has consisted of specialized language and area programs or theoretical political and economic studies that have not provided adequate opportunities to satisfy the needs and curiosity of students outside these specialties.

In fact, during the very period that a great increase in international studies has taken place, it is reported that the majority of students in American colleges and universities have had no contact in their courses with information on foreign societies.[1] I think we must agree with Maurice Harari that "a system of education which ignores the major problems of most of mankind is not acceptable."[2]

Let me cite the Swedish experience with this problem. In early 1972 the office of the chancellor of the Swedish universities appointed a committee to draft proposals for internationalizing university curricula, the motivation being to produce qualified manpower for the export industry and for development assistance. Once the committee got down to work, however, it discovered it had to abandon these limited objectives; the conclusion it reached, finally, was that internationalizing all education is necessary for the very survival of mankind. The main objective, the report said, must be "international solidarity and a sense of world citizenship." Sweden is now mounting a national educational program toward that goal.

Are Americans prepared to acknowledge such an objective? We know

1. Cf. Irwin T. Sanders and Jennifer C. Ward, *Bridges to Understanding: International Programs of American Colleges and Universities,* Sponsored by the Carnegie Commission on Higher Education (New York: McGraw-Hill, 1970).

2. *Global Dimensions in U.S. Education: The University* (New York: Center for War/Peace Studies, 1972), p. 9.

what a revolutionary idea this is and how difficult and costly its implementation would be. (Indeed, as one who has been president of a financially pressed university, I have no business making such an expensive proposal.) But I am far from being alone in this persuasion. Edwin O. Reischauer, for example, has written that education "is not moving rapidly enough in the right direction to produce knowledge about the outside world and the attitudes toward other peoples that may be essential for human survival within a generation or two." And he argues that "we need a profound reshaping of education if mankind is to survive in the sort of world that is fast evolving."[3]

The American Council on Education has proposed to Congress new legislative authority for a broad-based effort in schools, colleges, and universities to increase civic literacy in global problems. It would be difficult to overstress the importance of such congressional support if there is to be success in bringing about effective change. In saying this, however, I also urge that, in approaching this monumental obligation, we be mindful of the lessons we should have learned from recent experiences.

FINANCE AND THE ADMINISTRATIVE STRUCTURE

The accomplishments in the internationalization of American higher education since the Second World War were largely stimulated and maintained by foundation and federal initiatives and support. Of course, there were faculty instigators advising government and foundation officials, and there were willing administrators eager to introduce new programs for intellectual as well as institution-building reasons, particularly if they did not impose serious organizational rearrangements. But most of what has taken place in the name of international education has been add-ons rather than fundamental changes in traditional departmental structures and course content. In a superficial sense the device of add-ons was fortunate, for when the foundation and federal cutbacks came, and the institutional financial crunch was on, the surgery was somewhat less difficult. But it was—and is—damaging and painful, and the scars that remain are stern reminders that, no matter how beneficial government and foundation initiatives and support may be, we should be fully aware of the dangers inherent in such dependency.

Educators have, I hope, learned that outside initiatives and support must be combined with broadly based institutional commitments in mat-

3. *Toward the 21st Century: Education for a Changing World* (New York: Alfred A. Knopf, 1973), pp. 4, 3.

ters of curriculum change. Indeed, unless trustees, academic senates, deans, presidents, chancellors, provosts, department chairmen, and curriculum committees are all willing to acknowledge the deficiencies in the international education of American students, unless they can commit themselves to a new concept of education for world citizenship, no amount of federal or foundation support will be truly effective.

The post-Vietnam disillusionment provides an extraordinary opportunity to reexamine our values and performance and to find new directions for the international perspectives of Americans and their institutions. There is some evidence of a wish to withdraw from international commitments. But there is also evidence of a popular willingness to put faith in international agencies of cooperation. Now is certainly an appropriate time for a fresh appraisal of international education, not as peripheral to the educational experience but as a major preoccupation that will cut across the academic spectrum. As F. Champion Ward has written, "It is time for internationalism in higher education to be grounded in the very idea of a university, and this idea must rest in turn, on a universal view of knowledge and value."[4] Or as James A. Perkins has written: "Only as international perspectives become integrated into the work of most scholars and students will there be a full affirmation of the international dimensions of higher education."[5]

UNITED NATIONS UNIVERSITY: STRUCTURE AND FUNCTIONS

I now find myself, as rector of the United Nations University, among those charged with helping to advance the cause of international understanding through intellectual collaboration on a worldwide basis. I confess that I was not among the early advocates of the U.N. University. In fact, as the American member of the administrative board of the International Association of Universities, in early 1971 I voiced opposition to the original conception of the U.N. University, which was patterned like a traditional university, international only in purpose, staff, and student body. Along with others, I opposed that conception because I believed the United Nations should help to internationalize all higher education, rather than limiting the effort to one group of students and faculty mem-

4. Francis X. Sutton et al., *Internationalizing Higher Education: A United States Approach* (New York: International Council for Educational Development, 1974), p. 23.

5. *International Programs of U.S. Colleges and Universities: Priorities for the Seventies* (New York: International Council for Educational Development, 1971), p. 18.

bers. Therefore, when the concept of the U.N. University was changed to that of a worldwide network of advanced study and training institutes working in association with universities around the world, I felt genuinely enthusiastic about its potential value.

The creation of the United Nations University is a response to the growing recognition worldwide that the major problems confronting humanity are not the problems and responsibilities of single nations, however rich or poor, but of the entire interdependent world. It is a response to the same logic, the same imperative that calls on American education to embrace a new quality of internationalization.

The work of the United Nations University, according to its charter, will be focused on problems, "Global problems of human survival, development and welfare." And in keeping with this focus, the governing body of the university—twenty-four (mostly academic) people serving individually rather than as governmental representatives—has chosen world hunger, human and social development, and the use and management of natural resources as priority areas of study.

To devise strategies for the university's work on these problems, three small working meetings of world experts were held at the headquarters in Tokyo in the fall of 1975. The first, on world hunger, has produced achievements that are deeply reassuring to those of us charged with bringing the university to life. Nineteen experts from thirteen countries proposed for the university a most impressive set of urgent responsibilities which, according to their experience, no other institutions are fully equipped to handle.

In addition to research and advanced training, the university is mandated to disseminate knowledge. We intend that the United Nations University's scholarly output, as well as its methods of international intellectual collaboration, shall be of service to scholars around the world, particularly in strengthening their efforts to educate sensitive and effective world citizens. In keeping with this aim, the plans call for setting up a U.N. University press in Tokyo to be a source of reliable, unbiased transnational knowledge of the highest academic quality, which it is hoped will be of substantial value to colleges and universities everywhere in the internationalization of their curricula.

This ambitious undertaking was given its impetus by the enthusiastic support of many nations, and by the farsighted generosity of the government of Japan, which has pledged $100 million toward a $500 million international endowment fund and which is also providing headquarters and other facilities. The governments of Senegal, Ghana, Greece, Sweden, and Norway made contributions to the fund, and Venezuela has pledged $10 million.

The United States, no less than any other country, will gain knowledge about the world from the flow of information the university will provide. Data that have been lacking in matters of global interdependence—reliable worldwide statistics on energy, hydrology, agriculture, and oceans—are precisely the kinds of information that the university, as one of its purposes, is to collect and disseminate.

The concept of a worldwide network of advanced training and research institutes is unprecedented, and the use of the word *university*—for which there seems to be no adequate substitute—is confusing. But we are determined that this shall be a true university of the nations of the world in the most essential sense and spirit. The U.N. University will be concerned with universal problems of humanity, and it will examine them under conditions of the highest intellectual quality and objectivity. It is guaranteed academic freedom by its charter, and those of us developing the university are dedicated to protecting that freedom. Only by maintaining its freedom, autonomy, and intellectual integrity can we expect to create an institution that is of the highest quality and greatest usefulness and that is free from politics.

We are partners in the same effort—nationally and internationally—to change the old parochial curricula of mankind. Sir Eric Ashby once said that a university's greatest task is not to reflect yesterday but to illuminate tomorrow. That is the challenge before us in reshaping education and the institutions that serve it. It is an exhilarating task, and one in which we must succeed.

· 2 ·

Support for Emerging Universities

The African Case: Problems and Prospects

AGNES AKOSUA AIDOO

NEARLY ALL AFRICAN UNIVERSITIES today have been affected by the activities of international agencies interested in higher education. The agencies have served in advisory capacities or have actually helped to plan new universities. The greatest involvement, however, has been in areas of support, both financial and technical. It is natural that the international organizations expect returns from their investments, but the nature of these returns is sometimes difficult to define. Quite often the returns simply fail to materialize.

In part, the problem arises from the difficulties in establishing acceptable goals for the international investing agencies themselves (an area that others are more competent than I to explore). An equally important part of the problem of efficient international support is related to the nature and circumstances of the new universities receiving the support. Outside organizations that are willing to help need to consider the self-image of the emerging universities and the definition of their goals.

I summarize the problems of the African universities in this respect under two headings: the burden of history, and the hazards of politics. Major difficulties arising from these sources directly affect the operation and efficiency of international support programs.

THE BURDEN OF HISTORY

The universities in independent Africa are struggling with the burden of their colonial foundations and history—and a recent history it is.

12

There are now some forty-five universities in the Association of African Universities. None of them is more than fifty years old, and most of them date from the late 1950s or early 1960s. "Emerging" universities, therefore, aptly describes all but the oldest established institutions such as Khartoum, Makerere, Ibadan, and the University of Ghana at Legon.

Although the history of the foundation of African universities by departing European colonial powers is well known, certain aspects of that history which constitute what I term the "burden" need to be emphasized. First, the majority of the universities were established as optimistic institutions in the wake of African political independence. They were designed to be instruments of change and agents for the rapid fulfillment of the newly acquired freedom. It is significant that both foreign and African scholars for years predicated the rate of development of an independent country on the number of its university graduates.

Of itself, such a utilitarian definition of the African university poses no great difficulty. A problem arises when this definition is related to the second aspect of the history of the universities: their organic link with European countries, institutions, and traditions that gave them birth. In spite of rapid Africanization in the areas of curriculum, research, administration, and personnel found especially in the English-speaking universities, much remains that is a burden of history. All the African universities are constrained in some degree to maintaining the styles, structures, organizations, standards, and assumptions of their European parent institutions. The French-built universities have made woefully small modifications to suit the African context, whereas the English-founded institutions are straining through the dilemma of "Africanity" and international acceptability.

Since 1969, when I was first appointed a lecturer in the University of Cape Coast and later, as senior tutor, had the responsibility of administering the women's residence hall, I have been engaged in debates and discussions over goals and modalities in African universities. In Ghana our debates centered on such issues as the suitability of the fully residential university, academic gowns for undergraduates, moral tutors for students, prayers in Latin, exclusively male senior common rooms, and limited facilities for research on Africa. The minor points about Latin prayers and discriminating common rooms have been won. But the question of undergraduate gowns, for example, still engages university authorities. In November 1973 the acting vice-chancellor of Cape Coast (now vice-chancellor), Professor J. Yanney Ewusie, lamented that the ungowned students appearing before him at matriculation were "academically naked." He was happy to note, however, that plans were under way to design some new undergraduate gowns "which would reflect the culture of Ghana as well as symbolise the basic academic tradition of universities."[1] The gowns were to be worn by all incoming students in 1974. I consider the tradition of .undergraduate gowns unnecessary and economically wasteful in Africa.

A third historical burden, believe it or not, is the physical location of most of the African universities. The "campuses" were established as separate university towns built from scratch in bush tracts several miles from any city. The typical university plans in the 1950s and 1960s included not only academic buildings, laboratories, offices, and student residence halls but also heavily subsidized homes for faculty and staff, hospitals, elementary schools, post offices, shops, water supply, drainage, electricity, roads, and transport. Before the university itself could come into existence, a modern municipality had to be created for it. The university then assumed all the housekeeping responsibilities of the municipality. The vice-chancellor, who is the academic and administrative head of the university, becomes also a sort of lord mayor of the university town.[2]

This point about municipal responsibilities needs emphasis as it is not always fully understood by foreign experts visiting Africa. The situation materially affects the goals and priorities of the new universities as well as the allocation of their resources. The municipal costs of the residential university can be formidable, and they can and do severely constrain the development of the academic services. The municipal responsibilities of the universities urgently need to be reviewed and evaluated, and interested international agencies can assist in such reviews. Their financial and technical support given on the basis of knowledge of the reviewed situations can help to redirect the universities' energies.

THE HAZARDS OF POLITICS

The definition of the universities in Africa as "instruments of change" or "instruments of national development" has placed those institutions in some very precarious situations. The problem is complicated by the fact

1. University of Cape Coast *Gazette*, November/December 1973, p. 10.
2. See Alex A. Kwapong, "Universities in the Developing Countries of Africa: Some Problems and Prospects," Occasional Paper 13, University of California, Los Angeles (1973), pp. 2, 5–6.

that primary instruments of change and development in the postcolonial era are the states in which the universities are situated. A crucial question, therefore, concerns the proper relationship between the university and the state—a question that was not answered at the inception of the independent universities. A great anomaly actually exists in the English-founded universities where the state fully pays for the university but the latter is supposed to be an autonomous corporation.[3] Today, all the universities with African leadership recognize their responsibility and purpose with respect to relevance and responsiveness to the needs of their societies. They realize that they must produce graduates who will fulfill some definite economic, social, and cultural roles in their community. This point is always underscored in speeches by vice-chancellors at university matriculation, convocation, and graduation ceremonies. In one such speech the vice-chancellor of the University of Cape Coast declared:

> The whole world is watching the growth of this young University. Our task here does not end with the production of graduates; the graduates must at the same time be properly oriented to bring meaningful progress to the people of Ghana and Africa. Our aim here is not to please anyone. It is to serve the interests of this country and through it, Africa. We must recognize that a University anywhere, in spite of its universality of approach, should understand the society in which it operates and be understood by its countrymen in order to serve that country. We should never lose sight of that fact.[4]

African academics, university administrators, politicians, and statesmen agree on these sentiments and ideals. However, the achievement of the goals expressed greatly depends on the existence of a clearly formulated policy of national development and the ability of the universities to maintain a high level of intellectual vitality and innovativeness. Clear policies of national education and scientific research are essential. The universities cannot allow themselves to be devoured in the vortex of politics and short-term pragmatism.

Such a position is not an easy one to maintain in Africa. Most of the universities in their recent past have or have had the heads of state as chancellors. Some of these men like Presidents Kwame Nkrumah of Ghana, Kenneth Kaunda of Zambia, and Nnamdi Azikiwe of Nigeria were

3. For a good review of this problem, see Eric Ashby, *African Universities and Western Tradition* (Cambridge, Mass.: Harvard University Press, 1964).
4. "Matriculation Address by the Acting Vice-Chancellor (14 November 1973)," University of Cape Coast *Gazette*, November/December 1973, p. 14.

life chancellors of universities, and they did not act as mere ceremonial heads of the institutions. They frequently directed activities of the universities, from appointment of faculty to the selection of research projects. The assumption of chancellorships by heads of states may be a mark of the importance that the newly independent countries attach to the universities. It is also quite clearly a manifestation of the primacy of politics. As the major instrumentalities of national development and the principal financiers of the universities, African governments, whether civilian or military, exercise a vital control over the development of the universities. It is not surprising that most of the institutions have suffered from intermittent political intervention and from closures by state police and military forces. These kinds of intervention in university affairs make their situation precarious and hinder their growth.

How do institution-state relations affect international support for the universities? I believe that it is vitally important for the international agencies concerned with higher education in Africa to understand the historical burden and contemporary problems. The African universities are emerging in circumstances that in so many ways are quite different from those existing at the founding of similar institutions in the donor countries. Lack of understanding may produce insensitivity and impatience in foreign experts and agencies dealing with the African institutions and may adversely affect the efficiency of support programs.

The record of international support for African universities is encouraging. Fruitful programs of staff development, for example, have been sponsored in the past by international agencies. Several international (UNESCO, World Health Organization, Food and Agriculture Organization, and others) and binational arrangements have also provided much-needed specialized expertise and research facilities to African universities. Of particular help to faculty recruitment are the special arrangements such as the supplementation ("topping-up") schemes provided, for example, by the British Expatriate Supplementation Scheme of the Inter-University Council of the Overseas Development Agency. The Fulbright faculty exchange program in the United States has been valuable but it operates on too narrow a basis. Special "twin relationships" between African and foreign universities have also been effective. Such relationships exist, for example, between the University of Ghana at Legon and the Universities of Western Ontario and Guelph, Canada, in the fields of economics and agriculture. The programs here are deliberately limited but they have the advantage of being selective, well defined, and well funded. Their performance has been found to be efficient and beneficial to both sides.

The broad-based support programs of multinational agencies must be aware of their own special problems. They have to define their goals and modalities clearly in order to avoid presenting Africa with jigsaw puzzle or octopus forms of aid. If I may be permitted an analogy: it does not help to present Africa with cars hastily constructed from mixtures of component parts from Ford, Vauxhall, Peugeot, and Volkswagen!

Finally, it is necessary to state that the responsibility for real change, whether in structure, curriculum, research, or performance, rests with the Africans themselves. The kind of intellectual creativity and resourcefulness needed to advance the universities cannot come from outside agencies or sponsors. African academics and university graduates must establish in their growing institutions of higher learning a viable tradition for themselves. This tradition must have meaning and acceptability first in the African community. A viable tradition born out of a creative intellectual life will change the status of Africa in the world academic community; and this development must be encouraged. If fully developed, Africa's academic and intellectual life would cease to be a recipient and would become a donor of world knowledge to a world community. This goal must be achieved if Africa is to realize its truest emancipation.

Goals for International Support
of Emerging Universities

DUNCAN S. BALLANTINE

To UNDERSTAND how the World Bank or any other development financing and promoting agency looks at universities in developing countries, it is useful to examine first its vantage point. Successful development financing requires that *development* be the dominating criterion, towering above political, commercial, ideological, and other considerations which may also be present. In this context, the development objective is to use re-

Although the views in this paper are personal, I try to express the viewpoint of a development financing institution—specifically the World Bank—toward the support of emerging universities in the developing countries.

sources of the agency and the country to achieve a maximum improvement in the country's economic and social well-being and its capacity to create such well-being for itself—for all its people. This objective applies regardless of whether the assistance is directed to education, agriculture, transport, public utilities, water supply, or family planning.

For any given purpose, the resources that the World Bank can deploy together with those of its member countries are always limited to a fraction of what might be applied efficiently. The projects financed, therefore, represent a priority choice of one thing over another, whether the choice is between or within sectors. When the decision is taken to finance one project, a decision is also made *not* to finance a number of other projects. The choices are many and varied, for example, between the various sectors mentioned above (and others). Within a sector such as education, choices must be made whether to finance institutions of higher learning, secondary schools, primary education, nonformal programs, on-the-job training, technical institutions at various levels, literacy training, and other forms of adult education, perhaps employing radio or television or other media and delivery systems.

Behind the choice of specific areas and projects, there lie more fundamental choices of development objectives and requirements to be served. What balance between long-term and short-term needs? Is the objective to expand the modern sector rapidly and thus give emphasis to capital-intensive forms of production at the risk of unemployment, or is the aim to increase productivity in the traditional and transitional sectors with emphasis on fuller use of the labor force? What mix should there be between productivity and social welfare? What balance between rural and urban populations? The policy choices are complex. Among the choices and criteria pertinent to the support of emerging universities, the World Bank might consider: (1) the university as a national institution, (2) the production of high level manpower, (3) curriculum and teaching, (4) research and service, (5) social mobility and equity, (6) costs, (7) staffing.

This list of questions and criteria far from exhausts the issues confronting the emerging universities. Moreover, the exploration of each question and the conclusions reached will vary greatly between developed and developing countries and among world regions and countries within regions. But the questions do provide a way of talking about the emerging universities and especially about the active concern whether the new universities have lived up to the challenge of their developing societies and can justify continued support, both international and domestic.

THE UNIVERSITY AS A NATIONAL INSTITUTION

Perhaps the most severe and serious criticism leveled against the emerging universities has concerned its imported and irrelevant character. In its philosophy, curricula, and structure, the university is seen as responding to external criteria that are out of touch with the country's socioeconomic realities and culture. This condition is most apparent in former colonies, especially in Africa, but everywhere the spirit of non-engagement has been strong. Moreover, the university, shielded by traditions of autonomy and academic freedom, has been relatively untouchable. In addition, as Professor Babs Fafunwa of Nigeria has pointed out, during the years 1950–70, the governments and taxpayers supported the institutions generously and often uncritically, convinced that newly established institutions of higher learning modeled on those of the developed countries would help transform the economy and improve the lot of the people. As the decade of the 1970s approached, they came to feel that the universities had disappointed them: instead of transforming the economies, they were becoming too expensive for poor countries to support; and instead of benefiting all the people, they had become elitist "islands of privilege in a sea of poverty."[1] With habitual directness, Julius Nyerere declared earlier than most that, however desirable, his country was too poor in money and educated manpower to support an "ivory tower existence" for an intellectual elite and that, although the university must be concerned with the long future, the need was "now" (1963) to engage the three enemies of the people—poverty, ignorance, and disease.

The growing dissatisfaction with the borrowed and dysfunctional universities crystalized in 1972 in a statement by the Association of African Universities, representing forty-two countries, both Francophone and Anglophone:

> Modelled upon foreign institutions—the universities have not manifested the degree of flexibility essential to meet the ever changing aspirations and needs of the common man. The emerging university of the 1970's in Africa must, therefore, shed its foreign forms and cloak; it must not just pursue

1. Fafunwa, *The Growth and Development of Nigerian Universities*, OLC Paper, No. 4 (Washington: Overseas Liaison Committee, American Council on Education, 1974), pp. 31–33.

knowledge for its own sake, but for the sake of and the amelioration of the conditions of the life and work of the ordinary man and woman. It must be fully committed to active participation in social transformation, economic modernization, and the training and upgrading of the total human resources of the nation. Even in the pursuit of its traditional functions of promotion and dissemination of knowledge, as well as research, the university must place emphasis on that which is immediately relevant and useful.[2]

Although the African articulation of this changed attitude was the clearest, it typifies as well the emergence of new attitudes in Asia and Latin America. It was a call to the university, first, to identify with, and engage itself in, the affairs and culture of its own environment, to look more to internal criteria in defining its structure, curriculum, and philosophy and look less—less literally, at least—to the questionable concept of international equivalence. Second, it meant a new kind of relationship with the government and with other institutions of the society. In African countries where the one-party system prevails, some observers see a kind of triumvirate of administration, party, and university. This view may overstate the role of the university. Nevertheless, in all regions of the world there is a growing interaction between universities, governments, and other institutions, as seen in coordination of university and overall development planning, in the exchange of personnel, and, most of all, in the greater focusing of university attention on problems of health, agriculture, communication, education, and general welfare, which are the immediate concern of governments.

It would be wrong to say that this new movement has taken hold in all or even a majority of universities in the developing world. But as shown in a study of higher education and development, directed by the International Council for Educational Development, this new attitude and the conception of the university's role have become established everywhere and are taking concrete form in a variety of new specific programs and innovations, some of which are noted below.[3]

Manpower

Undoubtedly the most impressive achievement of the new universities in developing countries has been their quantitative contribution to the

2. *Creating the African University: Emerging Issues of the 1970's,* ed. T. M. Yesufu (Ibadan: Oxford University Press, 1973).

3. See *Higher Education and Social Change: Promising Experiments in Developing Countries,* vol. 1: *Reports,* ed. Kenneth W. Thompson and Barbara R. Fogel, and vol. 2: *Case Studies,* ed. Kenneth W. Thompson, Barbara R. Fogel, and Helen E. Danner (New York: Praeger, in press).

supply of educated, higher level manpower. From 1950 to 1971, third level (mainly university) enrollments increased from 0.9 million to 6.7 million students, an aggregate increase of more than 550 percent. As a result nationals with higher education credentials have substantially replaced expatriates in both private and public sector posts of leadership and management in the majority of countries. In the science-based and technical fields, including secondary and higher teaching, despite marked progress, the emergence of qualified cadres of nationals is still far from complete. In addition, despite the increased presence of university graduates in management posts, few of them have had training in modern management. In a sample of fifty-nine developing countries, for example, of total higher enrollments, the proportion in agriculture and engineering together averages only 15 percent. As a consequence of the heavy bias toward arts enrollments, the phenomenon persists that unemployment among the educated is accompanied by shortages of skilled manpower in particular fields. The reasons are various: the shortage of teachers at both the secondary and higher levels, the high cost of laboratory facilities for science and technology and the lack of experience in using them, the lower level of rewards in some fields such as agriculture, the lingering greater prestige of nontechnical employments, and, finally, the slower expansion of nonuniversity institutions and programs of higher education to produce in greater numbers the more readily usable operational engineer, agriculturist, and health auxiliary.

During the period of expanding enrollments, most of the students and degrees have been at the undergraduate or first degree level. At the time, this level of achievement was desirable and in most cases all that could be done. It meant, however, that the postgraduate training of university professors and other specialists had still to be pursued in developed countries, with the result that alienation problems discussed above were perpetuated and the day was postponed when university leadership could be exercised by sufficiently indigenous criteria.

The quantitative response to high level manpower needs has been the most important contribution that the universities could have made during these decades, and despite its qualitative deficiencies the record is commendable. In many countries it should now be possible to level off the increase in the number of students seeking first degrees and to concentrate attention in higher education as a whole on three aspects of manpower supply: (*a*) The distribution of enrollments among types of courses should be improved so that qualitatively as well as quantitatively a better balance is secured between supply and demand in high level manpower. Imperfect as the methodology may be, better manpower planning *and management* could still bring substantial benefits to most countries. (*b*) Postgraduate studies should be gradually and selectively built up to provide for local (or regional) training of researchers and specialists. (*c*) Higher, nonuniversity education and training, especially in the technical and applied science fields should be substantially expanded. In some cases, as in Mauritius, Cameroon, and Malawi, this development might take place within "umbrella" universities; in other countries, separate nonuniversity institutions would be the appropriate means. But it would be useful in all cases to consider higher education and training as a whole, distinguishing functionally from very early between the future operator and the researcher, rather than between university and nonuniversity or "higher" and "lower" levels.

CURRICULUM AND TEACHING

Criticism of university curricula and teaching is similar to the views on the university in general as described above. The curriculum is considered irrelevant to concerns and realities of the country, too rigidly disciplinary and fragmented, too dependent on materials and sources emanating from other societies and, in applied sciences and technology, too much based on sophisticated techniques that are not locally applicable. Teaching is descriptive rather than analytical, encourages rote learning rather than problem solving, and deals with abstract and theoretical constructs rather than human or physical phenomena observed here and now.

In many universities much of this indictment may still be valid, but even a cursory review around the world reveals significant changes and innovations. To mention a few examples, in Latin America and elsewhere, entrance directly into a self-contained professional faculty is being replaced by a preliminary year or two of basic studies common to all students, with choice of professional specialization postponed. Many professional courses have been radically transformed. At the Middle East Technical University in Turkey, architecture has been broadened into urban development. At a number of universities the emphasis in medical training has shifted from narrow therapeutic specialization to community and preventive health care, and at Bahia in Brazil and del Valle in Colombia these specialties have been combined with other disciplines into a multifaceted concern for community welfare and development. The

Maeklong rural development project in Thailand is an action-oriented research project which incorporates student participation and pools three universities' specialties in agriculture, medicine, and the social sciences. In many universities the social sciences are taught as related, rather than separate, disciplines. In Africa, to give effect to tribal custom, law and anthropology have become sister disciplines. The mounting concern for rural development has, of course, also encouraged both the multidisciplinary approach and engagement in immediate social problems.

It must be kept in mind that changes in curriculum and teaching in the university are often gradual and unspectacular and, therefore are not as readily identified as other kinds of university development. Changes in these areas are dependent on other factors which may change only slowly such as the availability of local reference materials in depth, relevant (perhaps intermediate) technologies, and—above all—professors who, whether trained abroad or not, retain a feel for the country's own conditions. There is also, one suspects, an important feedback relationship between the pace of curricular and pedagogical innovation and the amount of multidisciplinary and action-oriented research and service activity undertaken by the university.

Research and Service

As the ICED study of higher education and development reveals, interest has been mounting everywhere in using the university's resources for research and other services in a wide variety of sectors, but increasingly in problems of immediate, local concern that are often interdisciplinary in character.[4] Indeed, the identifiable opportunities for such work are so many and inviting that, considering the existing problems and constraints, danger exists either of diverting able staff from the still crucial task of teaching undergraduates or of producing a mass of high cost, low quality reports which in the long run prejudice potential users against university-based research.

There is, of course, a serious undersupply of people trained and experienced in the design and execution of research projects and feasibility studies. For this reason, research has become the last haven for the resident expatriate who, despite his research competence, normally cannot have the deep cultural sensitivity that is needed for the best results. Moreover, most local researchers have been abroad and habituated to

4. Examples are abundant and range from studies of harbor development in Istanbul to experiments in using the Yoruba language in primary education in Nigeria.

techniques and conditions not obtaining in the home country. Thus it has been suggested that an "intermediate technology" in research is needed. Finally, the inevitable gap between the viewpoint of the scholarly producer of applied research and the potential user and purchaser has been wider in the developing countries than elsewhere. As David Court has remarked in an essay on East Africa, "academic training in major universities in the United States and Europe did not always fit the scholar for responding easily to the demand for policy oriented research" while conversely "many of the policy makers . . . were not sufficiently familiar with the nature of research activity to know what kinds of requests they could justifiably make on the university." These shortcomings have contributed to a measure of disillusionment, which has inhibited the flow of funds and which, Court suggests, might be corrected in time by a "broad education in research appreciation."[5]

Despite all these qualifications, the obvious need for well-proportioned, selective research programs and the resulting benefits to government, society, and university are so great that strengthening and expansion of this sector of university life will have high priority in the next several decades.

SOCIAL MOBILITY AND EQUITY

To what extent has the university in developing countries been a mechanism for social mobility and through its admission practices, at least, counteracted the accumulated disadvantages of low income, inferior prior schooling, geography, social status, and home environment? In both developed and developing countries, evidence suggests that the university has not been highly effective as a mechanism for social mobility. Clearly, where (for all developing countries) only 5 percent of the age cohort are enrolled under conventional criteria, the cumulative gap between advantaged and disadvantaged will have an effect. Gradually, with expanded university enrollments and improved opportunity for secondary school preparation, some democratization of admission is taking place. But those developments are slow, and therefore experimentation with more flexible criteria and expansion of financial support *for the needy* seem called for.

The most promising development not only for equalizing opportunity but also for ameliorating many other problems discussed above is the

5. In *Higher Education and Social Change*, vol. 2.

adoption of a period of national service or other employment for all secondary school graduates before they can become eligible for university admission. Discussion of some form of mixing work and formal instruction is spreading rapidly (Kenya, Sierra Leone, Zaire, Zambia, Nigeria, Guyana are examples), but it is not yet clear whether the trend will be toward the Tanzanian model of service as a prerequisite to higher education or the earlier Ethiopian "year of service" performed during the university course. Although both models in part address similar problems, they are different in both objectives and application. A small sampling suggests that the Tanzanian model will be more favored, and even Ethiopia expects that when the present cohorts of university and upper secondary students return to classes, they will be replaced in time by others at the preuniversity level.

The Tanzanian model, which may have been influenced by events in the Chinese Peoples' Republic, stops far short of what appears to exist in China. Academic admission criteria are still used, but to them have been added an assessment by the employer of the candidate's work performance and by the party authorities of understanding and commitment to the country's system of "self-reliant" socialist development. Some may see these additional criteria as threats to the intellectual quality and autonomy of the university; others will see them as welcome correctives to the university's detachment from its social context.

This new approach to university entrance may not immediately alter the social origins of the student body, for the outcome will depend primarily on a host of determinants both inside and outside the education sector. It will permit a broader based selection from among those who possess the conventional academic qualifications. It may produce a better perspective on what qualities make for success in the university and, therefore, modification of the conventional qualifications. It will certainly produce a different kind of student with respect to what he brings to and expects to get from the university.

Costs

The cost of higher education bears heavily on all developing countries but, unfortunately, with increasing severity proportional to the poverty of the country. In a sample of forty-two countries, when the unit costs of university education as a multiple of the gross national product per capita are compared with GNP per capita, quite understandably the correlation is shown consistently to be inverse since unit costs vary much less than GNP. More significant is the almost quantum jump that the multiple takes as GNP per capita falls below the level of $250. The mean value of the multiple for nineteen countries below $250 is 13.7, whereas for countries above $250 it is 1.4. Stated more simply, in the poorest countries, university education of one student per year costs the country the average income of more than 13 persons. In the intermediate and better-off countries, it costs the average income of less than one and a half persons.

If further argument is needed, these figures again suggest that planning and management of universities and all other higher education, especially in the poorest countries, need to be flexible and closely related to the country's own needs and possibilities rather than to the standards and norms of other, differently situated countries. Are university graduates overqualified or misqualified for the roles they will play in the country's development, and are they therefore too costly? Would modification of structures and curricula reduce unit costs and conserve scarce resources for other priority uses without serious loss (possibly improvement) in the performance of the graduate? Ngee Ann Technical College in Singapore offers an instructive example. Should it be taken for granted that 50 percent of a faculty member's time is normally to be devoted to "research," or should it be argued that more than six hours per week is an excessive teaching load in a country whose higher education unit cost is twenty-five times the GNP per capita? Without subjecting a university to production line regimens, better management practices should still help to identify and correct many examples of waste and inefficiency.

STAFF

University staff development and use represent a problem both for the university and for the country's general development. In varying degrees, three aspects of the problem affect the universities of Asia, Africa, and Latin America: (a) localization of staff, (b) upgrading of qualifications, especially for research and postgraduate instruction, and (c) efficient use.

In Latin America and Asia, reliance on expatriates for routine tasks is no longer common practice (if, indeed, it ever was). In Africa, after a slow start, localization has increased rapidly but still has far to go. For example, in 1973–74 at the universities in Kenya, Tanzania, and Uganda (which formerly made up the University of East Africa), 35 percent of the established posts were occupied by East Africans, compared with 17 percent in 1964, most of them junior posts. This increase was a notable achievement considering that between 1964 and 1973 enrollments almost quintupled (4.5) and the number of established teaching posts increased by more than five times (5.2). Moreover, drainage of trained and experienced staff into more lucrative or influential posts outside the university, which is not entirely to be deplored, has been an additional obstacle.

However, if the data from the University of East Africa are representative, they raise the question whether economies of scale are being achieved as enrollments expand. In 1964, the overall ratio of students to established posts was 7.8; in 1973 it had declined to 6.8. If resources are to be available for essential needs in university development, seeking greater economy and efficiency in staff use might be a good place to begin.

OPPORTUNITIES FOR INTERNATIONAL SUPPORT

What then emerge as priorities for international support for developing universities and as conditions under which support would be most effective?

1. *Staffing*. Since, as Court has remarked, "Expatriates in an expatriate dominated university are almost always incapable of leading lasting innovation,"[6] the prerequisite for most of the changes desired may be the continuing localization and upgrading of staff. For newer universities, where localization is still insufficient, emphasis might be placed on rapid, even if incomplete, training of staff capable of providing undergraduate instruction. Indeed, it can be argued that staff training would be both more economical and effective if divided into several stages. In countries where the universities are using local staff and beginning to meet the most pressing demands for university-trained manpower, selective upgrading of teaching staff and in-depth training of researchers will have high priority, preferably in subject areas pertinent for the trainee's country. The training also should give greater attention to pedagogy. Overall, the development of education manpower to serve the society should prove a most rewarding and enduring investment in people.

2. *Management and costs*. Any government has the right to expect that a tax-supported university will be managed with maximum efficiency

6. Ibid.

and economy consistent with its tasks. Just how this maxim works out offers considerable latitude, but support of studies to improve fiscal self-knowledge can be helpful. If the university itself feels the need, management and planning studies—especially university planning related to education sector and national development planning—can produce a substantial return on a modest investment.

Donor agencies and universities should also consider whether the projects they support are likely to need recurring investment. Trying out an attractive idea may represent an unproductive investment unless there is continuing support in case it succeeds.

3. *Social equity.* Since many of the determinants lie beyond the reach of university policy or even educational policy, rapid improvement in the university as an instrument of social mobility should not be expected. Nonetheless, explorations toward flexible admission criteria, increased student aid, and revised structures and curricula such as streamlined and sandwich courses for operational people could offer a form of higher education to people otherwise excluded. Certainly a financing agency might hesitate to support a university that appeared to be unaware of the social equity dimension in development.

4. *Manpower.* The suggestion that some universities may shift emphasis from undergraduate to advanced training should not obscure the need in many countries to increase the number of people trained beyond the secondary education level. One hopes, first, that indiscriminate expansion in fields not directly contributing to development can be curbed. Second, one hopes that the needs for high level manpower and the response of all higher education—not just the "degree level" university—can be considered as a whole, with close attention to the roles for which people are being prepared. On these terms and subject to the best possible manpower estimates, support including physical facilities for expanded enrollments may often be justified.

5. *Teaching, research, and service.* In all three of these basic university functions, the most encouraging development of recent years in the emerging universities is the increased focus on "here and now" problems —problems of hunger, malnutrition, disease, poverty, equity, language development, nation building, education, population, and environment (to name a few). As concern continues to deepen and as capabilities to help solve these problems increase, one can envisage a powerful new instrument of development.

For this hope to be fulfilled, the university must come to embrace both thought and practice. Citing from history, both Harvey and Galileo were university men, and Tycho Brahe ran his equivalent of a university institute. But the remarkable advances of shipbuilding, seamanship, and navigation in fifteenth-century Portugal—which made possible an age of discovery—owed more to Prince Henry's captains, inching their way down the coast of Africa, than to the learned men of Coimbra. And where were the universities during some other major historical movements—the fourteenth-century development of banking institutions or the industrial and agricultural revolutions of the eighteenth century? Little purpose is served by extravagant claims that "the university is the conscience of the nation" (brushing aside the contributions of church, family, law, the media, even the popular vote) or that the university is "the engine of development" or "the author of political change."

Today's university and other forms of higher education have an important role to play. Moreover, it must be played in constructive interchange with the vast network of other institutions, most of which strike their roots far deeper into, and draw their nourishment more directly from, the social purpose of a nation. Unfortunately, until fairly recently most of the universities in the developing countries have been far indeed from this kind of constructive interaction with their country's institutions and mainsprings of development. A significant change is now taking place, with objectives clearly enough defined and widely enough expressed to merit credibility. As universities and other institutions of higher education move to assist the nation's development in these and other ways, international agencies may be expected to respond with support.

Evaluation of Purpose in Emerging Universities

HANS N. WEILER

BOTH IN ABSOLUTE terms and on a per institution or per capita basis, institutions of higher education in the Third World have received by far the largest share of financial assistance under both bilateral and multilateral assistance programs. Even allowing for the considerably higher unit costs involved in higher education, the international expenditure differential between higher education and the other levels and sectors of education is striking.

Partly as a result of this massive international assistance to higher education development, the growth of university systems in developing countries since the early 1960s has been phenomenal, both in number of institutions and number of students. Although social and political demands by national or regional populations have affected this growth, to a considerable extent it has been a response to urgent needs for university-trained manpower.

The growth process of higher education in developing countries has on the whole essentially perpetuated European models of higher education. Sporadic efforts at new departures toward more indigenous higher education notwithstanding, the structural and conceptual mold of the new universities in Africa and Asia has remained that of the classical European university in its French, British, Belgian, or Dutch varieties. Efforts to design new models more directly oriented to development problems[1] have not really moved beyond the design stage and may face tough political competition with the existing university establishment.

In the meantime, one of the stronger arguments for expanding higher education in developing countries, namely, the need to supply highly trained manpower for the key positions in the country's development effort, has lost in many countries a good deal of its force because of an increasing mismatch between university output and employment opportunities. Undersupply of graduates in some areas contrasts starkly with overabundance of unemployable graduates in other fields and dampens the exaggerated hopes that were once placed in manpower projections as a tool for planning in higher education.

Against this background, the questioning of international support for emerging institutions may not be heretic after all. Posing the question does not necessarily mean answering it in the negative, but some reflection about the relative place and rank of higher education in the overall priorities of international cooperation seems to be in order. For example, why not, instead, support rural community education centers, emerging alternatives to systems of primary education that have been too dependent on secondary school requirements, educational programs within work situations, other and perhaps much more needed efforts in the field of educational development.

I would like to raise several specific issues regarding the development

1. See, for example, the model described by Michael P. Todaro and colleagues in *Education and Development Reconsidered: The Bellagio Conference Papers,* ed. F. Champion Ward (New York: Praeger, 1974), pp. 204–13.

of universities in the Third World, issues that I believe will ultimately bear on the matter of international support and cooperation. I do so primarily in an attempt to examine critically some theses that appear to loom large in the discussion of university development in the Third World.

The major problem I see in most of the thinking about the development of universities in the Third World is that it puts these institutions in a category of their own and looks at their development in ways that differ substantially from how university development in Europe and North America has been conceived.

Battles have been fought and continue to be fought in the Western world over the autonomy of institutions of higher education vis-à-vis the institutions and interests of the state. Safeguards for the independence of the internal decision-making process in both private and public institutions of higher education have been skillfully developed and are being jealously guarded in the face of such threats as increasing reliance on government funding, taxpayers' concern over the rate of return on public expenditure in higher education, and downright interference in academic and personnel matters by boards that are supposedly set up to protect universities from such interference.

At the same time, the university in developing countries appears to be assessed with a different kind of measure. Autonomy, considered an indispensable condition for the exercise of the academic vocation at the Stanfords, Oxfords, and Heidelbergs, is considered more or less a luxury which developing countries in their "struggle for development" can ill afford. In the industrialized countries, the mismatch between the production of both knowledge and graduates is considered a worthwhile price for the academy's freedom from outside control and direction. In the case of universities in developing countries, such control and direction seem to be widely accepted as prerequisites for the most effective mobilization of higher education resources in the country's overall development strategy. Indeed, there even seems to be a tendency to look favorably at the increasingly frequent phenomenon of governments' bypassing existing higher education structures and setting up parauniversity institutions of the "development academy" type, where research and training can be much more closely geared to the state's development priorities.

This same dual standard appears to prevail in university teaching and research functions. Most of the European and North American universities I know would react indignantly to the suggestion that their policies of recruitment, enrollment, and graduation should be guided by externally developed projections of the country's manpower needs. Such restrictions as have lately been introduced in the enrollment practices of Western universities are confined to drawing the inescapable conclusions from existing limitations in study facilities (as with the *numerus clausus* in the Federal Republic of Germany) or from a shrinking academic job market (as in the Ph.D. social science and humanities programs in the United States). Yet in Western or international thinking about the Third World universities, it has been almost axiomatic that their development be governed closely by the kind of manpower projections that (with less rather than more accuracy) have been developed for a country's economic future. Accepting students according to their talents and intellectual passions (a highly cherished feature of European higher education) has been subsumed under the notion of "education for consumption" as distinct from the much more development-relevant "education for production."

The same double standard, I contend, also prevails in the field of research. Even though the time-honored tenet that academic research shall be unencumbered by considerations of utility and necessity is undergoing some revision in the universities of Europe and North America, it is still considered to be an important ingredient in the identity of Western academic institutions. By contrast, again, this principle is much less taken for granted in the case of institutions in the developing countries where "development needs" are construed as closely limiting the academics' choice of how they wish to spend their research energies and resources. Indeed, one question commonly raised in connection with "evaluating" the performance of universities in developing countries concerns the extent to which they have lived up to their role as suppliers of "development relevant" knowledge and skills. In discussions of university development in Europe and North America, this question, as far as I can see, has until very recently been conspicuous by its absence.

These few points simply highlight my concern about the tendency for Western "experts," in discussions of higher education in developing countries, to apply a perspective that varies markedly from that widely used for systems of higher education in the developed countries. Perhaps my work in the context of the heavily political discussion on the future of international cooperation in the field of education has made me overly sensitive to anything that may look like a double standard. It may well be, however, that political and intellectual leaders in the Third World find such a double standard as another ground for accusing bilateral and multilateral assistance agencies of engaging in new and subtle forms of cultural paternalism. I argue therefore for a major, deliberate effort on the part of everybody concerned to arrive at a common standard for the evaluation of whether or not an institution of higher education does its job well. As long as we are willing to accept constraints on universities in developing countries which we are not prepared to impose on our own universities, we face a credibility problem that even considerable funds in aid will do little to resolve.

Effectiveness of International Organizations in Higher Education

Public and Private Organizations: Their Differing Roles

KENNETH W. THOMPSON

LET ME SET OUT the assumptions that underlie my discussion. I believe that the large public international organization is subject to pressures unknown to private bodies. It must satisfy constituents who have their own constituencies. It can go so far but no further in analysis and criticism. It lives by certain dogmas and legitimacy myths which rise and fall in public favor. Its essential strengths, which are not inconsiderable, also encompass its weaknesses. It is by far the largest actor in the realm of education around the world, but has to meet the conditions for such large-scale funding. It must run to stand still, add staff to maintain staff, select personnel on the basis of national and regional quotas rather than strictly on merit, balance its ticket, change for the sake of change, spend much to be given much, ride the whirlwind of public opinion, and promise more than it can deliver.

The sympathetic observer, then, viewing the role of large public international organizations in higher education is caught up in a paradox. While they perform an indispensable role and must be preserved, they are also victims of their own limitations. On the one hand, the worldwide character and growing interdependence of science and learning invite international cooperation. Because knowledge is the patrimony of humanity—not of nations—advancement moves along a common front, drawing on the resources of all, not alone on the power and special privileges of the few. The late Raymond Fosdick, writing in 1941, saw this clearly, for to him internationalism in war no less than in peace had a wholly practical basis. No one nation monopolized scientific discovery, and new knowledge of basic human needs led men to seek help from one another, whatever their nationality or ideology. He wrote:

> An American soldier wounded on a battlefield in the Far East owes his life to the Japanese scientist Kitasato, who isolated the bacillus of tetanus. A Russian soldier saved by a blood transfusion is indebted to Landsteiner, an Austrian. A German soldier is shielded from typhoid fever with the help of a Russian, Metchnikoff. A Dutch marine in the East Indies is protected from malaria because of an Italian, Grassi, while a British aviator in North Africa escapes death from surgical infection because of a Frenchman, Pasteur.[1]

Nor in peace is the pattern any different for:

> Our children are guarded from diphtheria by what a Japanese and a German did; they are protected from smallpox by an Englishman's work; they are saved from rabies because of a Frenchman; they are cured of pellagra through the researches of an Austrian.[2]

From birth to death, we are surrounded by a host of invisible forces that serve and protect us and know no national boundaries. Can there be a more convincing statement of the need for internationalism in science and learning?

On the other hand, contributions to education by large, long-established, well-recognized public international organizations—given the scale and magnitude of their efforts—have been surprisingly modest. International bodies have, for the most part, not earned the full allegiance or respect of the scholarly community. They have produced few Nobel Prize laureates.[3] Their hallmark has been recurrent seminars and discussions, far-flung travel by short-term consultants, and a flood of papers and reports, few of which have had lasting influence. Public international organizations suffer from chronic bureaucratic illnesses: staffs whose most distinguishing characteristic has been quantity not quality, heavy turnover and rotation, serious political constraints, and more talk and planning than operational results. Seldom have they enjoyed the same

1. *The President's Review from the Annual Report 1941, The Rockefeller Foundation* (New York: The Foundation), p. 10.

2. Ibid.

3. It may well be said that research and discovery are not the business of international organizations. But why should they not be judged, as are private foundations or the National Science Foundation, by whether they single out and help the institutions that in turn provide for the growth and development of such people? Are they diverted from this search by the flux of program interests, from tube wells to basic education?

degree of independence and freedom as private organizations with international concerns or experienced the advantages of continuity and coherence. They have no "green revolution" to their credit, no transforming programs in public health, and no comprehensive attainments in overall university development.

LIMITATIONS OF INTERNATIONAL ORGANIZATIONS

The paradox, then, is that international cooperation in education is indispensable, but there is little consensus on the means by which this cooperation can be achieved. At least five sets of forces which appear to limit and restrict action indeed warrant study and attention by our best minds.

The first impediment is the state of flux in which international organizations find themselves. New organizations are coming into being; old ones are suffering far-reaching changes. Both new and old are assuming tasks the scale and urgency of which dwarf what has preceded. Thus, the United Nations University is undertaking a worldwide higher education mission that no previous international educational institution envisaged. In its planning, the World Food Council reaches beyond all earlier endeavors in international agricultural cooperation, whether by the U.N. Food and Agriculture Organization or the Consultative Group growing out of the Bellagio Conferences of donor agencies or through the far-reaching programs of individual private and public organizations such as the Ford and Rockefeller Foundations and the U.S. Agency for International Development. Similarly, the United Nations Environment Programme, under the direction of Maurice Strong, has eclipsed earlier organized international approaches to environmental problems.

No one reviewing the list of new international programs can believe that the work of the older international institutions is completed. The tasks are too great, the problems too numerous. The emergence of dynamic new bodies should come as no surprise: "new occasions bring new duties," and history throws up new organizations for coping with persistent problems. Viewing the landscape of work to be done, one remembers Winston S. Churchill's prudent response to Ernest Bevin in a House of Commons debate: "When there are so few of us and so many of them, we can ill afford to score points on one another." The problems to be faced call for mutual respect, not unending guerrilla warfare. A large amount of sorting out and division of labor lies ahead. It may be overly optimistic to hope that the process will be as free as possible from rancor, infighting, bitterness, and intrigue. Anything less, however, will reinforce the heavy doubts that have been expressed about the capacity of these institutions to serve educational development.

A second factor that complicates the relationship between international organizations and education is the difficulty of pigeonholing education into neat categories or programs. Education as such can neither be simply defined nor be restricted to a handful of international organizations. Almost every major worldwide or regional activity has its educational component: food, population, health, environment. Moreover, the lines of demarcation between education and action are unclear. Those who try to allocate the education expenditures of any international agency, as distinct from operating programs, are familiar with the problem. If the intention is to measure the educational output of international organizations, observers must look essentially at the full range of international agencies, public and private, responding to human need.

A third factor is rooted in the location of the education constituents, which are two steps removed from the international organizations. The genius of education, particularly higher education, at least in certain Western societies, stems from its autonomy. However much of the management and funding of higher education gravitates to the center and however much government budgets for education increase, higher education has preserved an independent status. National governments turn to international organizations for help in higher education, but the help requested is not for projects they themselves or governmental agencies are to carry out directly, as in most environmental or technological fields. The aid—and this makes the difference—is for educational institutions, whether dependent on or independent of their governments. For international organizations, giving this kind of help means funding programs at institutions which must be dealt with at arm's length—through intermediaries, not directly as educators to educators. This distance makes for an uneasy alliance, some uncertainty, and recurrent doubts. Yet both international organizations and educational institutions must learn to live within this relationship and draw on each other's intellectual and material resources without either expecting to dominate.

A fourth factor limiting action arises because the goals and purposes of education around the world are under serious review. The last three decades have been ones of intense activity and expansion throughout the world. Now there is a call for examination and study to make clear what has been done and what remains to be done. Although the task is urgent

and the work long overdue, it fairly bristles with perplexities and difficulties. Few—if any—measuring rods exist for determining effectiveness,
and there is dissension over fundamental aims and purposes. The debate
over the ends of education is illustrated by the controversy that arose
within the Latin American team of the recent Review of Higher Education for Development (HED), a study sponsored by twelve major multilateral and bilateral assistance agencies.[4] One group insisted the goal
should be "the development of education," that is, the building of stronger
and more relevant programs and institutions and, through them, the
training of qualified people. Its members insisted that the building of
cadres of trained professionals must precede development programs. Another group maintained that education must direct itself to society's most
urgent needs, not in some distant future but here and now. It must
answer the question, "Education for what?" by a clear but comprehensive
definition of development. This debate is going on in every educational
forum and restricts the precision with which a review, handicapped by
the absence of any consensus on ends, can measure the effectiveness of
means.

A fifth and final limitation is the position in which public international
agencies find themselves. They are, after all, political bodies and need
constituent support. Apparently it is not enough that they serve the
well-being of mankind in deliberate, long-paced efforts. Their dilemma
may not be as acute as that of one bilateral foreign assistance program
whose task was described as meeting twenty-year needs with two-year
personnel and one-year appropriations. Yet the pressures are the heart of
their problem. Political and economic forces crowd in upon them and
prompt them to claims of unrivaled know-how and prescience, move
them toward positions of sovereignty approaching that of the nation-
state, and can result in a psychology of self-sufficiency which divides the
world into "we" and "they." To survive, they need a clear and well-
perceived identity; to earn their keep, administrative and operational
personnel feel they must prove that no one else can perform international
tasks so well. The drive to protect their turf is compounded by the difficulty and uncertainty of defining or quantifying education compared,

4. The study was conducted by the International Council for Educational Development at the request of a consortium of the twelve large donor organizations. The
ICED, which is funded by grants from foundations and national and international
agencies, was created to serve as a bridge between universities and donor organizations
at work in the field of international education.

say, with agricultural production. (The international agriculture research institutes are alone in being able to point unequivocally to break-throughs.) These are the pressures with which all international agency workers must cope. Devoted supporters no less than mischievous critics must recognize them in considering the role of international organizations in education.

COOPERATIVE PUBLIC-PRIVATE ENDEAVORS

One way out for the public international agency, I suggest, is to couple its strengths with those of the private organization which has international activities and concerns. These two types of international organizations need each other, but more often than not they weaken and detract, each from the other. The time has come when the larger public international organization must, in its own interest, help and encourage the private organization. An analogy is the relationship between the private foundation and the university. Foundations for the most part have not tried to be universities but have given universities the support necessary to do things foundations could not do. Private international organizations are trying, experimentally, to fill the gap between what international organizations can do and what needs doing. In the case of the ICED's HED study, some of the larger agencies drew back in astonishment from the candid criticisms made by developing country educators they had helped, but the criticism was voiced because a private organization gave the educators confidence that they would be listened to. A sense of partnership grew up across north-south boundary lines because the private organization was viewed as a neutral, nonpolitical body whose only purpose was to conduct the study objectively and assure that developing country educators would be freely heard.

THE PROMISE OF INTERNATIONAL ORGANIZATIONS

Roberto Guyer, Under Secretary of the United Nations, has said: "Abandoning international organizations because their internal and external worlds are full of problems is like jettisoning a ship because the seas in which it sails are stormy and turbulent." Quite clearly, the international organizations have entered what Professor Toynbee called "a time of troubles"—more talk of expulsion of members, more use of vetoes from unaccustomed sources, more harsh and bitter language than at any time since the height of the cold war. A recent topic proposed for a discussion meeting graphically portrays the problem: "Can UNESCO survive international politics?" From the beginning, it was illustory to believe that international organizations, as some utopian defenders proclaimed, could exist independent of the play of world politics. It is false to imagine we live in two worlds, one dominated by rivalry, contests for influence, and struggles for power and the other blessed with harmony, rationality, and truth. International organizations are a forum, an arena in which personalities and ideas compete, and a framework for contending principles and groups. There are not two worlds but one, where vaulting ideas, if they are to be realized, must come down to earth.

Yet international agencies, despite their inherent problems, have certain comparative advantages. Within their walls, the strong and the weak, great powers and small, compete on more nearly equal terms. National sensitivities can coexist. Fears and resentment of imperialism and colonialism surface less often, especially when majorities owe their existence to policies of decolonialization. And if a single international organization is less subject to such complaints, a consortium of international agencies can be even freer. The HED study group (of which I was a member) found this increased openness in working with and for a consortium of twelve organizations; my colleagues in agriculture have had similar experiences in working with an even larger consultative group. It is at this point that a unique role for the private international organization can be perceived. It made a substantial difference for agriculture, more than four years ago, that two private foundations with flexibility and freedom to innovate and to commit funds quickly took the lead in drawing others together. In education, the International Council for Educational Development has enjoyed some of these advantages, although without the accompanying leverage of the two foundations.

The case for international organizations working together is best argued from personal experience. As I have traveled the world, I have heard more about what international organizations have not done than what they have done. Almost every international organization suffers from an ambiguous image. The word is out that some are too narrowly political, some too specialized, some infected by constraints of doctrine, some too elitist, and some too populist in their view of things. The way out, I suggest, is to cultivate a more comprehensive image—to combine approaches and doctrines, to exchange the unacceptable image, say, of being merely the world's banker or only the school for training professionals in just one skill a nation needs. By joining forces and combining skills, international organizations can prove they recognize that the problems are many-sided and that they compete with one another on every nation's agenda for the future. It is no longer enough for donor groups to commit themselves to train developers or agronomists or basic educators. They cannot be *for* or *against* higher education, or primary and secondary education, or technical training, because hard-pressed national governments have shortages in every field. The nation's leadership, rather than well-intentioned outsiders, must work out national priorities. For organizations with resources, the best corrective to a universal tendency to impose answers on others is to see the problem whole. Some form of consultative group of international organizations provides the mechanism for pursuing international cooperation on the same broad, complex front that national policy makers must use. The task is far simpler in well-defined sectorial efforts, but the mechanism is not ruled out in spheres as all-inclusive as education.

VALUES IN COOPERATIVE EFFORTS

The promise of international organizations, public and private, lies in their joining efforts and striving to be complementary, not competitive. This statement can be said to ignore a fundamental trait of human nature: men and organizations act not from ideals alone but from self-interest or, in Churchill's telling phrase, "Pride and ambition are the prod of every worthy act." To that I would answer parochial interest is not enough. Worldwide human need is at stake, not American self-interest or the self-interest of any single national or international organization, however powerful and important. In education and development, the challenge to be faced is that of mankind's survival, not any narrow question of national or institutional survival.

Let me draw on four lessons from the HED study, in which I have been engaged, to make this proposition concrete. First, in the twenty-five case studies of selected higher education institutions which contributed significantly to the definition of urgent development needs, no one donor agency emerged as the dominant catalytic agent. (I, for one, had expected a different result.) Thus we found that the World Health Organization and the U.N. Development Program, and somewhat later UNICEF, took the lead along with an outstanding young Cameroon medical scientist, Dr. Monekosso, in bringing to fulfillment an innovative rural health program at the University of Yaoundé. UNESCO joined with the government of Mali to institute a program of higher education lodged in institutes linked with key ministries of government. The Development

Academy of the Philippines, committed to training leaders and studying rural development, land reform, and land settlement, drew on earlier training programs funded by the Ford and Rockefeller Foundations and the U.S. Agency for International Development. An innovative program in rural development in Thailand capitalized on a World Bank loan to Kasetsart University and Rockefeller Foundation assistance to the three participating universities contributing in the fields of agriculture, public health, and the social sciences. A public health program for low-income Colombians inaugurated at the Universidad del Valle (Cali) was helped by the Kellogg and Rockefeller Foundations. The Monterrey Institute of Technology and Advanced Studies in Mexico has received 95–98 percent of its support from local sources, but the Ford, Rockefeller, and Tinker Foundations and AID and the U.N. Food and Agriculture Organization have supplied valuable external assistance. It is tempting to claim unique professional competence for a handful of international organizations in given sectors of education, but the evidence does not support that conclusion.

Second, the time has passed—if it ever existed—when outsiders could speak for the needs and priorities of a particular educational system. In the HED study, we determined "to listen to" the educators from Africa, Asia, and Latin America. The regional leaders whom we selected in turn organized regional teams, picked team members, and chose case study institutions. They were given far greater access than any outsiders could have obtained. Their studies are products of insiders looking out, rather than outsiders looking in. The combination of insiders and a broad-based representative group of international sponsors gives a unique authority to their work.

Third, the studies were free and open inquiries because no single doctrinal position colored the investigations. The work did not start with the assumption that the institutions studied were doing either little or much for their people. The teams represented planners for development, institution builders, and professional specialists. For example, the African participants included a Tanzanian who saw education and social revolution as closely linked, as well as several university vice-chancellors whose major concern was institutional development. The results reflect their diversity. Some emphasize the union of governmental and educational planning while others argue for more independence and separation of the two sectors. The findings, therefore, do not match predetermined monolithic ways of thinking.

Fourth and last, the beginnings of an exciting adventure in mutual education took place, which it would be difficult to overstate. The process was sometimes painful: the intellectual and political differences were all too apparent. The educators from less developed countries learned what was on the minds of the leaders of the international organizations—their changing priorities and what they would and would not do. The agency administrators may, in turn, have heard things, statements made in all candor, from which they had been shielded in the past. It is often difficult for those who seek help to speak freely to those who have the means of helping. A forum is needed which encourages honesty rather than withdrawal or blind confrontation. Existing political forums need to be replaced by forums in which the quiet talk of educators speaking with educators replaces strident political debates. Most of all, the process requires time, patience, and some ongoing effort marked by continuity and responsible thought.

EMPHASIS ON EDUCATION

There is a lesson beyond these four lessons, as Berdyaev spoke of a morality beyond moralities. It is that education is more important than the sum of a collection of problem-oriented educational missions. In dealing with education, all international organizations can be parochial. They tend to believe that the best way to deal with the whole educational and social problem is by concentrating in one sector, whether it be health or agriculture or population. As yet no international agency, public or private, has said unequivocally, in the comprehensive terms of this paper, that "education is our agenda." At present, those who would bring education effectively to the attention of the international organization must mask it under science or manpower training or the welfare of children or the cold war. In every case, the effort must be indirect, justified on grounds other than education in its historical meaning. Is the time approaching when some international organization should address education as such, with its perennial and recurrent problems? In the words of Mr. Soedjatmoko, former Indonesian ambassador to the United States:

> The universities in developing countries should be capable, more effectively than they have been so far, of relating the study of the humanities to both the "little" and the "great" moral questions regarding social purpose and national goals, in a national, regional and global context. These questions must include the search for a more humane society in an increasingly technology-dominated environment, even in the Third World, created by

the pursuit of development goals. This means, in short, the need to strengthen the national capacity for moral reasoning in relation to the development effort.

In addition, the viability of many developing nations on the road of development, as well as their capacity for increased self reliance, will to a large extent depend on the nation's capacity to provide for a meaningful and culturally satisfactory life at what for a long period will inevitably have to be low levels of per capita income. Similarly the social cohesion of these nations will depend on the gradual transformation of traditional social structures into modern communities, in the urban as well as in the rural setting, capable of cultural self-entertainment and enjoyment. The effort to stimulate creative participation in the arts, traditional as well as modern, and to use the communications media towards these ends will also fall to an important extent, on the universities in these developing nations, especially in terms of experimentation.[5]

There is need for a commitment by some international organization to continue the discussions and to further inquiry and study without being bound by the ongoing operations of well-known organized programs of existing international bodies. For the immediate future, an independent private organization may best be able to further the interests of all without promoting the program aims of any one international agency. With these considerations in mind, the Board of Trustees of the International Council for Educational Development has taken two important steps: announced its continuing commitment to higher education for development as a major program interest; and appointed an advisory committee of distinguished educators from developed and developing countries to guide its efforts—leaders such as Sir Eric Ashby, Felippe Herrera, Roberto Santos, Soedjatmoko, Puey Ungphakorn, John Hannah, and the Reverend Theodore Hesburgh.

Without prejudging the directions in which this group of leaders may move, they will undoubtedly urge that conversations be continued between developing country educators and leaders within and outside the international agencies. They will undoubtedly organize forums, particularly in the developing countries, for larger groups of educators to discuss, in depth, the ICED HED reports (three regional reports, twenty-five institutional case studies, and four special studies).[6] They will wish

5. Personal letter to the author, commenting on the ICED study.
6. *Higher Education and Social Change: Promising Experiments in Developing Countries*, vol. 1: *Reports*, ed. Kenneth W. Thompson and Barbara R. Fogel, and vol. 2: *Case Studies*, ed. Kenneth W. Thompson, Barbara R. Fogel, and Helen E. Danner (New York: Praeger, in press).

to consider ways in which the lessons learned can be applied more widely. They may call for studies in other regions or for a few more in-depth studies within the present three regions. Or it may be they will see more urgent needs that have not been foreshadowed by the present work. A common goal for the International Council for Educational Development and similar organizations will be to serve as important resources to the international community, helping to collect and organize facts, sharpening focus and discussion, bringing leaders together, and contributing on the private, independent side to the larger public international effort.

The American University and Its International Relations

RALPH H. SMUCKLER

FOR THE PAST TWENTY YEARS, I have participated actively in the development of international activities at Michigan State University and have observed—from various perspectives—similar developments at other institutions. Our work at MSU preceded the issuance of the 1960 Morrill Committee report, which helped to stimulate the growth of an international dimension throughout American higher education.[1]

The two decades have seen many changes. In the mid-1950s, only a few institutions acknowledged the importance of broad international concerns within higher education. The Ford Foundation's International Training and Research Division (out of existence since the mid-1960s) had yet to make its first major grants. Education and World Affairs and the Overseas Education Service (both organizations now defunct) were not yet created. We had no title vi of the National Defense Act, no National Endowment for the Humanities; in fact, except for the very important Fulbright program, colleges and universities had little federal support for their new international directions. Experience with the predecessors of the Agency for International Development, which supported a wide range of research and institution-building activity abroad, was still in its infancy. Area and other international study centers at American

1. *The University and World Affairs,* A Report by the Committee on the University and World Affairs, J. L. Morrill, chairman (New York: Ford Foundation).

universities were few in number, as also were specialists on Asia, Africa, and other distant, newly "discovered" world areas. Our experience with international associations and relationships with institutions in other societies was meager although a few institutions had long-standing ties with universities in China, western Europe, and other places. The American Council on Education had no Overseas Liaison Committee and was just beginning to define its international interests. In the newly emerging countries, there were few higher education institutions with which we might associate and there were relatively few alumni of American institutions in those countries to whom we could comfortably relate. We were inexperienced in most aspects of international relationships in higher education. We lacked academic commitment to foreign areas and foreign relations except possibly with the more advanced institutions in the large cities of Europe.

Looking back, we have traveled a long way—both literally and figuratively. After twenty years we have had a wide range of international contacts and a depth of experience. In my opinion, American universities are now at a new plateau of international involvement in higher education, a plateau that is potentially downward sloping, but nevertheless far above the plain of international activity and concern that prevailed twenty years ago.

Let me take Michigan State University as an example. Over the years we have worked closely with at least forty or fifty institutions in various regions of the world. At the present time, we have ties with institutions in the United Kingdom, France, Japan, Africa, the Soviet Union, Asia, and Latin America. These ties are in the form of agreements to exchange faculty or students, to provide technical assistance, to participate in joint research activity, or to join in developing programs in the future. We have a Peace Corps Internship Program which sends a good number of our graduates into foreign settings; on campus each year we have more than 1,200 foreign students from eighty-five or more countries and about 150 foreign scholars in one department or another. In addition, we offer opportunities for undergraduate study abroad and a good range of area study programs which reflect a general evolution of courses with increased international emphasis. At any given time, we have forty or more faculty members overseas on university assignments, attending international congresses or consulting within their specialized fields. Above all, the university leadership and many, but not all, faculty members appear to accept that a strong commitment to international concerns and a direction which keeps us in contact with developments in many parts of the world—not just western Europe—are important assets and integral components of the university in 1975.

That Michigan State University is not unique in its array of international concerns became clear to me when, in 1975, I participated in the sixth congress of the International Association of Universities. Many other institutions in this country, as well as in Europe and other regions, have had parallel experience and growth. Discussion at the IAU meetings revealed that universities in most countries are now looking for effective means of cooperating and of establishing links with institutions in other countries. The "plateau" to which I referred is well populated, and universities generally are looking for new modes of working together and advancing the quality and universality of their programs through international cooperation. New directions for international cooperation are clearly being sought and not alone by American institutions.

In this quest, American higher education has entered a new era, an era devoted to mutuality, not tutelage. The IAU meetings and similar gatherings underline mutual benefit as the basis of international cooperation among universities. Each side must gain. For the most part, we are beyond the point of being asked to "give," to help build up institutions or build new institutions in newly emerging countries, although this need is still clearly present in some. We are being led in the direction of acknowledging the need for mutually advantageous relationships, and thus we in the United States should approach international contacts to gain as well as give—as should be the case for our colleagues abroad.

UNIVERSITY PURPOSES IN INTERNATIONAL RELATIONSHIPS

In this new era, therefore, one important question to be considered is, What should *we*—American higher education—expect to gain through international associations, international organization activity, and institutional linkages across national boundaries? It is no longer merely a question of helping others. What can these international associations and the organizations to which academics or academic institutions belong, or to which our nation belongs, be doing for *us?* We can assume that institutions in other countries are asking the same question from their vantage points. Posing the question does not reflect a selfish view of the world. It means knowing our own interest well enough to present it effectively and to lead in directions that will serve our interests, as others are leading in directions to serve other interests. From these efforts, intelligently pursued, will come the broad compromises and relationships based on mutual understanding which can be productive over the years, in ways beneficial for all parties.

Our universities vary greatly, and each should have its own projection of needs and goals as it enters into relationships internationally. The further that needs and goals are generalized, the further they stray from the institutional realities which govern at each campus. Nevertheless, the institutions' commonalities are sufficiently great to project some broad national purposes.

The first, and foremost, reason for pursuing international institutional relationships is to promote a flow of knowledge, which is usually reflected in exchange of materials and, particularly, in movement of scholars. Such movement is crucial to the quality of work in various disciplines within our institutions. Our relationships and associations should somehow facilitate and expand this flow.

A second purpose, one of increasing importance, concerns our ability to perform our defined roles more effectively. Our international relationships should be such that our educational purposes are served: research, teaching, and service programs should become more effective as a result of these associations. Mere access to foreign areas is important. For example, cannot foreign languages be taught and learned more effectively by establishing relationships with institutions in other countries where a given language can be practiced on its home ground? Are our graduate students not more effectively served if they can conduct field research at whatever sites are most appropriate, rather than being limited only to American settings? Is our research and teaching approach to energy and environmental issues not best served through a global framework? There are many other examples. They tend to include an expanding range of disciplines and subjects within our university programs.

A third gain relates to innovation—educational and administrative innovations that apply to the university in general. (Innovation or creativity within a particular field is, of course, served by movement of knowledge or individual scholars.) This third purpose is highly important, but less critical than the first two. The United States is a large country with many institutions, which tend to learn from each other. Nevertheless, they gain from the "spark" of new ideas from abroad, and this purpose ought to be served by international relationships.

A fourth purpose is to reinforce the value status of higher education. Through well-managed, effective international organizations, we can advance the role and image of higher education worldwide, an advance that might be reflected in a broader support within our own society.

If these are the purposes which American higher education seeks to serve through our international relationships, how well are they now being served? My own review suggests that these purposes are being achieved in a very mixed fashion—some well; others, not at all.

The first and most important goal—the expanded flow of knowledge—is the best served, particularly in the natural sciences and in technical fields. International scientific meetings, the widespread distribution of materials and journals in the natural sciences, the visiting scholars and postdoctoral fellows, international seminars in specialized fields—all of these tend to assure us that within these disciplines there is a good flow of knowledge. The situation is far from perfect, however. In many fields of the social sciences, in some professional areas, and in the humanities, there is a great need for a flow of knowledge, which is not now being achieved. As for the other three purposes, the performance is even more questionable. Our international relationships and organizations are not serving us particularly well. Access to foreign settings, for example, is becoming more, not less, difficult. The prestige of higher education is not being enhanced through the actions of its international organizations.

Some Guidelines to International Relationships

If higher education's purposes in international relationships are to be achieved to better effect, we need to make good use of the knowledge we now have about university participation in international associations and linkages. I had an opportunity to reflect on some of these matters during the 1975 International Association of Universities meetings in the Soviet Union. About 900 people from more than 700 institutions and organizations in eighty-four countries participated.

The diverse definitions of *university* are apparent at a large international gathering. The institutions differ greatly in concept, structure, purpose, administration, and relationship to government and society. The very universality of membership in a group such as the IAU lessens the chances of a sustained program effort. Inevitably, programs and process become encumbered by broad generalizations, by national rivalries, by lack of time to delve into issues from several viewpoints, and by the constant problem of communication. Something other than *universal* organizations is needed—whether it be regional groupings of institutions, focus within subject matters, or groupings of similarly committed universities. I urge the last.

Along the same line, the trend toward specialization and the strong disciplinary forces within universities suggest that institutional linkages should be designed to reflect the same forces. Rather than university participation, departmental or disciplinary participation in international conferences and in international linkages might prove effective. Meetings such as the broad, universal sessions of the IAU are useful if held about once in five years. Meetings of sociologists or biophysicists or linguists should occur more often. Beyond this device, interinstitutional linkages along department or college lines should be encouraged. "University linkage" should mean and strive to expand department or college ties. University ties should facilitate interchange among specific groups within the universities.

A new element in international intellectual cooperation is the United Nations University. Its program, however, is not yet sufficiently defined to contribute fully to American higher education's development of ideas about its own international cooperative needs. Several years from now, the UNU should be a force of genuine value to university programs.

At the IAU meetings, nation identification was emphasized, and even the participants' name tags identified the country but not the institution represented. UNESCO and other international organizations are governmentally sponsored, and their dealings with higher education institutions reflect a constant awareness of national identities. As we Americans associate internationally, I hope that we can maintain our institutional identities, which reflect the pluralism of our higher education system. The alternative is to move toward participation in international relations through our institutions in a carefully structured framework under the national aegis. Emphasis on nation identity will not be easy to avoid, but some balance is certainly needed.

Inevitably, at the Moscow gathering, the universities reflected their national ideologies. Most of the institutions appeared to be identified with the goals of planned economies and therefore they emphasize training of technical manpower and specialist scientific personnel rather than broad educational goals. They will seek access to our advanced scientific settings. But our American institutions will have difficulty in establishing *mutually beneficial* ties with these institutions unless in our negotiations we have some clear ideas about what our universities want to gain as well as to give.

As we proceed, all of these factors and others as well must be taken into account. Diversity of definition, trends toward specialization, the new United Nations University, and national differences are all ingredients in the new design. At the IAU meetings, it was clear that universities today are jealous of their "sovereign" equality, that is, their individual need to be considered as equal. This factor is an extremely important part of the formula. This feeling prevails even though *inequality* in a reservoir of talent or accomplishment exists in reality. This need for equality in spite of inequality in academic strength adds to the delicacy of negotiated relationships and argues strongly for taking a long-term view.

Steps are being taken in the United States to pave the way for a new initiative in this country for establishing higher education relationships, in the form of a new association named the Association for International Cooperation in Higher Education and Research (AICHER). Its aim would be to serve American higher education internationally, to lead toward new forms of working on the international scene, and to assist in negotiating institutional linkages and forming new bridges to institutions in other countries. The new association would serve as the entry point for institutions abroad which want to relate to American universities in mutually desired ways. A study is being launched to examine new ways of working internationally. It will include a series of seminars, meetings with institutional leaders here and in other countries, gathering of data on institutional cooperation and other activities that should measure views and test the feasibility of new arrangements and, indeed, whether other means which already exist will be more appropriate and should be encouraged.[2]

The review comes at a good time. Some of the trends referred to earlier, including the beginning of the new United Nations University, will serve as backdrops against which the review can take place. There were many statements at the IAU congress about the need for greater international cooperation among universities, a thought conveyed over and over at the meetings, both formally and informally. Although the Russians were referring to it as "the spirit of Helsinki," the idea does seem to be a persistent and basic value held by universities in general and by institutions from most regions. In my judgment, this attitude provides us with a genuine opportunity to realize our needs as others achieve theirs.

2. For a fuller discussion of the proposed organization—its background, aegis, and study of structure and aims—see "Association for International Cooperation in Higher Education and Research," by Glen L. Taggart, in the present volume.

Functions for International Organizations in Higher Education

DRAGOLJUB NAJMAN

WHENEVER THE EFFECTIVENESS of international higher education organizations is discussed, the first question raised is, Should international organizations play any role in higher education? The question is neither academic nor rhetorical. International organizations, by definition, can deal either with questions that concern the international *intergovernmental* community or with those that are raised by members of international *nongovernmental* organizations. In the field of higher education, the latter category includes the universities themselves, students' and teachers' associations, and similar groups. UNESCO is an international intergovernmental organization that has close and extensive contacts with the international nongovernmental community through the network of nongovernmental organizations associated with it in a variety of relationships. UNESCO's status being thus defined, we face two questions. First, does the subject of higher education come within UNESCO's terms of reference? Second, do those who are involved in one way or another with higher education want UNESCO to deal with their concerns?

Higher education has only recently emerged as one of the major problems on which world attention has focused. For example, UNESCO was created thirty years ago to deal with problems of education in the world, but until about ten years ago it had no meaningful program concerned with *higher* education. In effect, the governments of UNESCO's member states, which determine the organization's program, came to feel only recently that higher education was a subject to be studied, discussed, and developed through international cooperation. Given this situation, how could one discuss the effectiveness of international organizations whose constituent members had not felt that they should be dealing with problems of higher education?

This question raises another question. How can an intergovernmental organization deal with problems of higher education when its point of contact at the national level is usually the ministry of foreign affairs or

This paper is submitted by the author in his personal capacity and is not intended to represent the views of UNESCO.

ministries of education that often have a limited influence on higher education institutions? A further question is often asked: Can technical and professional aspects of a program of an international and intergovernmental organization be kept separate from some of the political problems that are often discussed in general conferences or assemblies of international organizations? Both questions require candid answers.

In my view, international organizations, and especially intergovernmental organizations, should confine their activities in higher education to those problems that, by definition, bridge frontiers; that is, they should take up only those questions that can best be answered or treated by international cooperation, by international exposure, through international methods of comparison. In these cases, the international (more specifically, intergovernmental) organizations deal with governments (more specifically, ministries of foreign affairs or ministries of education), and the dealings constitute no serious obstacle either to international cooperation in the field of higher education or to activities of international organizations related to problems of higher education. In practice, at assemblies, general conferences, and meetings where governments are represented, if the discussions pertain to higher education, the government representatives are usually specialists in the field of higher education or administrators and managers of systems of higher education.

As for the relationships between professional and political concerns, I think that, just as it is impossible at the national level to consider problems of higher education in isolation from political, social, and economic concerns, the same applies, *mutatis mutandi,* to the discussion or analysis of problems related to higher education at the international level. International cooperation in general cannot be conceived to be purely professional and technical because in the world of interdependence all aspects of social, political, economic, and educational life are closely interlinked. In particular, the role that higher education plays in the economic, social, and political development of all countries is so important that no rational person can isolate educational developments from any given set of social, economic, and political conditions. At the same time, although the political aspects play a major role in international cooperation, international cooperation cannot be confined to political objectives. Therefore, higher education, with its growing impact on national development around the world, appears increasingly to be an area in which international cooperation is considered not only desirable but also necessary.

"Systems" of Higher Education

Before pursuing further the possible role and effectiveness of international organizations in higher education, one should ask what is happening at the national level and whether higher education actually exists as a system in the various countries. There is, of course, no universal answer to the question. For a variety of reasons, there is a tendency at the national level to create and develop educational systems, and this tendency influences the development of higher education as systems. This world tendency nonetheless meets serious resistance in many countries and in many universities for reasons that are perhaps understandable but that will be difficult to overcome, no matter what the general tendency is.

Universities have not yet overcome what I call their "original sin." They are supposed to play a crucial role on the late twentieth-century stage, yet they are still heavily encumbered by the medieval mores that gave them birth. Born in feudal societies where artisan production prevailed, universities adapt themselves only with great difficulty to the ever-changing dynamics of contemporary production systems and social structures.

Their medieval origin still marks, for example, the relationship between students and teachers and between teachers and knowledge. The teacher-student relationship is still largely modeled on priest-layman or master-disciple relations, whereby the one is entrusted with "revealing" the truth or the dogma to the other. This relationship can be illustrated in brief: in most higher education institutions, teachers still require the students to prove at examinations that they have digested and assimilated the pronouncements of the teachers, whether delivered from the lectern or the pages of a text. As for the second relationship, that of teachers and knowledge, one cannot help comparing the Ph.D.'s of today and the ceremonies which conditioned membership in craft guilds in the Middle Ages. Today in the university hierarchy, the person without a Ph.D. knows that only on the day he is invested with the doctoral gown and certificate will he obtain all the rights, privileges, and immunities of the university establishment—above all, the supreme right of becoming a university teacher, a full-fledged member of that all-powerful modern guild.

I realize that when anyone starts discussing the evolution of the modern feudal fortresses called universities into up-to-date systems of higher education, many teachers invoke the concept of autonomy. In my recent book on autonomy, I said,

> The independent nature of higher education historically has certainly played a positive role; it has allowed the development of science and research and has often given rise to training protected from outside pressure. This is now, however, a part of the past. The present system cannot insist upon such liberty and the following question can, in fact, be asked: in respect to what does a university today require autonomy? If it is with regard to the government, then we have seen and probably will see in the future that today the government has sufficient means to limit, in practice, an autonomy that is even legally recognized. If it is with regard to society, then we wonder if higher education can really be independent in relation to those who support, pay for and finance it. Can the institutions, then, claim an autonomy in relation to the labour market? No more so because, on the contrary, they ought to try by every possible means to tighten the existing links with those who have an influence on the labour market and who use the finished products of "higher education." If sovereignty is required in the name of freedom of research, we can, rightly, ask the question why it is not granted to all similar institutions existing in all countries, which often obtain results far superior to those obtained at universities.
>
> If we wish to orient ourselves in the direction of a reform which will result in the creation of a true system of higher education in each country, then the concept of autonomy for each of these institutions must be given up for the benefit of a system in which the objective will be, not the quest for an extra-territoriality, henceforth obsolete, but of a grafting into the social fabric of each country.[1]

I realize that my opinion on the subject is far from being shared by all the interested parties and, without attempting to analyze the wide variety of opinions existing throughout the world, I will quote two American authors. In the early 1970s, James Perkins, in "The Drive for Coordination," wrote that "the traditional independence and autonomy of [higher educational] institutions [in the United States] is giving way to state or national coordinating bodies."[2]

However, in 1974, John D. Millett wrote in support of financial independence for higher education: "It seems to me that *if we do not want a national system of higher education* [emphasis added], we would do well to confine our financial expectations for federal government as-

---

1. *L'enseignement supérieur, pour quoi faire?* (Paris: Fayard, 1974), p. 167.
2. In *Higher Education: From Autonomy to Systems*, ed. James A. Perkins and Barbara Baird Israel (New York: International Council for Educational Development, 1972), p. 3.

sistance to two primary areas of activity: the financing of student access to higher education and the support of research."[3]

To say that there are as yet no national systems of higher education and that, consequently, it is difficult to conceive of an international or world system of higher learning, is not to say that there are no international or world problems affecting higher education. The years 1967–69 witnessed a world crisis of education and especially in higher education. The consequences of that crisis are still being felt.

Therefore we can legitimately ask whether we should wait for another world crisis before concluding that there is a need to conceive of higher education as a system. Incidentally, every crisis is not necessarily violent. In the field of education our concepts have been somewhat biased by the happenchance that, no sooner did the word "crisis" appear in the excellent and still absolutely up-to-date analysis made by Phillip Coombs and submitted to the Williamsburg Conference in 1967,[4] than we witnessed an outbreak of violence on the campus.

WORLD PROBLEMS FACING HIGHER EDUCATION

To my mind, the concept of educational crisis has, most unfortunately, too often been linked to the violent external manifestations of the crisis. The crisis, as illustrated by the financial difficulties of higher education institutions in many countries today, may be relatively nonviolent, but still extremely serious. The financial problems of higher education are important, but represent only one of the international, if not global, problems facing higher education.

Another problem facing higher education—one that to my mind holds much greater significance—is the quantitative growth of higher education. Let me quote again from my recent book:

> I would now like to proceed further and try to predict for the next 20 years the evolution of the student population by a careful examination of the last two decades. In 1950, there were in the world 6,317,000 higher education students, less than 3% of the population between the ages of 20 and 24. In 1960, with 11,174,000, this number had nearly doubled, thus reaching, 10 years later, 6% of the population between the ages of 20 and 24. In 1965, 18,007,000 were counted, representing 6.8% of the same age group of the population. Finally, in 1970, the corresponding figures were 26,065,000 and 11% . . .

3. "Institutional Accountability," *Management Forum*, April 1974, p. 4.
4. *The World Educational Crisis: A Systems Analysis* (New York, London, Toronto: Oxford University Press, 1968).

. . . if one takes into account the fact that the growth of the student population throughout the world for the years 1965 to 1970 was at a yearly rate of 7.7%, it becomes simple to establish, with a high likelihood of accuracy, what their total number will be in the years to come. For 1975, it is estimated at about 38,000,000 and at some 11% of the population within the 20 to 24 age group.

It is interesting to note that in 1950 there were 38,040,000 secondary students and to draw, with 25 years hindsight, all the lessons which such a numerical equivalence implies. First of all, let us examine the secondary education figures. In 1950: 38,040,000 in the world; in 1960: almost 69,000,000; in 1965: more than 93,700,000; in 1970 (the last year for which exact figures exist): 113,197,000. If we now compare these statistics with the development of higher education and with the forecast which I have attempted to make, one comes again to very significant conclusions. Thus the 7.7% growth rate of higher education leads us, in 1980, to over 54 million students; in 1985 to 79,130,000 and finally, in 1990, to 115 million.

These figures are interesting because one can easily conclude from them that if in 1970 we had just over 113,000,000 secondary school students, there is every chance that in 1990, i.e. in 20 years' time, we will have 115 million higher education students, who represent more than 25% of the total population in the 20 to 24 age group.[5]

This quantitative growth of higher education will not, of course, follow the same pattern in every country. But, on the whole, I think my projections may be low and that we may see much more rapid growth.

The word "interdependence" has recently acquired such status that it is difficult to imagine the world of today without it. It has become a fashionable word because it says what it should say and accurately describes the situation in a variety of fields—energy, civil aviation, meteorology, control of infectious diseases. Interdependence will increasingly become the key word in fields like employment and population. To come closer to higher education concerns, I submit that interdependence is *an acknowledged fact* in the field of economic development and relationships (regardless of the difficulties involved). Interdependence is certainly a *recognized need* in the field of scientific research, as evidenced by the growing number of joint international research programs. But interdependence in the field of training highly qualified personnel is *an idea* yet to be recognized even as a project, despite the glaring need in this shrinking world for exchange and movement of highly trained personnel.

5. *L'enseignement supérieur*, pp. 67–68.

For brevity's sake, let me put aside other important functions of universities and other higher education institutions and address the single function that I consider to be essential, that is, the training of highly qualified people who will be working, but above all *living,* in tomorrow's societies. Here, too, we must radically change our conceptual approach to what is and what should be the *content* of higher education. A year ago I wrote: "If, within the different educational systems, and particularly at the higher education level, we consider today that 80% of time is devoted to the transmission of knowledge and 20% to the acquisition of learning and research methodologies, it becomes clear that this ratio should change radically in the future. I would even go so far as to imply that it must be inverted."[6]

Now I shall go a step further. In an unchanging society, there is little difference between the past, the present, and the future. Therefore, for long periods of time, higher education institutions could be content with training people for tomorrow by teaching them about what was happening yesterday. In slowly changing societies, tomorrow looks much like today, and, again, too many universities are more than satisfied if they train people for tomorrow by studying, analyzing, and doing research on what is happening today.

But today's era is one of fast and telescoping development in the sciences and in technology. Moreover, for better or for worse, basic social values are changing at the same speed. Therefore, higher education institutions, national systems of higher education, and, I venture to say, the international system of higher education to be, all will have to come to terms with what should be the content of education and training in higher education institutions designed to prepare people for tomorrow. The task is far from easy. Therefore I submit that we need not only national and international systems, but also international cooperation among the best brains capable of imagining the alternative futures for which higher education institutions should prepare people.

Let me not be misunderstood on one aspect of higher education that I consider as extremely important. Although I advocate an international or world system, in my view this world system cannot exist without being based on national systems of higher education that are firmly rooted in the socioeconomic circumstances of the countries they are supposed to serve. In a national education system, higher education is an

6. Ibid., p. 62.

integral component and also the apex because it trains all those who are active in the system, is often in charge of designing the curricula, and so on. This being said, there is a vast area of problems and issues that can profit from international cooperation but also in which, often, no progress can or will be achieved until international cooperation becomes a routine fact of life.

I mentioned the financial difficulties confronting higher educational institutions. I believe that while many solutions can be found inside national systems of higher education, many others will require international cooperation. For example, it will probably become necessary to move much further in developing educational technologies such as computer-assisted instruction for institutions of higher learning. Some programs, for instance, would probably be economically feasible only through international cooperation.

The quantitative growth of higher education, noted above, will certainly require much greater mobility of both graduates and teachers. This development, in turn, will necessitate much greater efforts to establish the comparability and equivalence of university degrees. Although there seems to be an overall consensus on this point, the resistance must not be underrated. Despite some results achieved through international organizations, nonacademic circles are becoming impatient, for easily understandable reasons. The recent Helsinki Conference on Security and Cooperation in Europe, in its Final Act signed by heads of state and governments of the whole of Europe, plus the United States and Canada, recommended to the appropriate international organizations that "they should intensify their efforts to reach a generally acceptable solution to the problems of comparison and equivalence between academic degrees and diplomas."

I have mentioned a number of problems linked to the content of higher education, many of which, I think, can be solved only through international cooperation.

THE ROLE AND WORK OF INTERNATIONAL ORGANIZATIONS

Since international organizations have increased their attention to problems of higher education, it is appropriate to ask whether they have adequate contacts with educators, professors, university administrators, and private and public institutions dealing with problems of higher education at national, regional, and even local levels. International organizations have tried to establish those links and also to develop them as they expand their programs in the field of higher education. On the personal level, there are a great number of contacts between the staff members of international organizations (usually termed secretariats) and educators, professors, and administrators of higher education institutions. Contacts are also developed in other forums through which international organizations work. A few examples will be useful. Major problems are usually submitted to expert committees composed of persons in the categories cited above. Some international organizations have at times created consultative committees to advise them on their programs in the fields of higher education, and persons so appointed are directly engaged in higher education activities. Finally, associations acting in consultative status with international organizations—particularly *intergovernmental* international organizations—bring the voices of the academic community and of administrators of public and private institutions concerned with problems of higher education to the attention of governing bodies of international organizations.

The international organizations—both governmental like UNESCO, the United Nations University, the Organization for Economic Cooperation and Development, the Council of Europe, the Council for Mutual Economic Assistance, and nongovernmental like the International Association of Universities and regional associations of universities—already exist. The cooperation among them is extremely good: there are many examples of joint meetings, projects, and activities, and consultations among them on problems of higher education are permanent and almost daily occurrences. Each has accumulated knowledge and experience in its own field, and, with the emergence of higher education as a world problem, each has been involved in numerous activities in that field. Collectively, they represent an infrastructure able to respond to changing needs and constitute an essential instrument for the further development of higher learning. But their effectiveness should not be fully judged until they are allowed to deal with key problems of higher education today for which, to my mind, solutions can be found only through international cooperation.

I shall summarize types of activities in which international organizations have been involved and which may become major areas where the organizations can play an effective, sometimes crucial role.

Normative activities. International organizations have in the past attempted to establish some basic norms as guidelines for development of universities and other institutions of higher learning. As international cooperation increases, it is imperative that normative activities of the international organizations—especially intergovernmental international organizations—be given greater emphasis. One obvious normative activity is the elaboration of international conventions on the comparability and equivalencies of university degrees, an area in which international organizations—especially UNESCO—have been active in the past. One example is the recently adopted convention on comparability and equivalencies of university degrees for Latin America. Other subjects that will soon call for international cooperation and the establishment of international criteria and norms will include the status of university teachers and of part-time university lecturers and professors.

Comparative studies. Decision makers at national levels and at the level of higher education institutions are finding increasing need to make comparisons with similar systems or institutions in other countries. The most efficient way to gather the kinds of information needed—on the status and development of higher education as a system—is through the international organizations. Among the decision maker's essential tools are comparative studies on the costs of higher education, on curricula, on methods used at institutions and in departments, on the average length of studies in various countries, on the number of dropouts from universities. Comparative studies by international organizations, it appears, are activities that can advantageously be further developed.

Dissemination of information. International organizations, by their nature, are repositories of information from many sources and also are the best equipped entities to disseminate the data brought to their attention. Currently, there is both an overabundance of unsystematized information and a lack of clear presentations on specific subjects. The international organizations should assume an important role in higher education by delivering well-organized information to all those who are interested in a given subject.

Neutral meeting grounds. As a singular service, international organizations have provided opportunities where persons in charge of national systems of higher education can compare and discuss their experiences acquired in the systems. UNESCO, for example, organized the fruitful first and second conferences of ministers of education of European countries, at which the *only* subject of discussion was the development of higher education in the European member states of the organization. But exchange of information and experiences should not be the only goal of such gatherings. As already indicated, some areas will require not only exchange of information and experience at the international level, but also some form of joint action in order to overcome the problems that higher education is facing in the different parts of the world.

Cooperation for development. A final essential task of international organizations in the field of higher education lies in development—for many years called "assistance." Higher education is now a worldwide phenomenon. Indisputably, some universities and some systems of higher education are more highly developed than others, just as some countries are more developed or less developed than others. Assistance to the less developed systems and institutions of higher education will continue to constitute important work for international organizations.

We in the international education community are overcoming the concept of "assistance." We are moving into an era of cooperation in which international organizations should help establish links between systems of higher learning and between institutions of higher education so that they may help each other and also achieve through cooperation the common objectives of the academic community.

· 4 ·

Higher Education and the Food Crisis

*Applying American Science and Technology
in Developing Countries*

DALE E. HATHAWAY

As THE WORLD FOOD CONFERENCE opened in Rome in November 1974, there were numerous well-publicized statements that millions would die of starvation before the 1975 harvest was available. But widespread famine did not occur in 1975; and if the supplies are distributed equitably, major famine is unlikely during the 1975–76 crop year. However, the predictions of 1974 could be realized in some year immediately ahead and are highly probable unless the world, including the higher education community in the United States, takes immediate steps to deal with the problems involved in what is commonly known as the "world food crisis."

In the 1960s, the world, and especially Americans, became largely complacent about food supplies. This complacency was not shared by millions who have never enjoyed an adequate diet and have always lived in the margin of inadequate food supplies. However, plenitude was the perception of most of the world's leaders and of most of the informed public, including those in higher education. Indeed, as the 1970s opened, a psychology of surplus prevailed in developed and developing countries alike. In the developed countries it was caused by the chronic surplus capacity of our high-technology agriculture, and in the developing countries it was the promise of "Green Revolution."

Until the early 1970s, the world food situation did appear to most informed observers to be well under control. Production of grains—the foundation of the food supply for most of the world's population—rose almost every year from 1960 to 1972, interrupted only by poor crops in

63

the U.S.S.R. in 1961 and 1963 and the great Indian drought in the mid-1960s. This steady growth in world output occurred despite large-scale production control programs in the United States.

As background, one must remember the importance of grains as a measure of world food supply. Except in the poorest parts of the developing world, where starchy root crops are the staple diet, grains in one way or another are crucial as a source of the world's food supply. In the poor countries the grains are consumed directly as human food, supplemented by modest quantities of meat, poultry, and fish. In the richer countries only a small portion of grains are consumed directly, and most are fed to meat-producing and dairy animals and to poultry. The products derived from these sources are the major elements in the diet in rich countries. The events that affect grain supplies and prices create a feeling of crisis or confidence about food supplies among rich and poor countries alike.

Demand for Grain

Two factors affect the demand for grains: population growth and income growth. Each needs some examination.

The world's population is about four billion at present. Nearly three-fourths of these people live in the developing countries, and, of these, half live in Asia. The population of the developed world is only a little over one billion persons. In the developing world, the population growth rate is about 2.5 percent a year; in the developed world, about 0.8 percent a year. Thus *each year there are eighty million more people to feed and over seventy million of them are in the developing countries.*

If all of the world's growing population consumed grain at a rate of 180 kilograms per capita annually, as did the population of the developing countries during their years of highest consumption (1969–71), an additional output of about 15 million metric tons of grain would be needed annually just to keep up with current population growth. But, in the developed world in 1972 the consumption was 550 kilograms per capita, and in the United States it was 850 kilograms per capita (four and one-half times that in the developing world in 1967–71). Thus in the early 1970s the population growth in the *developed* world required another five million tons of grain annually to maintain its high consumption levels. For the world merely to sustain its consumption patterns at the beginning of the decade required an annual increase in output of over 20 million tons. And as the population base grows, this figure increases.

But population is not the only factor. In the world economy, generally there has been a slow but steady growth in per capita income, and with it comes a rise in the demand for food. (The years 1974 and 1975, when most of the world's population has been suffering a loss of real income, do not represent typical years.) In the poor countries and among the poorest in all countries, as income increases, the proportion of additional income spent on food is relatively high. Thus increased affluence adds to the demand for grains. In the poor countries, as people grow wealthier, they eat more grain directly and increasingly shift to more meat, dairy, and poultry products. In the wealthier countries, as incomes rise, the consumption of poultry and red meat rises.

If calculations allow for a modest rise in income in addition to population growth, one can easily project an increase of nearly 3 percent a year in food output needed to meet world demand without a sharp increase in food prices. And a 3 percent rise annually means food production must rise by nearly 30 million tons per year and double every twenty-three years.

In general, the world did not do badly in keeping up with the increase in demand from 1950 to 1970. World food output increased by 0.75 percent per capita per year, about 1.5 percent in the developed countries and about 0.5 percent in the developing countries. But this increase was not enough. The U.N. Food and Agriculture Organization estimated that in 1974 there were at least 400 million persons whose food intake was too low to maintain their health. These people suffered from malnutrition if not from the starvation so widely predicted. World food production had kept pace with world consumption increases until 1970. The great Indian drought and the corn blight in the United States in 1970 slowed the growth in world output in some years, but since the United States had huge stocks of grain accumulated under previous price support programs, these stocks could be drawn upon to meet the deficit between production and expanding demand.

Then in 1972 a nearly unprecedented event occurred in world crop production. Adverse weather in the Soviet Union, Asia, and Africa occurred simultaneously, and world grain production dropped by nearly 40 million metric tons. In comparison, in the preceding year production had increased by nearly 85 million tons and over the previous decade had increased by an average of 28 million tons per year. As a result of this decline and the Russian decision to purchase from U.S. markets, world stocks, largely held by the United States, plummeted. By the beginning of 1973 grain stocks were down to 10 percent of annual consumption and prices began to rise, sharply in the United States and wildly in some of the food-deficit developing countries.

In 1973 world production recovered, with over half the increase in the United States and the U.S.S.R., but still output only balanced consumption and stocks were not rebuilt. Then in 1974 catastrophe struck again. World output declined again in 1974 by more than 50 million tons, with the decline largely in the United States and the U.S.S.R. By fall 1974, grain prices were at record levels and climbing, the United States had de facto export controls, and no significant reserve stocks were available in the non-Communist world to draw upon. The developing countries, buffeted by high fuel prices, fertilizer shortages, and inadequate grain supplies, were frightened, and rightfully so. Some, like India and Bangladesh, faced severe shortages if not starvation for portions of their population. India and several other developing countries used precious foreign exchange to buy high-priced food grains, and thereby set back their development plans for years. Concessionary food aid, which had been ample when food was available and low priced, was sharply reduced; and the largest source of such aid, the United States, refused to commit its food aid in late 1974 when it was most needed. While the world was waiting for the U.S. government to act, some of the developing countries and especially India bought in world commercial markets. As a result of the combination of these purchases and the eventual increase in food aid, most of the developing countries scraped through early 1975. No major famine developed.

Now the end of the 1975 crop production season is near, and, again, largely as a result of adverse crop conditions in the U.S.S.R. and in parts of western and eastern Europe, grain consumption will again about equal current production.

The most optimistic projections for world production for the 1975–76 crop year are somewhere under 1,300 million metric tons for all grains. That is about the 1973–74 level and well below the trend line of the last decade. Assuming that the Soviets get a major portion of the supplies necessary to maintain their livestock herds, there will be little or no rebuilding of world stocks, and the 1976–77 crop year will bring the same uncertainty as the last two years.

The world has consumed more grain than it has produced in five of the last six years, and world stocks are at an all-time low relative to consumption. Until there have been at least two or three years of good harvests distributed around the world, stocks will not be in a position of safety to withstand a large drop in output without a serious reduction in someone's consumption. This situation could lead to more food price inflation in the United States or serious shortages in those parts of the world where diets are already inadequate. The prospect of serious famine is not imminent in 1975–76, but neither is it impossible during the next few years.

Over the longer run, the task of feeding the world is formidable indeed. The statistics quoted earlier are worth repeating. To keep up with prospective population growth will require a sustained increase in world output of 2.5–3 percent per year and most of it must occur in the developing countries. Most of the easy gains are gone, especially in Asia where the problems loom largest. Most of the available land is already under cultivation. In fact, in some areas, farming on land that is too dry and too steep threatens irreversible ecological damage. Thus, despite high fuel and fertilizer prices, most of the expanded output must come from higher output per area of land, which means more irrigation, better varieties, more intensive cultivation, and better farming practices. In order to achieve the higher output, there must be research, large-scale internal and external investment, vastly improved education for scientists, research workers, extension workers, and farmers, and the mobilization of national and international efforts to achieve these ends. The margin of safety is too narrow and the price too high to allow any lagging in the efforts to increase food production in developing countries.

MAGNITUDE OF THE PROBLEM AHEAD

The statistics regarding population and income growth and the demands that these put on the pressure for food supplies in the developing countries are awesome. The FAO in its assessment document of the world food situation prepared for the 1974 World Food Conference estimated that if food production growth rates in developing countries continued at the rate of the past decade, by 1985 the food deficit in the developing countries would amount to 85 million metric tons in average years and would increase to more than 100 million tons during years of bad crops.

The magnitude of the income transfers and the drain on balance of payments plus the sheer complexity involved in distributing such quantities of food aid indicate that the major problems over the next decade in meeting the world food supply needs lie within the developing countries. To meet these needs the FAO indicated that growth rates in agriculture in the developing countries must increase by 30–50 percent over those of the past decade. The importance of the developing countries in solving these problems is emphasized because the production of additional food is a major factor in increasing their overall national growth rate. Additionally, the rural sectors in developing countries must by necessity absorb, and also provide employment and productive income for, a substantially larger population than now resides in rural areas. It is in the context of meeting this challenge in the developing countries that the role of the American university must be considered.

I shall discuss American universities' competence in three areas: (1) the application of American science and technology to food production, (2) the experience of American universities in institution building related to food production in developing countries, and (3) the training of students from developing countries to improve food production in their own countries.

APPLICATION OF AMERICAN SCIENCE AND TECHNOLOGY

I think there is little question that the United States holds technological superiority and has the best scientific base for its agriculture of any nation in the world. Moreover, I think it is generally agreed that much of the American scientific base and the applied technology is based in the American university system. A number of studies regarding American agricultural sciences have particularly stressed that the scientific base in the American university system is by far the best base that exists in the American food production system.

At this point let me distinguish between science and technology. By *science*, I mean the basic knowledge of soil, water, economic, and other relationships, whereas *technology* is the use of this knowledge to produce a particular seed, plant, machine, or irrigation system that will work in the context of the country or area concerned. It is important to understand what is applicable and transferable and what is not in light of the developing countries' needs and views. Thus, I argue that the American scientific base in agriculture is a world asset which can have significant effect if correctly applied to meeting the problems of the developing countries. From my evaluations, I believe that most of our attempts—by universities and others—to transfer American technology directly, through university personnel abroad, into a sharply differing ecological, institutional, social, and economic framework have been less than successful in aiding developing countries with their agricultural problems. Too often the American technology has been inappropriate, irrelevant, or unprofitable.

Regarding institutional arrangements, I would like to note the rapid, impressive development of the International Agricultural Research System, which is now financed through the Consultative Group on International Agricultural Research—an institution of thirty-one members including governments, international and regional organizations, and private foundations. The IARS, comprising twelve research institutes and several affiliated organizations, now provides a major link between the scientific base in modern agriculture and the applied technology needed to meet the needs of the developing countries. This highly innovative institutional structure, which grew out of the activities of two major foundations, is in a sense a measure of the shortcomings of the American university system in applying its scientific base to develop a usable technology to increase food production in the developing countries.

AMERICAN UNIVERSITIES AND INSTITUTION BUILDING ABROAD

It is generally acknowledged by American university leadership, although it may be questioned by people in other countries, that the American university system has produced the best set of existing educational institutions for the development of a productive and expanding agriculture. Thus, one of the major activities of American universities abroad has been institution building that attempts to transplant the American system of land-grant universities, agriculture experiment stations, and extension services to developing countries. In the American system, the functions of research, teaching, and adult education of farmers and related persons are combined into a single institution. This institutional structure has worked successfully for American agriculture. There is substantial question, however, whether or not it is transferable. There is evidence that it is not only not transferable but also perhaps has little relevance in many developing countries with major food problems. I am not asserting that all American university efforts at institution building abroad in the field of agriculture have been a failure. Indeed one can point proudly to many successes.

I do suggest that the American universities' efforts at institution building have been substantially less than successful because relatively few societies have a social and economic structure where an American type of university system can survive, thrive, and produce technology for the agricultural sector as it has in the United States. The developing countries have histories and structures of government and of society quite different from ours. Often the social structure and the economic structure determine who enters the university system—their backgrounds, their interests, and the values which determine their studies and the ways in which they pursue them. Similarly, the reward systems in many of the countries give very low rewards to people who contribute substantially to the development process and give substantially higher rewards to the cautious, bureaucratic civil servant whose main object is to produce balanced books, multitudinous organized files that have been collected for decades and sometimes centuries of colonial rule, and carefully avoid any decision that will implement change.

Thus, perhaps as is the case with democratic government, the concept of the transfer of American institutions into foreign cultures is a dream, a dream fostered by the illusion that our institutions are not intimately related to our own history, social and economic system, and development. I suggest that this belief is a result of our ignorance, both of the evolution of our own agricultural educational systems and an even greater ignorance about the institutional, social, and economic structures of the developing countries and the paths that they may wish to pursue.

RESEARCH AND TRAINING

The third major activity of American universities that makes a substantial contribution to the development of increased food production in developing countries is training in agricultural research, extension, and the other activities relating to increasing production. Again, I argue that our record is varied and that we can do better in almost all respects.

However, in spite of elaborate protestations by American institutions about their ability to train foreign students in agriculture, I believe the American higher education system is second to none in training for the development of improved agricultural production in developing countries. The sheer numbers of foreign students who gain admission to American universities for undergraduate and graduate education in agriculture and related sciences are testimony. Of course there are many things they can and should do better. However, they underestimate their ability in the training function, perhaps in part because that function has been limited more than is necessary, given the history of the American university in relation to agriculture.

The ability to train foreign students has varied among subject-matter areas, and this variance shows up with respect to the food problems of developing countries. In the areas of plant and animal sciences, soils, and crop production, and in the application of economics to the problems of agriculture, the rigor and depth of training in American universities, with their heavy emphasis on applying basic scientific knowledge to farmers' problems, is probably the best education in the world. However, one shortcoming is the nature of the applications that foreign students are asked to make. If American universities are to be serious in the training of foreign scientists for problem solving in the developing countries, the students should have in their training, classroom, and field experience more opportunities than now afforded to apply the techniques, scientific knowledge, and tools they have acquired to the kinds of problems faced in developing countries.

In addition, our training assumes too much about what scientists know. A general observation in many developing countries is that their agricultural experimental work fails less because of the ability of the scientists to do good laboratory work than because of their lack of understanding about simple elements of public administration and management of an agricultural experiment station. As far as I know, no university in the United States has ever offered, as part of a degree program in an agricultural science, a series of lectures (let alone a curriculum) on the management and operation of applied agricultural research. Somehow, we assume that the development of scientists and researchers inherently educates them in how to manage and develop scientific enterprises. This situation is ridiculous. With a huge establishment, science managers can be trained on the job. The developing countries cannot afford to have well-trained scientists who totally lack training or experience in managing the laboratories, experiment stations, or research systems that are a crucial link in applying science knowledge to the problems of the farmers.

American universities are especially ill-equipped to deal with certain problems which arise in my own field—economics applied to policy planning—and related fields such as political science. The United States has had little experience in centralized or even decentralized public planning and management. Foreign scholars come to the United States assuming that they will learn government planning techniques and other tools related to the problems of centrally managed economic systems in which the government plays a major role. Here again, there is a gap between science and technology. I do not argue that the tools of the social scientist as commonly taught in American universities are irrelevant or inapplicable to the problems of developing countries or centralized decision making. I do suggest that most American social scientists have little experience in applying these tools to the particular kinds of problems of developing countries. A major drawback in the development of improved agricultural production in developing countries is the inability of the social scientists, wherever they are trained, to deal effectively with the policy issues and problems faced by the government decision makers in those economies. Thus, the gap between our social science base and its application abroad is wide indeed.

FUTURE CONTRIBUTIONS

What can American universities do to meet the challenge? I have stressed problems because I think the American university system has tended to overrate both its past contribution and its potential contribution to solution of the world food problem. But I assert also that our contribution can be very great—greater than it has been at any time in the past.

In order for the American higher education system to make its maximum contribution, it must continue to provide general education to American young people and to the American public regarding the nature of the world and the problems which its people must face. The food problem is certainly one of those. Thus, the American university system has a major educational responsibility to bring undergraduate and graduate students, regardless of discipline, to understand that one of the major problems the world faces is related to the race between population and food supply on this planet.

Granted this general educational function, more specifically, what can American universities do to help the developing countries in their race to deal with food supply relative to their population and income growth?

First, I suggest that the institutions can do a much better job of making the American scientific capability available to developing countries without tying that scientific capability to American technology, and therefore work more on the application of our science to the problems of developing countries. There appears to be a strong relationship between the American universities' attempt at institution building and their attempt to transfer the technology itself rather than the scientific base which underlies the technology. Thus, whether or not American universities like it, if they are to play a major role, that role is more likely to be in technical assistance than in institution building. In other words, I suggest that American universities must make their best scientists available to work—

either in their own laboratories or in conjunction with colleagues in laboratories abroad—both on the problems of basic science related to world food production and, specifically, on the problems of applying that science to develop a technology applicable to the economic, social, and institutional conditions in developing countries.

As for training, I believe that U.S. training is by and large good, but I argue that American universities need to do much more than they have historically in the agricultural sciences to train both domestic and foreign students (and perhaps retrain their faculties) in some simple matters like comparative economic systems and in other, more complex matters that may sound simple, regarding the development, administration, and organization of research and its application.

The American universities do have a major contribution to make to the solution of the world food problem. Most of that contribution will not be made simply by continuing what they generally do at home except occasionally doing it abroad. Our contribution can be made only by a commitment to the application of our scientific base to the problems of developing countries. Yet that commitment may not be readily desired, accepted, and deemed as worthy of American higher education, particularly by public bodies that fund American higher education and tend to view it as serving primarily the American public.

Second, there must be a continuing financial base for the American university commitment and involvement abroad. But the mission must be carried out on a different basis from that in the past and frequently suggested recently. Long gone are the days when American universities and their professors would go abroad and suggest to other countries that, if they would allow it, the American specialists would show them how to build American-type institutions and thereby solve their problems. Now we must recognize that the American scientific base in agriculture must go abroad to serve in a collegial fashion with colleagues around the world, saying in essence, Let us apply our scientific knowledge together with your scientific knowledge within your institutional, social, and economic structure in order to improve your agricultural production and food supply. In other words, we have a right to be proud of our system and of our scientific base that undergirds it, but we must be humble when we apply this system in other countries and institutional settings.

Relevancy in Agriculture Education Systems

ISHAYA S. AUDU

THE RELATIONSHIP between population and a sufficient food supply has always been tenuous because of its dynamics and the influence of external factors. On the population side, spectacular medical developments and humanitarian provision of medical facilities have led in the less developed countries to lowered infant mortality rates and longer life for adults. The result has been rising population growth rates, for example, reputedly 3 percent in Nigeria. Yet population growth has not always been offset by increases in food production. This imbalance has been highlighted by the director-general of the Food and Agriculture Organization who stated that 10–15 percent of the world's population does not get enough calories to lead healthy lives and that a far greater proportion suffer from protein deficiency. The percentages have changed little over the last ten years so that there are now, in numbers, more hungry people. In addition to this alarming trend, short-term disasters exacerbate suffering. For example, West Africa has recently experienced the Sahelian drought, which has brought suffering to so many people and has threatened the future viability of seven national economies.

Can these problems be overcome? Have we really reached the situation predicted by Malthus? Is man overtaxing his environment? I believe that these problems can be overcome if correct strategies are employed.

There is evidence that over the last twenty years total food production increased at about the same rate in both the developed and developing countries. However, because the population growth rate in the developing countries has been the higher, the per capita increase in their production has averaged less than 0.5 percent per annum, compared with 1.5 percent in the developed countries. Thus many people argue that the food crisis is more one of distribution than of production. Although this argument has some merit, in the long run the developing countries must become more self-supporting in their food production. For example, surpluses of food production in the developed countries cannot realistically be expected to increase rapidly enough to feed the growing population of the less developed countries. In any case, the fragile economies of many less developed countries will not be able indefinitely to use their limited foreign exchange earnings to import food.

Finally, in the developing world as a whole, 50–80 percent of the population is now and will probably continue to be engaged in agriculture. For national governments not to harness this vast labor force for the production of food would be economically irrational and a quick way to generate social and, therefore, political instability. In addition, governments in the less developed countries are becoming increasingly occupied with the importance of increasing employment in order to provide people with income to purchase food and other necessities of life. Inasmuch as agriculture is and will continue to be the main "employer" for many years to come, increased food production and employment generation are goals consistent with each other.

The problem is how this labor force can best be harnessed to increase food production in the less developed countries. In the past, agriculture production has been increased through using indigenous or traditional technologies together with more land and labor. Nigeria is a good example: prior to the discovery of oil, most of the foreign exchange earnings came from export cash crops produced by small farmers using traditional technology. However, as the population grows and (as in many developing countries) land becomes scarcer, further increases in production must come from the use of improved technology—improved seeds, fertilizer, sprays, and the like. Indeed, improved technology in the form of tractors, herbicides, et cetera, has relevance in those areas where labor rather than land is the constraint. The increasing necessity for the less developed countries to turn to improved or modern technology has important implications for the development of their higher education facilities for agriculture.[1]

The Role of Education

The human element is, of course, a key factor in agricultural change and progress. Education to bring human capacities to their maximum potential therefore becomes a vital element in increasing productivity and bringing about progress. The relationship between education—intellectual investment—and the rate of economic growth and development has been a subject of many investigations. A positive relationship between the two is not in doubt, but the strength and efficiency of the relationship is greatly influenced by the type and relevancy of that intellectual investment.

1. One may argue desirability as well since educated people are unlikely to be attracted to agriculture that continues to use traditional technology.

It is worth noting that even in many developed countries—the United States and Japan, for example—the average length of training for those engaged in farming is generally less than that for other social and professional categories. Similarly, the amount spent in training a person in agriculture is much less than in nonagricultural areas. In most developing countries, where much higher proportions of the population are based in agriculture, the imbalance of emphasis between agricultural training and nonagricultural training appears to be even greater, and is further exaggerated by the fact that agricultural training is almost completely publicly financed. (In the developed countries such financing is supplemented from private, usually commercial, sources.) Fortunately, in most developing countries, Nigeria included, increasing attention is being paid to the balance of support for training in areas *not* immediately related to national needs. Unfortunately, there is a limit to the extent to which people can be persuaded to undertake certain training programs. The limited numbers of qualified persons, the unattractiveness of agriculture as a career, and in some cases limited training facilities have all combined to produce a chronic manpower shortage in agriculture in many developing countries, particularly those in Africa. In Nigeria, for instance, it was estimated a few years ago that in the establishment at that time 42 percent of the positions for agriculture graduates were vacant whereas at the intermediate level—certificate or diploma level—11 percent of the positions were vacant.

The test of relevancy of education to national needs does not, however, stop with the disciplines such as medicine, engineering, and agriculture. Relevancy goes much further. For example, it is becoming recognized that higher educational institutions, such as universities, can no longer afford the luxury of being academic ivory towers, but must relate to the environment around them. As only one segment in the educational program, the institutions must develop in balance with other parts of the program. In agriculture, training proceeds at three levels: farmer education programs, intermediate-level programs for extension workers, and university programs in agriculture. Vertical continuity from one program to the next is essential, for, in the relationship between higher education and the food crisis, without these other programs there is no hope of solving the crisis.

In pursuing relevancy, universities will have to adjust the curricula in each subject area—medicine, agriculture, engineering, whatever—to the needs of the society. In certain areas, a relevant curriculum may be quite different from its counterpart in the developed world, and here lies one of the strongest arguments for indigenous universities in the developing countries. However, this test of relevance is not always given sufficient attention by those who hold preconceived ideas formulated during training overseas and by expatriates working in the indigenous institutions. Two means can help make the test of relevancy operative: careful scrutiny of the syllabus by knowledgeable persons outside the university,[2] and the development of peer group review, which would give professional attention to relevancy. The latter should be encouraged within the developing countries themselves.

RELEVANT SYLLABI

University graduates in agriculture are expected to be a link in getting farmers to achieve the targets laid down by government, targets that the graduates often help formulate. At present, agriculture graduates in developing countries are employed chiefly in four areas: (1) administrative, particularly planning, posts mainly in government, although increasingly in commercial organizations; (2) research; (3) teaching, at the intermediate agricultural staff level and sometimes in practical extension itself; and (4) teaching of undergraduate and graduate students.

The development of relevant syllabi for teaching at both the undergraduate and graduate levels can be advanced by close examination of the types of functions graduates will be expected to serve. It should be emphasized that human and environmental situations change continuously, and syllabi contents should be reviewed and altered as necessary to reflect the changes. Let us look at a few kinds of factors that are important in constructing relevant syllabi designed to develop graduates who have the potential for an important role in overcoming the food crisis. But first, one warning. Higher education cannot by itself overcome the food crisis; it can only create the preconditions in terms of relevantly qualified graduates who can tackle the problem in a pragmatic manner.

In agricultural education, the most basic essential is that students obtain a detailed, intimate knowledge of both the physical and human[3] environment with emphasis on the existing situation, the potential of the environment, and the constraints to be overcome in achieving progress. Such an approach stresses the multidisciplinary nature of agriculture and, at the undergraduate level at least, a general rather than

2. Of course, the scrutiny would have to be managed carefully to avoid undue outside interference.

3. Human in this context includes economic, attitudinal, political, and institutional elements.

a highly specialized degree. The principal types of jobs in agricultural programs require such background knowledge. Administrators and planners require it in order to arrive at realistic targets and some idea of the costs involved; research workers require it for developing realistic, pragmatic research programs; and extension-level people need the overview in order to relate and assess the problems and repercussions of suggesting a particular change in the farming system. Time and time again, targets have not been achieved, research programs have been irrelevant, and changes have not been adopted by farmers. All these manifestations indicate a failure to understand or analyze the existing situation properly and then synthesize the knowledge gained to arrive at relevant, realistic strategies.

The farmer himself is the kingpin in the production of agricultural products. Without his cooperation, nothing will change.[4] An intimate understanding of his total—physical and human—environment is absolutely essential in order to introduce changes that are relevant. In many less developed countries, for example, the farmer has thus far adopted little in the way of modern technology, and the technology therefore must be simple rather than complex; he has received little or no formal education, and therefore the instructions for adopting the improved technology must be conveyed verbally and by demonstration; he lives very close to the subsistence level of income and therefore is likely to have a conservative attitude to change because he cannot afford to take risks; and he often lives in remote areas with poor access to markets and improved inputs, a circumstance that implies special intervention by government. These and many other characteristics have great ramifications for persons in any job connected with agriculture and so deserve careful, detailed study at the undergraduate level.

Administrators and planners need such information if they are to derive realistic targets and are to design and implement the related support systems necessary to the goal—extension staff, credit program, distribution system for materials and supplies, and market for products. In the Zaria area it is technically and economically feasible to bring about five- to tenfold increases in yields of maize and cowpeas if the relevant structure to support the farming is available—improved seed, fertilizer, spray materials, and so on.

4. It is assumed, as is the case of most less developed countries, the cooperation of farmers is to be achieved by persuasion rather than through compulsory programs.

RESEARCH AND DEVELOPMENT—FOR PRACTICAL APPLICATION

In the case of research, priorities need to be determined in line with the targets or plans laid down by government. However, the type of technology developed by the technical scientists must be closely attuned to the total environment of the farmer and take into consideration the type and degree of infrastructural support likely to be provided by government. It is essential that such research be undertaken in the local setting. Basic scientific knowledge, primarily a product of fundamental research, is usually readily transferable. Adaptive research—the application of science to solve real-world problems—which is necessarily the major responsibility of research workers in the less developed countries, tends not to be transferable because of differences in the total environment. Thus, in much of northern Nigeria, the technology that would be most relevant to farmers would involve little change in their farming systems—such as changes in the crop mixtures, that is, two or more crops on the same plot of land—would provide a dependable return, and would require relatively little infrastructural support from the government. Relevancy thus is a function of (1) fitting the technology to the physical environment, for example, breeding crop varieties whose growing season fits into the rainy season or is insensitive to wide variations in weather, and (2) fitting the technology to the human environment and infrastructural support systems available. It is, therefore, desirable to consider the development of more than one level of technology in order to suit different situations.

In addition to the role played by the technical scientist, the social scientist has an important function in such research areas as delineating the constraints faced by farmers, working with technical scientists to produce appropriate technology, working with policy makers to help formulate targets and policies, evaluating the feasibility of different infrastructural support systems, and so on. Thus relevant research in agriculture, because of the complexities in the physical and human environment which can only partially be influenced by man, tends to be location specific. Imposing technologies from outside without due consideration to the environment can have dire consequences. Again an example: boreholes in the Sahel area provided water for more animals but did not provide a corresponding increase in pastures. When pasture lands suffered from lack of rain, the consequences in terms of starving livestock were probably graver than they would have been with fewer boreholes.

Finally, there are the people who are responsible for getting the technology into use, whose function is to reduce the time between its discovery or invention and practical adoption. Their role will depend on the type of governmental program being advocated. Examples range from complex types of technology accompanied by concentrated infrastructural support systems such as are envisioned in the agricultural development projects of the International Bank for Reconstruction and Development, compared with simpler types of technology and lower infrastructural support systems. Whatever the level, a basic knowledge of the farmers' environment remains an essential. In addition, such people must be able to communicate with the users of the technology, an important point in most developing countries, where literacy rates are low.

In this discussion I have not attempted to detail what relevant syllabi should contain. Rather, I have illustrated two points: (1) syllabi, in order to be relevant, must be attuned to the environment, and (2) the environment is extremely complex, involves many disciplines, and thus necessitates a multidisciplinary approach in the study of agriculture. These two criteria in turn imply a generalist rather than specialist approach at the undergraduate level. In addition, administrators and planners, research workers, and extension workers, if they are to be truly effective in their work, need additional courses especially pertinent to their work. Unless the length of the B.Sc. agriculture degree is lengthened, such studies are best pursued at the graduate level.

Ensuring Relevancy in Higher Education

As already noted, higher education alone cannot solve the food crisis, but it can contribute training that is potentially relevant. Is it possible within a university to create conditions to ensure that the teaching will be relevant? Unfortunately, in the instance of the developing countries, staff members in agriculture faculties have been confined to teaching functions. This restriction is particularly regrettable for two reasons: first, persons highly trained in agriculture are generally limited in numbers and therefore are not being utilized with optimum efficiency; and second, if staff members of agriculture faculties could be given additional functions in the areas of government-funded research, representation on governmental policy boards, and training of extension workers, the knowledge so gained could promote relevancy in the teaching program inasmuch as the staff members would become much more attuned to the current situation in the country.

In Africa, Ahmadu Bello University has an unusual arrangement in its agriculture complex which appears to overcome many of the problems discussed above. The agricultural complex covers a number of areas: (1) the Division of Agricultural and Livestock Services Training (DALST) consists of four Schools of Agriculture offering training at the subdegree—intermediate—level for extension workers; (2) the Faculties of Veterinary Medicine and Agriculture offer undergraduate and graduate training; (3) the Institute for Agricultural Research (IAR) provides the agricultural research function for the northern states of Nigeria; and (4) the Extension Research Liaison Section (ERLS) provides two-way communication between the states' Ministries of Natural Resources and IAR, by writing extension leaflets based on the research work, providing in-service training courses for extension workers, and channeling research problems of the states to research workers.

In many respects the arrangement at ABU resembles the land-grant system in the United States. The system, although admittedly not perfect, does help create conditions that promote relevancy in the teaching program while maximizing the utilization of the limited skilled manpower available in agriculture through exploiting the complementary relationships of research and teaching. In addition, the system has encouraged input from the social sciences into research, a practice that is usual in teaching programs but rare until recently in governmental research institutions in the developing world. Finally, staff members in the agricultural complex are constantly reminded of the various components necessary to bring about agricultural development and the resulting necessity for interdisciplinary cooperation. There appears therefore to be a great deal to recommend the setting-up of agricultural complexes analogous to the ABU pattern in other parts of the developing world. The structure of the ABU complex ensures that the university relates to the community, rather than operating in isolation. For example, IAR programs are approved by a board consisting predominantly of representatives of various state ministries. As a result, in recent years priorities have become oriented more toward food crops, with the result that the imbalance in favor of export cash crops, which existed prior to independence, has been corrected. Significant results have been obtained in developing profitable modern technologies for some food crops that are consistent with the total environment of the farmer and, if provided with the relevant infrastructural support systems set up by government, could have significant effect on food production.

Education, especially relevant education, is a long-term investment which, if properly made now, should result in a substantial payoff in the long run in reducing the probability of further food crises. At the same time the probability of further food crises can be reduced by a simultaneous attack on the other side of the population and food supply equation, by encouraging more vigorous family planning programs concomitant with improved medical programs to reduce infant mortality rates and enhance longevity. Perhaps the advocacy for such a program implies partial failure on the part of the agriculturists to ensure adequate food supplies, but human lives are too valuable to permit the advantages to be ignored. At the same time the burden still lies with the agriculturists to increase food production substantially, both to improve the diets of people today and to feed future generations. Relevant higher education in training agriculturists must play a key role in enabling them to execute this responsibility.

Education: An Economic Necessity
to Developing Countries

ALI MOHAMMED KHUSRO

THE LAST TEN YEARS have seen many studies on the dimensions of the world food-population problem.[1] All of them suggest a catastrophe in the offing. Other crises are brewing simultaneously—the crises of emerging ecological imbalances, of environment, of energy. Such crises have occurred in the past, for example, when, with Malthus, humanity feared a massive death toll owing to a food-population imbalance. But, as important as any crisis is, man, through his ingenuity and through his sympathy and cooperation with his fellows, can devise means to surmount crisis.

By all accounts, the food-population crisis now unfolding is very serious. The population of industrialized countries has been growing at a rate of less than 1 percent per year. But the population of less developed countries, already two billion, has been growing about 2.5 percent per

1. See, for example, *The World Food Problem: A Report of the President's Science Advisory Committee*, vol. 2 (Washington: Government Printing Office, 1967); Donella H. Meadows et al., *The Limits to Growth*, First Report for the Club of Rome (Washington: Potomac Associates, 1972); Mihajlo Mesarovic and Edward Pestel, *Mankind at the Turning Point*, Second Report to the Club of Rome (New York: Dutton, 1974).

year. The chances are that the less developed countries will have a population of about four billion around the turn of the century.

However, the developed world is highly productive in terms of grain yields: yields per hectare are five times higher and yields per farmer are eleven times higher than those in the Third World. As Guernier has shown recently, it is precisely in the Third World, where population growth is highest, that the per capita availability of food is static or increasing only slowly; in the industrialized countries, where population is growing more slowly, the per capita rations are increasing at 1.5–2 percent per year.[2]

There is, thus, a serious regional crisis and not a worldwide crisis. Despite high productivity, the developed world does not have sufficient surpluses to meet the enormous demand from the Third World.

The countries with substantial food surpluses are the United States, Canada, and New Zealand, which typically export about 100 million tons annually. The main importers are the countries of western Europe and Japan (41 million tons), eastern Europe and the U.S.S.R. (10 million tons), China (7.7 million tons), and the Third World (30 million tons); and the trend has been upward. However, when bad years in the food-importing regions coincide with droughts in the surplus regions, there emerges a serious food crisis such as that in 1972–74. Even in 1975, bad harvests in Russia and a major purchase program by that country have shaken the world grain markets and exerted serious upward influence on grain prices, making it difficult for poorer countries to buy. Between September 1972 and January 1974 the prices of wheat increased threefold, to $235–$250 per metric ton;[3] the price of corn more than doubled, and that of soybeans increased by about 90 percent. More recently the prices have declined but are still much higher than their 1972 levels.

These crises are expected to repeat themselves all too frequently in the period immediately ahead, when population growth rates in developing countries are not expected to fall below 2 percent and their grain production will not have risen much above 3 percent.

The world's carry-over stocks of grain have been declining over the years. Toward the end of 1973 the world total of grain carry-over stocks, at 100 million tons, was equivalent only to 8 percent of annual world

2. Maurice Guernier, "The World Food Problem" (Paper presented at the international conference of the Club of Rome, Guanajato, Mexico, July 1975).

3. T. H. Lee, "The Present Situation and Future Prospects of World Food Production," *Industry of Free China*, May 1975.

grain consumption—less than one month's consumption. Toward the end of 1974 it had declined to be equal to a mere three weeks' consumption.[4] Again a crisis was close. In years of a food crisis, the normal 100 million tons per year grain transfer through exports and imports become totally insufficient, and the transfer requirements rise to 150–200 million tons. This magnitude of demand cannot be met from the surpluses of the exporting countries. Additionally, it is most unhealthy for the Third World to live off charity and be fed by others; it will generate apathy and lack of effort. Thus, it has been argued that the Third World countries must grow as much of their own food as possible and make the least possible demand, either through trade or aid, on the food products of the industrialized countries.[5] Each major region should thus attempt to meet its own nutritional needs within a narrow margin, and each region should be responsible for its own food and agricultural policies.

APPROACH TO SOLUTION

The developed world has the advanced technology for agriculture as well as food surpluses (at any rate in some countries), and the developing world has food deficits but some technology and (often) labor surpluses. Therefore, the following set of solutions suggests itself.

1. The developing countries must attempt to lift themselves through their own efforts and undertake investment, to the best of their ability, in agricultural and food technology, in resource development—land development, prevention of soil erosion, afforestation, irrigation, seeds, fertilizers, manures, pesticides, and implements—and indeed in human skill development for agricultural requirements.

2. The developed countries must undertake more rather than less food production, help build up world food stocks, and resort to food trade and food aid—more trade than aid.

3. There should be a transfer of agricultural technology and a transfer of resources—including trained manpower resources—from the developed to the developing world.

What might be some major implications of these solutions? Given widespread understanding of the problem and given human ingenuity, resourcefulness, and will, the food-population crisis is a time-bound crisis. If in the developing world the annual increase in food production stays at 3 percent and the annual increase in population declines from 2.5 per-

4. Ibid.
5. Guernier, "The World Food Problem."

cent to 2 percent and then to 1.5 percent, the increase in per capita food consumption in the developing world will go up from 0.5 percent to 1 percent and then to 1.5 percent. The crisis will then be at an end, for food availability in the developing world would thereafter be doubled in less than fifty years.

NEED FOR EDUCATION IN RELATION TO FOOD AND AGRICULTURE

In order to reach the goal of sufficiency, the developing countries must undertake massive investments in population control and in agriculture. The meaning of the crisis must be brought home. Illiteracy prevents real understanding of the crisis and of the urgency of adopting family planning and new agricultural technology. In the early 1960s, out of a population of 1.3 billion in the developing countries, about 750 million persons of school age or older could not read or write. Even if the developing countries devoutly wish to undertake investment in agricultural technology and resource development, the shortage of skilled manpower prevents them from having their wish. Lack of sufficient higher education thus becomes a bottleneck to all agricultural development.

The need for higher education appears at all levels of agricultural expansion. The need is not merely for agricultural scientists to introduce and adapt new technology. Farmers must be persuaded that there is a crisis and that they should adopt the new inputs and new methods. It might be thought that people with middle-level education—the village-level workers, block-development officers, extension workers, and the like—can persuade them. But as these middle-level workers are themselves required by the millions (India alone has 500,000 villages with about 80 million farmers and 400 million farm people to be persuaded), a vast body of people with higher education in public communication is required to train the persuaders. Highly educated manpower, working through radio, television, the press, and all publicity media, is needed before the middle-level people can do their job.

Then comes higher education for the creation and adaptation of agricultural technology. Knowledge and its further discovery through research is one essential; the application of that knowledge and its adaptation in a particular sociocultural environment and to a particular resource base is another. The market is a cruel place as well as a benevolent one. Many a scientific discovery of great sophistication is rejected either because of cultural resistance or because of cost-return calculations. Trained manpower is required to develop knowledge and to adapt and apply it widely. The geneticist, the soil scientist, the agronomist, the entymologist, the economist, and a host of other scientists are needed.

There is, then, the need for highly educated manpower in the realm of resource creation—land development, irrigation, afforestation, prevention of erosion, an infrastructure of institutions (for example, banks to promote savings, service and extension organizations) and many others. Thus, the demands are fantastically high; there is an absolute shortage of *relevant* highly educated manpower in the world—especially in the developing world.

Some of the most glaring deficiencies in higher education, especially agricultural higher education, in developing countries are revealed in the 1969 report of the President's Science Advisory Committee.[6] These countries have a vast modern-knowledge gap, low student enrollment, lower enrollments and graduation of agricultural students, a high dropout rate, and a low rate of literacy. Moreover, they have shortages of qualified teachers, books, and teaching aids; the relevancy of curricula needs improvement; and, on top of all this, there is a "brain drain."

By categorizing seventy countries of the world into four levels—underdeveloped, partially developed, semiadvanced, and advanced—some significant conclusions may be reached.

> As one scales the educational heights in developing countries, the student population appears especially minute in relation to the nation's manpower needs. In terms of these needs, the proportion of students studying agriculture in higher education is abysmally low . . . [Table 1].
>
> College graduating classes in six Level I countries with a combined population of 116 million in 1964 included only 144 agricultural students. Moreover, the entire college student body in these six countries as well as the other nine in Level I includes only 5.6 percent studying agriculture. In contrast, about 20 percent are studying humanities and fine arts. Obviously food supply has not been accepted as a problem worthy of their study at the college level.[7]

Per student cost of higher education being relatively high in developing countries, there is a preference for study in the United States and Europe. There are, of course, distinguished universities in Mexico, India, Egypt, and Chile, but the quality of education is uneven.

In 1966, out of 82,709 foreign students in the United States, only 3,064 (3.7 percent) studied agriculture. The foreign students then in this country were enrolled in the following fields of study: engineering, 21.9 per-

6. *World Food Problem*, 2:601–14.
7. Ibid., p. 607.

TABLE 1: *Enrollments in Higher Level Institutions, by Field of Study*

Field of Study	Percentage Distribution			
	Level 1: 15 Under-developed Countries	Level 2: 20 Partially Developed Countries	Level 3: 20 Semi-advanced Countries	Level 4: 14 Advanced Countries
Enrollment (thousands)	29	991	2,922	2,802
Humanities and fine arts	20.2	14.9	26.7	23.3
Education	9.3	13.0	6.8	6.9
Law	16.9	9.2	6.2	8.1
Social sciences	15.5	11.7	16.0	16.7
Natural science	13.0	7.6	16.8	11.2
Engineering	8.2	24.3	13.3	14.5
Medical sciences	9.7	12.7	8.4	11.2
Agriculture	4.9	6.0	5.0	2.3
Not specified	2.3	.6	.8	5.8

SOURCE: Adapted from United Nations Educational, Scientific and Cultural Organization, *Statistical Yearbook, 1965* (Paris: Unesco, 1965).

cent; humanities, 20 percent; natural and physical sciences, 17.6 percent; social sciences, 14.9 percent; business administration, 9.6 percent; medical sciences, 5 percent; education, 5.1 percent; and, as already noted, agriculture, 3.7 percent.[8] Obviously, neither their higher education abroad nor their education at home was closely related to national needs.

THE "BRAIN DRAIN"

The report of the President's Science Advisory Committee quotes a study which documents the proportion of foreign students who remain in the United States after receiving their degrees: B.S. degree, 39 percent; M.S., 43.5 percent; Ph.D., 32.9 percent.[9] Contributing factors are both the higher earnings in advanced countries and unsatisfactory working conditions in developing countries. In classical economic theory, if the supply of skills improves, the wage rate falls and the drain comes to a halt or is even reversed. Under present world conditions, however, the difference in earnings, initially already large, increases to widen the gap, and continuous technical change and faster economic development in the already developed countries never reverses the drain.

The obvious answer in the developing countries is that they should recognize the key role of agriculture by adding more higher educational facilities and realloting existing facilities in line with requirements. They should consider higher stipends, larger numbers of scholarships, and, in

8. Institute of International Education, *Open Doors, 1966* (New York: The Institute, 1966), p. 13.
9. *World Food Problem,* 2:611.

fact, differential wage payments favorable to those areas of the economy which are nationally crucial and in which there is a shortage of manpower. The economic policies of developing countries would do well to incorporate manpower shortages in their considerations and, through wage, price, and other incentives, divert resources toward shortage areas. Furthermore, in sending students abroad, they should lay down some guidelines about fields of study. And absolutely necessary are wider contracts between scientists and educationists of developing and developed countries to accelerate the transfer of knowledge that impinges on standards, syllabi, and research and its applications. Multinational institutions—if necessary, under the auspices of international organizations—can be set up in line with needs.

MORE FOOD FROM DEVELOPING COUNTRIES

To say that the developing countries should concentrate a great deal more on growing their own food is not to say that the developed countries must not grow food for themselves and for others. There has long been a facile assumption that the nonindustrial (agricultural) countries have a comparative advantage in agricultural products and the industrialized countries, in industrial products. It follows that nonindustrialized countries must grow their own food and not import it, while a country like the United States should concentrate on industrial output and put little emphasis on food surpluses for trade. Hence, U.S. policy, under many successive presidential administrations, has been to make payments ("farm subsidies") to farmers for leaving some of their lands fallow, thus reducing production and export sales.

However, with the rapid advance in agricultural technology in North America, Europe, and Australia–New Zealand, and a great scarcity of industrial labor in the developed world, it has become clear that the developed world has a comparative advantage in agricultural products, and the developing Third World, with its vast labor surpluses, has a comparative advantage in many types of industrial production. Thus, situating much more industry in the Third World countries and massive exporting of agricultural products from the developed countries are by no means a farfetched possibility. It is happening already. The United States, Canada, New Zealand, and other developed countries need not hesitate in producing and exporting larger and larger quantities of agricultural products, inasmuch as comparative advantage lies in that direction. Nor need the Third World countries hesitate to import food from abroad if they can pay for it through industrial exports.

· 5 ·

New Exchange Opportunities

Exchange Opportunities in a No-Growth Period

BARBARA B. BURN

A PRINCIPAL ELEMENT in international education is the movement of scholars between institutions and across national borders. Although the international movement of scholars is hardly a new phenomenon, what is relatively new is that faculty exchanges can be carried out at low cost, at least with western European countries.

The migration of scholars (and of universities, themselves) dates from the Middle Ages. Cambridge University, for example, received a critical infusion in 1209 when, as a result of disturbances at Oxford, a number of Oxford scholars migrated to Cambridge. In the nineteenth century, some hundreds of American scholars traveled to Germany to engage in study and research, and brought back concepts of the Von Humboldt research university. This migration had much to do with grafting the German model for graduate research onto the Oxbridge collegial pattern of higher education in the United States, as modified by this nation's land-grant service orientation.

The wandering scholar, whether student or teacher, is integral to more than the history of university development. If the pursuit of academic excellence is not to be restrained by national borders or defined by national objectives, the free flow of scholars, sometimes referred to as the "brain drain," is essential. The Fulbright-Hays program, established shortly after World War II, has contributed significantly to this scholar migration. Under its sponsorship, more than 150,000 Fulbright scholars and graduate students from the United States and the 110 other participating countries have studied, taught, or pursued research abroad.[1]

1. "Address by John Richardson, Jr.," *Selected Speeches,* National Association for Foreign Student Affairs, 27th Annual Conference, Washington, D.C., Summer 1975 (Washington: The Association, 1975), p. 45.

Unfortunately, international education in general and the international exchange of professors, researchers, and teachers is regarded in some quarters as a luxury, better afforded in periods of affluence than in a situation of tightening resources. Institutional administrators too often see such exchanges as an exotic frill, to be reduced in scope—and funding—along with other such allegedly nonessential activities as interdisciplinary studies, faculty travel, and various kinds of experimental programs, especially those not firmly embedded in departmental niches.

Restrictive Measures

In a situation of no-growth or much-slowed growth in higher education, which today, in the United States and in some other countries, is compounded by a high unemployment rate, there is the added pressure against offering appointments to foreign faculty—a pressure that might be called "Buy American." This attitude is reflected by the increase in restrictive regulations of the U.S. Department of Labor on permitting foreign citizens to work in the United States and for foreign citizens to obtain permanent resident status here. This pressure is also exacerbated—perhaps more elsewhere than in the United States—by an increased nationalistic mood, exemplified perhaps in Canada. At its May 1975 meeting, the Canadian Association of University Teachers endorsed the "head-and-shoulders" theory of faculty recruitment according to which a non-Canadian should be hired only if he/she were head and shoulders above all Canadian candidates. It should be explained that in 1973–74 about one-third of all professors at Canadian universities were not Canadian citizens, and nearly 15 percent were U.S. citizens.

Another example is Switzerland's restrictions on hiring foreign faculty during the last year. Devised to stabilize the foreign population, quotas now limit foreign faculty recruitment, and these limits apply to faculty members, researchers, and technical staff staying in Switzerland for more than three months.[2]

Given the declining growth rate of higher education enrollments and hence of faculty recruitment in the United States, Canada, and some European countries, the increased nationalism, and the pressure against hiring nonnationals, are there then any new exchange opportunities for scholars? I am convinced that there are and that they are more necessary and feasible than ever, although not free of obstacles. The past lack of

2. Association for the European University Community, *European University News* (Paris), April 1975, p. 9.

support for international exchanges by American colleges and universities does not mean they cannot be expanded in the future. As a recent study by the American Council on Education noted:

> Few, if any, universities have directly encouraged the movement of their faculties across national boundaries as a conscious act of institutional policy; too often the implicit policy of most universities is that it is the responsibility of the individual to pay his own way or to find external resources for trips abroad, while trips within the boundaries of the United States are legitimate professional expenses which may be reimbursed directly. In any event, college administrators, state legislators, and the United States Congress tend . . . to look at foreign trips for faculty as pleasure junkets rather than as investments in academic competence.[3]

VALUES OF EXCHANGES IN A NO-GROWTH PERIOD

In a no- or low-growth situation where few new faculty members can be hired, when grants for overseas (and domestic) research have shrunk, and when the already high and probably rising proportion of tenured faculty offers little scope for faculty diversification, planned programs of international (and domestic) faculty exchanges offer one of the few ways to diversify faculty at the home institution. Exchanges abroad also offer an institution's faculty members opportunities for professional growth. By planned programs, I mean a careful meshing of faculty resources to support existing or developing programs. Such exchanges are one of the few ways to allow faculty members to go elsewhere and at the same time keep their departmental positions occupied. By contrast, a one-way exchange implies that the college or university can afford to get along without its faculty member for a year, and, therefore, his/her department may even have a position it does not need. At a time when departments need to hold fast to their positions or at least to be seen as needing to do so, a two-way exchange of faculty members provides a mechanism both for holding onto positions and for achieving faculty diversification. The reciprocity of the exchange is thus critical to its practicality.

International faculty interchange is also a strategy for strengthening or developing new specialties in a period when shrunken resources preclude hiring the new faculty typically recruited for this purpose. For example, three British higher education institutions are developing American studies programs, for which they intend to lean on faculty

3. International Education Project, American Council on Education, *Education for Global Interdependence: A Report with Recommendations to the Government/Academic Interface Committee* (Washington: IEP, 1975), pp. 58–59.

exchanges with U.S. colleges and universities. Again, a U.K. university plans to use international faculty exchanges to strengthen its offerings in folklore. Thus, when financial resources are limited or diminishing, international faculty exchanges constitute an important strategy for program development. Yet the financial problems of British universities are such that not only can they recruit few new faculty, but also they have had to postpone filling vacant positions. A survey conducted there in 1975 showed that "at least 1,000 academic posts in universities were left vacant during the past academic year as an economy measure."[4]

THE FINANCES OF EXCHANGE

What do international faculty exchanges cost? It is commonly thought that inviting foreign faculty members to a U.S. campus or sending U.S. faculty members abroad requires substantial funding. If so, current financial pressures on American colleges and universities would make exchanges less possible today than in more affluent times. However, from my experience over the last several years with the University of Massachusetts' international faculty exchanges, those with western Europe (my principal focus) require only modest funding and significantly less than they did a few years ago.

In contrast, international faculty exchanges with developing countries are prohibitively expensive—for a number of reasons. Travel costs to almost all other world regions are high. Salary levels in the developing world are so much lower than in the United States that the cost of providing U.S. faculty members with salaries equal to or near their home salary becomes very high. Moreover, in my experience, relatively few American faculty members seem inclined to participate in faculty exchanges with the developing world. To attract an American professor, such an international exchange ordinarily must provide a salary that is equivalent or nearly equivalent to his or her U.S. salary; at the same time, the visiting foreign professor must receive an American-level salary that is appropriate to his/her rank and experience in the American context.

In international exchanges, the closer the foreign salary schedule is to the American salary, the less are the funds needed for topping. Salary scales in the United States and Europe are now much closer than they were a few years ago, mainly as a result of the dollar devaluation and the high inflation rates in some European countries; therefore less funds

4. *Times Higher Education Supplement* (London), July 25, 1975, p. 1.

are needed for topping. For example, in 1974 the average British university professor was paid about $18,650; in October 1975 the average figure was around $19,500. The full professor in Sweden in 1973 was paid the equivalent of about $20,200, and receives something more now. In the United Kingdom, the lecturer (somewhat equivalent to the U.S. rank of assistant professor) received in 1974 the equivalent of $5,800–$12,700, compared with a fall 1975 range of $6,600–$13,500. The difference between U.S. and European salary levels has been diminishing, and the foreign university comes closer to offering the American exchange teacher a salary corresponding to his/her U.S. salary. To be more concrete, four years ago two faculty exchanges at the assistant professor level between the University of Massachusetts at Amherst and universities in Germany and England required salary-topping funds of $5,000 and $4,000 respectively, whereas during the current year they require only about $2,500 and $1,600 each.

Let me illustrate the finance of international faculty exchange with a hypothetical exchange between my own institution, the University of Massachusetts, and the University of Ruritania. If we send a $20,000-a-year person to Ruritania U. and it pays him $15,000, he continues to draw $5,000 of his UMass salary but frees $15,000 for the professor from Ruritania U. If the appropriate salary level for the latter is fixed at $16,500 (we normally seem to invite faculty requiring lesser salary than the UMass counterpart going abroad), we need to find an extra $1,500. This is a modest investment to give our person the experience of teaching in Ruritania and having the Ruritanian professor teach at UMass for the year. On a per capita basis, the cost comes to only $750 per person exchanged.

Leaving aside salaries, there are certain financial and other benefits for foreigners and Americans in teaching abroad. If a professor from England teaches in the United States for an academic year, is paid by a U.S. college or university, and is out of England for 365 days, he pays no British income tax, nor does he pay U.S. income tax. The American teaching in England does not have to pay British income tax on salary paid by a British university. Tax agreements between the United States and a number of other countries contain similar provisions. Americans teaching in a number of European countries also have the advantage of generous health insurance, special allowances for dependents, and so on.

Faculty exchanges with French universities merit special mention. The Franco-American Commission on Educational Exchange in 1975 announced a new Exchange Agreement Project. Under this project French and American institutions of higher education are encouraged to enter into formal exchange agreements under which faculty exchanged can continue to be paid their regular salaries from their home institutions, will be exempt from income tax in the foreign country, and will have their round-trip international travel paid by the commission. The disciplines in which French universities have indicated an interest in faculty exchanges include American and French literature, law, economics, anthropology, and theater arts. While it is obviously desirable for Americans teaching at French universities to have proficiency in French, in some subjects—for example, the sciences and business—it is not essential.

Foreign Faculty on the American Campus: Suggestions

Although international faculty exchanges with western Europe are less costly today than several years ago, they require considerable staff time to arrange. It is therefore important to examine whether the effort is worthwhile. Certainly exchanges involve problems. Many American faculty members will testify to their frustration in teaching abroad, of feeling isolated or peripheral at the foreign institution. Foreign faculty members teaching at an American college or university may find it difficult to adapt to teaching American undergraduates. In the United States, close to 40 percent of the age group attend college or university; in most European countries the proportion is 20 percent or lower. Thus, in this country we have a more diversified and in many cases less rigorously prepared student body than do the European institutions. American students are also likely to be younger than their European counterparts. The high school graduate in most European countries has had a longer period of schooling than the American and has completed the equivalent of at least the American college freshman year. Whereas European professors typically react positively to the outgoing and active class participation of American undergraduates, they may be understandably frustrated at the lower level of writing ability and less analytical approach on the part of many American students. A visiting professor from Germany who taught literature at the University of Massachusetts last year referred to the inclination of students in class discussion "to refer immediately and sometimes almost exclusively to their own personal experiences." Another problem is that visiting foreign faculty may be needed to teach lower division courses when they would much prefer to teach graduate courses in their specialties. With the decline in graduate enrollments in some fields, this problem may increase.

To gain maximum return from international faculty exchanges, it is vital to involve visiting foreign faculty in a variety of campus activities. Obvious suitable activities include advising students on study in the foreign countries, lecturing or giving seminars on topics falling within their expertise, and making them members of faculty committees on foreign area studies programs. Some visiting foreign faculty may be interested in serving as a faculty member in residence in a student dormitory. When this arrangement is possible, it not only may reduce the rent but also gives to many students special contact with a person from another country and culture. Putting foreign faculty on committees that are not directly concerned with international education also can be rewarding; for example, a Swedish or British professor can contribute a perspective on scholarships and financial aid, which are handled so differently in Sweden and Great Britain. As the Council for International Exchange of Scholars has learned through long experience in administering the Fulbright Scholar program, visiting foreign faculty have a much more rewarding experience personally and professionally in the United States if efforts are made to involve them in a range of ongoing college or university activities.

Continuity in international faculty exchanges helps solve many of the problems that crop up. Perhaps most important, it encourages direct knowledge of the foreign faculty proposed for exchange a year ahead. Evaluating candidates on the basis of curriculum vitae and exchanges of correspondence is obviously less successful than having a person on the spot who can write his colleagues back home about the candidate proposed for the U.S. institution the next year. Continuity is also helpful in the orientation of faculty on both sides of the Atlantic. It ensures the flow of information in both directions that is essential to making exchanges successful: the departments involved keep 'in practice" on how to handle visiting foreign faculty, anticipate their needs, and integrate them into the department and community life.

It is of interest that the Henry Luce Foundation launched in fall 1975 a program to support faculty exchange among the countries of Asia. The foundation has set aside up to $20,000 for the exchange of leading Asian academicians among Asian colleges and universities, the funds to be used to defray travel costs and other unusual expenses associated with the exchange. The aid is "to make more effective regional use of academic talent,"[5] the underlying idea being to have the exchanges draw on the resources of foreign universities for program development, a purpose mentioned above as an important exchange contribution.

COMPARATIVE EDUCATION IN ACTION

Overall international faculty exchanges offer important benefits in enabling faculty at American colleges and universities to learn something of higher education systems elsewhere and to see American problems in an international perspective. For example, in the United States we seem to be moving toward an increasing enrollment of older students. As Martin Trow has pointed out, 48 percent of U.S. college and university students are over twenty-two years of age.[6] However, I doubt that the institutions have done much to adapt to this trend or have thought through its implications for our higher education institutions. In Sweden, enrollment of older students is expanding as a consequence of the policy which gives access to higher education to anyone who has worked for four years and is at least twenty-five years old. At the University of Stockholm, 25 percent of the students are now in this category. The university is having to grapple with how to handle this new clientele in terms of curriculum, teaching loads, the preservation of research in the face of increasingly vocational interests on the part of these new students, and the life of the university.

My final observation, therefore, is that visiting foreign faculty should be made members of college or university committees that are concerned with future problems and directions. Some countries have problems more acute in some areas than those in U.S. higher education institutions. It helps to hear occasionally that our problems are not unique and may even be less acute than those faced in other countries.

5. Henry Luce Foundation, Inc., *1974–75 Annual Report* (New York: The Foundation, 1975), p. 16.
6. "The Implications of Low Growth Rates for Higher Education" (Paper delivered at the conference "Implications of Low Economic Growth for Higher Education," London, May 1975), p. 17.

Association for International Cooperation in Higher Education and Research

GLEN L. TAGGART

IN TODAY'S WORLD, where so many seemingly insolvable problems are arising, where the needs and ambitions of nations clash fiercely, where a fresh crisis arrives as regularly as the morning paper, where the danger approaches the infinite, education and research have assumed an increasingly important place in the resolution of the ills which affront mankind.

For the past eleven centuries, the basic idea behind the university has never changed. Like many of the really achromatic ideas which have altered the course of thinking man, the idea behind the university is simple: a group of people whose main objective is the discovery, gathering, sharing, and extension of knowledge—*all* knowledge everywhere. The realm of the intellect for any university worthy of the name cannot be fenced by any artificial barriers. Certainly, the search for truth cannot be circumscribed by national boundaries.

• A basic component of a liberal education must be an intelligent understanding of our changing world. There is a growing need to impress our college and university students with a knowledge of other world cultures since the security of this country is dependent on a citizenry capable of helping to evolve a more harmonious world environment, a citizenry who understand the basic and underlying sources of conflict and who are sympathetic to the compulsions which animate the other peoples of this globe.

• Then, too, we in the universities must vastly increase the number of specialists we train for international service, specialists with skills that include a knowledge of institution building in foreign cultures. As problems common to all nations escalate, the shortage in America of trained scientists, teachers, engineers, and others who have an international capability becomes ever more acute.

• Still another need is to develop a spirit of educational cooperation among the scholars of the world and to interrelate educational programs of American colleges with those of institutions in other countries.

• We in the universities need to build additional world problem-solving activities into the service arms of our institutions. We need this increased component not only because we have a responsibility to ad-

vance learning wherever it is needed, but also because it will enrich our
programs and enable us to do a better job of educating Americans.

• We need to assemble in our faculties scholars from every discipline
and culture that we may explore together the questions that man finds so
troublesome. Our research personnel should not be fearful of tackling
problems international in scope, for they are precisely the problems that
demand the best minds for their solution.

These are some of the important roles which the universities must
play. Some we are carrying out now, though admittedly there is a need
to do so with greater effectiveness. Others we have yet to undertake.

THE PAST OF INTERNATIONAL EDUCATION AS PROLOGUE

Perhaps by tracing what the universities have already done, we can
better understand where we are today and find a sense of perspective
and direction. After all, international education is not a new concept.
Some of our nation's religious and private organizations were founding
colleges and schools in China, Japan, the Philippines, the Middle East,
and Africa as long ago as the nineteenth century. The Robert College in
Turkey and the American University in Egypt are two laudable examples
of these pioneering overseas efforts. Students from foreign lands have
been enrolling in American colleges and universities for many years (as
we have been sending students abroad), but until recently their numbers
were relatively few and their influence on our system of higher education was negligible.

Both geography and the course of history in the nineteenth century
inclined the United States toward an isolationist view of world affairs. A
land blessed with almost every requisite for an abundant life and
separated from the major world centers by broad oceans left little
incentive for involvement abroad. This insular viewpoint of the 1800s
extended into the twentieth century, and even our nation's involvement
in the First World War did little to change these attitudes. The failure
to join the League of Nations was evidence that Congress felt the
isolationist pulse of the American people was still beating strongly. It
was not until World War II that the strategy of isolationism was
abandoned, perhaps forever.

The United States emerged from the war ill-suited for the role of
leadership in which she found herself. The events of 1939 to 1945
presented the nation not only with a different world, but also with a

series of extraordinarily difficult, indeed perplexing, problems in the conduct of her international affairs. Those in positions of leadership found themselves grappling with the necessity to maintain a strong military posture to contend with the spread of communism. They found it necessary to encounter successfully the fantastic developments of worldwide scientific and technical advances. Those in business and industry were faced with demands to keep pace in productivity and development with competing countries and with opportunities to develop profitable markets abroad. And as the world's most affluent nation, we learned we could not ignore the yearnings of millions in the less developed nations who aspired to a modern standard of living.

To the credit of the universities, they saw the challenge and responded. Many universities joined in the new projects of technical assistance allied originally with the Point Four program, and in the intervening years the underdeveloped regions of the world have savored a rate of unexcelled educational growth. The American university has been loudly and deservedly extolled for its impresive achievements in the technical assistance programs, though there is still much left to do in relating the university to the fundamental task of developing in its students and faculty the desired competence in the international arena.

Our nation is no stranger to international education, including the exchange of scholars with other nations. Virtually every major university has developed fundamental ties with institutions abroad. But given the complexities and dangers of today's world, we must find means to continue these relationships and to accelerate such efforts. We must seek new avenues through which the higher educational community in the United States can effectively relate—in a bona fide way—to the institutions of a similar nature in other countries, and do so in a mode and style that will be in keeping with the tone and necessities of our present era. During the last quarter of the twentieth century, the American university community will face many crucial issues. Significant among these will be questions concerning the ability of our universities to discharge their responsibilities to the society they serve. The university community abroad will face a similar set of questions. The manner in which the world's network of institutions of higher education relate to each other in resolving these issues will be of critical importance to all.

There is today an urgent need within the world academic community for the interchange of ideas on an institution-to-institution, department-to-department, and individual-to-individual basis. Unfortunately the costs and complexity of intergovernmental relations have made the exchange a difficult task indeed. All too often the fluctuating relationships between nations have crippled exchange programs just as they have reached the productive stage.

A New Intermediary for International Cooperation

A few years ago the International Affairs Committee of the National Association of State Universities and Land-Grant Colleges began deliberating the issues associated with the international aspirations of the world academic community. The committee developed a line of discussion and planning which then led to the establishment of a task force consisting of institutional representatives and personnel of various higher education associations. The task force was asked to explore issues relating to the broad concern for international education and to the development of a suitable national approach. The associations involved in the task force were the American Council on Education, the National Association of State Universities and Land-Grant Colleges, the American Association of Universities, the American Association of State Colleges and Universities, the Association of American Colleges, and the American Association of Community and Junior Colleges.

Out of the task force's study came a proposal for the creation of a national organization, sponsored by the six associations, which would perform a number of functions in the international higher education field. The proposed organization was named the Association for International Cooperation in Higher Education and Research. Briefly, its main purpose would be to develop ways of tying together the institutional needs and interests in this country with those of other countries. It would be designed to provide a new focus and a new entry point for contacts between institutions. The aim and hope are that AICHER will serve as a dynamic force in the creation of new exchange opportunities.

AICHER is envisioned as building upon existing relations with institutions in the less developed countries and encouraging them to maintain or establish strong ties with advanced departments of colleges and universities in the United States. This approach could promote development of mutually beneficial long-term relationships and be a means of moving from the contract type of assistance to a new style of collaboration.

Assumptions and Functions

The AICHER proposal includes some basic assumptions that require further study. The assumptions fall into two clusters, related respectively to the lesser developed countries and to American higher education.

It is assumed, and substantial evidence says, that in many of the developing nations governments really want their higher education institutions to become deeply involved in development. Further, it is postulated that significant numbers of the governments are prepared to invest substantial sums in their universities for important development-oriented activities and that a significant number of universities abroad possess the capability and determination to engage vigorously in national development. It is assumed that the governments and their institutions will accept an association of the kind proposed in AICHER as an important, continuing resource in their national planning and development and regard such an intermediary association as needed—an association that would not be viewed as any attempt to exert American political and economic influence abroad. AICHER's character would be established by ensuring that it is an expression of the higher educational community and not of business or government.

The second cluster of assumptions, related to American higher education, includes the premise that American higher education has entered an era of interaction and cooperation across national boundaries which will be characterized by a spirit of partnership in exploring mutual interests and in achieving mutually determined goals. (The association proposal itself may well be one concrete sign.)

It is also assumed that American higher education institutions are genuinely interested in and capable of establishing or strengthening relationships that will help higher education in the developing nations to engage in problem solving and national development on an enduring basis, and that they are willing to do so through such an association as AICHER. It is believed that such an association could lead American institutions to increase their own investment of institutional resources and could gain significant, increasing support from both the public and private sectors to strengthen the linkages between American higher education institutions and those in the developing nations. American higher education, it is claimed, through its diverse institutions with experience in development at home and abroad, can appropriately join with higher education institutions in developing nations in a partnership to strengthen the role of higher education in development.

Declarations of interest from associations and institutions in the new era of international higher education cooperation are encouraging but are only a beginning. It is important to test the new cooperative style of working and the readiness of American higher education to invest its own quality institutional resources. Specifically, AICHER would serve as:

- An easily identified, responsive ingress for institutions abroad seeking contact with American higher education.
- An operational channel through which American higher education and research institutions may have ready access to the foreign university community.
- A source of information about opportunities for interinstitutional interaction, and a mechanism for establishing the parameters of mutually beneficial cooperation.
- A vehicle for providing new resources and for assisting U.S. and foreign institutions in mobilizing their own resources for cooperative activities.
- A linkage mechanism between U.S. and foreign institutions that are actively pursuing similar knowledge or solutions to common problems or that have other congruent academic and scientific interests.
- A forum for national and international agencies that are interested in or responsible for expanding the educational and research capacity of colleges, universities, and scientific institutions, worldwide.
- An avenue for exploring new opportunities for the exchange of scholars—both students and faculty members.

Proposal Activities

Although AICHER's initial program emphasis would be on the less advantaged regions, its operational devices would be adaptable to broader ranges of international intellectual communication and cooperation. For example, AICHER could attempt to provide topping-up grants to cover the difference between the remuneration that a foreign institution could provide a visiting U.S. academician and the sum necessary to make the desired arrangement possible. Such grants would be available for U.S. academicians on sabbatical leave, visiting professors at foreign universities, American scientists on short-term assignments, and distinguished lecturers from the United States and other developed nations.

In addition, AICHER might try to obtain funds to make up salary differences for American college and university personnel serving under country contracts for technical assistance projects.

Another operational device would help provide travel grants for U.S. and foreign scholars for professional interaction and joint scholarly research activities. The beneficiaries would be established, intermediate, and young scholars; graduate students; and foreign institutions desiring short-term consultants on scientific, academic, and administrative issues. Other contemplated operation devices would help support salary, travel, and subsistence costs of foreign scholars while they are in residence at U.S. educational institutions; provide for the promotion, organization, and funding of international seminars, symposia, workshops, and conferences; assist in financing special missions for planning and evaluating educational and research projects; and fund grants for research projects on priority issues of international significance such as population control and improved production methods. As funds would permit, AICHER could expand its activities to include cooperative programs with other developed nations and to other problem areas not directly concerned with development.

ADMINISTRATIVE ORGANIZATION

As presently conceived, AICHER would be an incorporated nonprofit organization. The founding sponsors (the six associations that participated in the task force) have designated the National Association of State Universities and Land-Grant Colleges to assume responsibility for exploring the feasibility of AICHER and determine whether the new association could serve as the chosen instrument for advancing enduring linkages between American and foreign universities. The Agency for International Development has awarded a $175,000 grant for additional exploration of the concept.

As currently planned, the new organization would eventually become an independent entity. Its ownership would reside in twelve trustees, of whom six would be the executive officers and six the elected heads of the sponsoring associations. AICHER would be governed by a board of directors appointed by the trustees to be broadly representative of American higher education. The new organization's funding would come from both public and private entities in the form of donations, grants, gifts, agreements, contracts, and appropriations.

EXPLORATION OF THE CONCEPT

There are many questions about AICHER still to be explored. The first is whether there is a demonstrable need for a new organization to serve university interests in America and abroad and, if so, how it might best be organized. In addressing these questions, a number of major concerns need to be examined:

• What are the priority needs that stimulate lesser developed countries to involve their universities more effectively in development problems? What are the constraints? And to what degree do these needs and constraints relate to U.S. university interests, resources, and operational styles?

• What needs and interests are shared by the developing nations and U.S. university communities to serve as a firm foundation on which to plan, implement, and achieve by means of the development process?

• What are the strengths as well as the weaknesses and inefficiencies of existing institutions, agencies, linkages, and networks with respect to the promotion of development abroad?

• What appear to be the most effective forms or modes of meeting the needs: institutional linkages, professional associations, or problem-oriented organizations?

• How do the alternative approaches compare in effectiveness, acceptability, financial requirements, and management arrangements for implementation and evaluation?

• How can institutional arrangements be organized and managed to emphasize priority development problems and to stay on target?

• What safeguards are essential to ensure programming that focuses directly on fundamental development goals?

• What incentives should be provided to promote a true collaborative style between U.S. institutions and those abroad in developing interdisciplinary resources useful in programming in a multisector context?

• Will the institutional arrangements under study (AICHER or other alternatives), which represent primarily the administrative levels of higher education, effectively marshal and support top-quality faculty expertise and other university resources relevant to the needs of the developing nations? And will the quality services be maintained as the direct university-to-university linkages continue?

• What arrangements should be made for periodic evaluations, particularly where policy permits any institutional arrangement to operate with a minimum of continuing supervision?

• What assurance can be provided for maintenance of quality and strength in the management of any institutional arrangement?

Those who have participated in planning AICHER are enthusiastic about its potential as a major institutional intermediary between American higher education and higher education in other areas of the world. Although there are other organizations with similar interests, AICHER is not envisioned as encroaching on their efforts. Pluralism in international education is probably highly desirable. As the next step, others who are interested in international education and the exchange of scholars need to evaluate the concept and interact with AICHER's planners in order to achieve an organization that is fully capable of doing all we would have it do.

Thoreau once said; "If you have built castles in the air, your work need not be lost; that is where they should be. Now put the foundations under them." Perhaps it is a deserved criticism that American higher education has too often—at least in international education programs— built castles without providing the necessary underpinnings. AICHER, it is to be hoped, can serve as a vantage ground for our future endeavors, the bed rock upon which we can fashion programs both significant and enduring. And in the process, we can be true to the calling of American higher education.

Professional Manpower Needs in Venezuela

RAMÓN MANCILLA H.

VENEZUELA is a developing country where new international exchange opportunities are closely related to its scholarship program and to its great need to train human resources within the country. In nations growing as rapidly as Venezuela is, one serious challenge is to guide economic and educational policy to the maximum benefit of the nation and its individual citizens.

The changes that have taken place during this century will illustrate the enormous effects on our manpower needs and, therefore, on the education program entailed. At the beginning of the century, Venezuela was an agricultural country of 2.5 million people, most of whom lived in the rural areas. Its chief exports were cocoa and coffee, in which it ranked second only to giant Brazil. In 1920, it produced only 0.1 percent of the world's petroleum; by 1937, it produced as much petroleum as Russia—10 percent of the world's annual production. In the last fifty years, petroleum has become the most important element in our national life, influencing the economy, urban development, education, and everyday life. Since 1921, the country has become dependent on the extraction of that nonrenewable raw material. Inasmuch as the petroleum produced was extracted, processed, and commercially handled by powerful international consortia, Venezuela's economy is based on a sizable foreign influence.

The first national enterprise within the petroleum industry appeared in 1960. By that time, oil industry products represented 90 percent of our exports and more than 60 percent of the nation's income—one-third of the gross national product. At the time of General Gomez's death in 1935, only 7 percent of the oil companies' profits were taxable and became royalties for Venezuela. By 1970, the situation was quite different: 67 percent of the profits were being returned to Venezuela. The industry has now been nationalized.

DEVELOPING A NEW ECONOMY

The radical change from an agricultural to an oil economy has meant a radical change in our labor sources, technical needs, financial capacity, and so on. Our long-time practice of importing much of our consumer goods has held back Venezuelan economic development and stifled progress toward reaching equality in the world markets. Nevertheless, since 1936 much thought has gone into the critical need to transform the economy so as to put an end to our dependence on a single product. And we must develop all possible of our national resources in order to take advantage of the consumption capacity of our international markets.

We have established the organizational structure to start development projects. For example, our irrigation system is capable of supplying water to thousands of hectares but is now operating at only 30 percent of capacity. We also have the social organization necessary to developing a national income distribution program.

Our economic policy has been developed in two stages. The first stage has concentrated on substituting Venezuelan products for imported goods: since 1940, we have succeeded in creating a protective climate for national industry and credit policies, under which, for example, we were able, by 1961, to reduce agricultural imports to 10 percent of all imports. The second stage, somewhat more complex, is concentrated on creating and developing export-oriented industries that in the future will provide for the country's foreign currency needs.

In the first stage, it is evident that the policy of substituting Venezuelan products for imports can be developed without depending to any great extent on international considerations. For the second stage, related to the export industry, development will have to take into consideration such factors as price and quality, which, in turn, depend on achieving capacity which is technologically and technically competitive with that of other nations.

POPULATION: IMPLICATIONS FOR EDUCATION

The efforts to carry out economic policies have sometimes been complicated by our population growth. During the 1960s, the population grew at an annual rate of 3.3 percent, which gives us a preponderantly young population. We estimate our population at 12.5 million, and of these, 8.5 million are under age twenty-six; in general terms, two-thirds of our population is under age twenty-five. This configuration is of great significance in the development of an independent economy. It makes the Venezuelan state responsible for achieving a coherent and integrated development that will favor all social sectors equally. Therefore, any model for socioeconomic development must be planned with its main variable as the social element. Such a model poses a new conception of the economic element and, consequently, of the scientific and technological elements. Thus we must evaluate the scarce resources going into technological and scientific activities and create within them developments linked to plans for socioeconomic development. Further, such a conception of the future must anticipate the consequences of innovations in areas such as employment, urban planning, resource conservation, the quality of life of our people, and the meaningful participation of different sectors in the national life.

A statement made by Frederick Harbison about Venezuela still holds much truth:

> Let us put aside once and forever the idea that Venezuela is an underdeveloped country. Venezuela is in the process of becoming a very advanced country, and Venezuelans should be conscious and proud of that fact. However, I take the liberty to suggest that the real wealth of this nation is not its mineral resources, its assets in foreign currency but the stage of mental development of its population.

If a country does not develop its population or its human resources, economic development projects will be condemned to failure.

Harbison's statement indeed challenges us to serious thought about the future. When we talk about training human resources, we are really talking about the nation's urgent need to plan for its educational system. In this sense, we have a series of problems related to quantitative and qualitative assessment of that system. Let me take up briefly some of our main concerns in this area.

In 1959, Professor Angel Rosemblat raised serious questions about the quality of our high school system. Not only do troublesome problems (which I shall not pursue here) remain unresolved, but also we can see ahead that our young population will pose even deeper problems for our educational system. We worry that we move slowly in developing our system and that we shall soon face a mass of demanding young people who must be channeled within the education system lest they be unemployed, in dissatisfaction or anarchy. Professor Reyes Baenas has reflected about this development as a motivation for education: "The only thing left to us is to wish that all those things happening now may become a subject for reflection, and that some day there will be a firm purpose to start from where we ought to start, because we have been asking for many years for an ordering of the educational system and the removal of those factors impeding our development."

Quantitatively, we observe with astonishment that from 1901 to 1970 there were only 48,000 university graduates. Of these, 54 percent were in the traditional fields of medicine, law, and civil engineering. Within the fields now considered as priority—that is, essential for the nation's development—there were only 244 chemical engineers, 393 petroleum engineers, 63 metallurgical engineers, 1,400 agronomists, and 1,247 educators.

Other figures requiring consideration relate to our educational population. In 1958 we had a population of 7.5 million, of whom 900,000 were elementary school students, 120,000 were in secondary school, and 16,000 were university students. In 1968, we had a population of 9.5 million, of whom 1.7 million were elementary school students, 360,000 were in secondary school, and 59,000 were in higher education. In 1974, the population was 12.5 million, of whom 2.5 million were primary school students, 1.5 million were in secondary school, and 150,000 were college students. Despite the surprising increases in enrollments, a large and growing number of youngsters are not within the educational system. Of the four-to-fifteen age group, 1.82 million are not in the educational system; of those fourteen to eighteen, only 516,000 are enrolled, whereas the nonenrolled number more than 1.1 million.

At the same time, academic records are alarming: only two out of every 100 who enroll in elementary school obtain a university degree. Yet we live in a world that needs a large proportion of postgraduates among the young professionals. We face a difficult situation: the increasing demand by industry for university graduates makes further specialization less attractive than immediate monetary and job gratification.

Whatever the pitfalls of our educational system, a process of change is taking place: we are starting a complex activity—an opportunity that few countries have had.

Need for Professional Manpower

Traditionally, immigration has been used as a means to help compensate for the lack of talent (the so-called brain drain). However, such countries as Japan, Canada, India, Germany, and even the United States have developed significant programs of transnational collaboration. In Venezuela's case, we have embarked on broad and detailed research on human resources in a collaborative effort by the staff of the Research Department of the Programa de Becas (scholarship program) "Gran Mariscal de Ayacucho" and a research team at the Massachusetts Institute of Technology. The study's purpose is to provide guidelines to policies for allocating scholarships, with the priority fields of study being chosen carefully so as to avoid unproductive investment in educating professionals who will later be unemployed or underemployed.

In the award of scholarships, we need a precise program derived from systematic research on demand and supply in the professional labor force market for the various sectors of the economy. It should be noted that research on human resources of the specificity needed by the Programa de Becas "GMA" has never before been undertaken. Earlier discussions about educating professionals have been centered on training "professionals with national consciousness" and linked to national needs without ever defining "national consciousness" or "national needs." Neither have these discussions produced specific recommendations about implementation policies designed to create the "ideal professional." As a result, analysis of the technical education needed by professionals has been overlooked. It is, of course, impossible to educate a future professional in all the techniques, knowledge, and information of that discipline. At the same time, the increase in knowledge and information exceeds the teaching capacity of our institutions. Stated another way, the crux of professional education is, not the quantity of knowledge taught, but the efficiency and selection of that knowledge for its applicability as a transforming agent for things not taught and for subsequent new knowledge. From this perspective, it is valid to consider institutional solutions, that is, to create new institutions and to reorganize existing institutions to maximize the selected functions.

PROFESSIONAL MANPOWER IN A DEVELOPING NATION

When we come to maximizing our profits from investment in training human resources, the model becomes more complex. In any given industry, the kinds of professionals needed from a given discipline are unlikely to be the same throughout the industry. The professional knowledge and abilities required by the industry will improve by defining them as a function of three elements: the speed of innovation and of generation of knowledge in the discipline; the speed of innovation and technological change in the industry; and the stage of the development cycle of the industry. In certain cases, the first and second elements coincide: when the degrees of specialization and specificity are in proportion in the profession and the industry concerned.

In cases where there is no specialization, the situation is as follows. The discipline of the professional develops so that in a short time he becomes distant from that discipline. The fields of industrial activity in which the professional works are also in a process of technological innovation; when technological innovation is combined with continued expansion of the industry, the type of professional needed becomes unstable.

As yet no analysis has been made of the quantitative and qualitative variations in the demand for professionals in an industry during its life cycle. We can distinguish four stages in the life of an industry: (1) the starting point, (2) the takeoff, or acceleration growth, (3) expansion, and (4) stabilization. The first stage includes establishment, search for staff, design of activities, and so forth. From here, the industry moves to takeoff, where the emphasis is on production operations and sales and all functions related to them. As the second stage reaches its maximum, stress shifts into the expansion stage. At the third stage, growth lessens up to the entrance into the stabilization stage. (There could, of course, be a contraction stage, which could end with closing down the industry.)

It is evident that the professional's activities change in each stage of a cycle of the industry. The managerial professional can serve as an example. In the first phase he will develop activities related to the design of administrative systems, study and evaluation of markets, hiring of staff, and so on. In the second stage, he will be concerned with activities related to production and sales. In the third stage, the activities will turn to financial planning, budgets, market strategies, and so on. The stabilization stage will call for professional specialists in project assessment, high management, and planning—that is, the search for new markets.

According to the traditional concept, professionals should adapt to the different functions they are required to perform at different stages. This conception is partly valid, but as a matter of efficiency, the problem, on analysis, becomes more difficult to handle. The activities mentioned in the examples have acquired—as a result of an increasing division of labor—the characteristics of particular disciplines, each with its individual methods, techniques, and knowledge. The problem becomes still more complex from the view that analyses similar to those applied above to managerial professionals are also relevant in all other professions-applied industries.

The problems posed by the empirical adaptation of professionals to functions for which they have not been trained makes it clear that the types of institutional solutions mentioned above lose whatever validity they could have.

In Venezuela, the limitations of our university sector combined with structural characteristics reduce the opportunities for a substantial part of our population to enter the universities and technical colleges. Even if our universities and technological institutes were overloaded with students, it is unrealistic to assume that they, with their limited academic staffs, could solve, with the needed efficiency and urgency, the problems of training professionals.

Both the limited access to higher education and our economic policies indicate that the search for solutions lies outside the university sector and will entail a nontraditional strategy. For these reasons, an international effort, such as the Programa de Becas "Gran Mariscal de Ayacucho" seems not only possible, but, we believe, also a creative solution for Venezuela's challenge. Our youth represent an immense and valuable natural resource. It is our goal to develop that resource to the greatest good of the nation and the greatest good of the individual.

· 6 ·

The Changing Employment Market

Too Many College Graduates for Traditional Jobs

BETTY M. VETTER

A CAREFUL LOOK at recent projections of the supply of and demand for college-trained people in the labor market can be depressing. Yet such an examination should stimulate ideas for educating and utilizing practitioners in fields where supply now or potentially exceeds the number of jobs that require training in those specialties. Those who are in positions to do something about the situation can, of course, let a crisis arrive before they decide how to avert or allay catastrophe, and sometimes they choose this path even when the coming crisis is apparent. In other cases, as they see the problem approaching, they try to make changes in advance that will alleviate or ameliorate the conditions foreseen. Objectively, most of them would choose to act before a crisis; in actuality, they usually do not.

A case in point is the perception of the job market for college-trained people over the next decade. Graduates are now emerging from our colleges and universities in numbers greater than the number of job openings that require the kind and level of training they have achieved. Among the reasons for oversupply are the many years of a rising birth rate (now leveling off), and the generally rising expectations about the proportions of young people who should go to college and the proportions of graduates who should continue into graduate school. By now, most people are aware that the condition of oversupply will not disappear as the nation pulls out of recession; rather, it is likely to worsen over at least the next decade.

Some recent projections of manpower trends tell the story. The Bureau of Labor Statistics estimates that new college graduates will exceed

112

available jobs requiring their skills by about 800,000 by the year 1985.[1] The problem will be less severe in some fields than in others because the professions and the technical, managerial, and clerical areas will, in general, be the fields of faster growing demand. For a number of reasons not fully understood, large proportions of young people have chosen to concentrate their higher education in fields where the demand is expected to be least. This situation is already beginning to change, as more graduates fail to find jobs in their field of preparation.

The Bureau of Labor Statistics says that between 1972 and 1985 about 13.2 million people are expected to enter the labor force after receiving their degrees. This includes 11.2 million at the bachelor's level, 1.2 million at the master's level, 40,000 Ph.D.'s not previously in the labor force at a lower degree level, and 750,000 persons with first professional degrees. In addition, more than 2.1 million college graduates who have not entered the labor force immediately after college will add to the supply of new graduates seeking opportunity. In this group are immigrants, delayed entrants, and reentrants, the latter two categories being composed principally of women. Thus, the new supply of college graduates expected to enter the labor force will total 15.3 million by 1985.

On the demand side, growth, replacement, and rising entry requirements are expected to open up about 14.5 million jobs, of which 7.7 million will be needed for growth and higher entry requirements and 6.8 million for replacement. The difference between supply and demand leaves 800,000 more college graduates than job openings, and these estimates, particularly at the doctorate level, probably are too low.

Doctorate Projections

According to another recent study by the Bureau of Labor Statistics, 580,000 new doctorates will graduate between 1972 and 1985.[2] But if present trends continue, only 187,000 openings requiring the doctorate are expected. In other words, only one-third of the new doctorates will find employment in traditional jobs. There is, of course, variation among fields (Table 1) with the greatest oversupply expected in business and

1. This figure and succeeding figures in this section are from U.S. Department of Labor, Bureau of Labor Statistics, *Occupational Manpower and Training Needs, Revised 1974*, Bulletin 1824 (Washington: Government Printing Office, 1974), p. 26.

2. U.S. Department of Labor, Bureau of Labor Statistics, *Ph.D. Manpower: Employment, Demand and Supply 1972–85*, Bulletin 1860 (Washington: Government Printing Office, 1975), p. 14. BLS estimates that all but 40,000 of these will have been in the labor force at some lower degree level before receipt of the doctorate.

TABLE 1: *Doctorate Supply in 1972 and 1985; Demand, 1985*

Field	1972 Supply	1985		Surplus	
		Supply	Demand	No.	%
Physical sciences	63,800	118,700	91,700	27,000	22.7
Chemistry	[35,900]	[61,500]	[50,500]	[11,000]	[17.9]
Physics	[22,600]	[41,500]	[29,400]	[12,100]	[29.2]
Engineering	31,000	80,100	59,100	21,000	26.2
Mathematics	12,400	31,400	19,800	11,600	36.9
Life sciences	54,500	137,700	73,100	64,600	46.9
Social sciences	63,800	153,700	87,100	66,600	43.3
Psychology	[22,700]	[57,100]	[34,400]	[22,700]	39.8
Total, science/ engineering	225,500	521,600	330,800	190,800	36.6
Arts and humanities	38,800	109,300	49,400	59,900	54.8
Education	58,300	201,200	79,200	122,000	60.6
Business and commerce	5,400	23,500	6,300	17,200	73.2
Other fields	6,700	15,200	9,100	6,100	40.1
Grand total	334,600	870,900	474,900	396,000	45.5

SOURCE: U.S. Department of Labor, Bureau of Labor Statistics, *Ph.D. Manpower: Employment, Demand and Supply 1972–85*, Bulletin 1860 (Washington: Government Printing Office, 1975), pp. 7, 11, 13, 14.
NOTE: Details will not add to totals because of rounding.

commerce, education, arts and humanities, life sciences, and the social sciences. The smallest oversupply is expected in the physical sciences and engineering, but even in those fields more doctorates are expected to be produced than there will be jobs available that have traditionally required a Ph.D.

Another recent projection of doctorate supply and utilization by the National Science Foundation has examined the picture to 1985 for the science and engineering doctorate population, a group that makes up nearly half of all doctorates. The probable model for 1985 (Table 2)

TABLE 2: *Science and Engineering Doctorate Supply, 1972 and 1985; Demand, 1985*

Field	1972 Supply	1985		Surplus	
		Supply	Demand	No.	%
Physical sciences	65,300	85,200	76,000	9,200	10.8
Engineering	34,000	63,300	45,000	18,300	28.9
Mathematics	12,900	21,600	16,000	5,600	25.9
Life sciences	56,700	92,100	85,000	7,100	7.7
Social sciences	52,500	112,700	71,000	41,700	37.0
Total	221,400	374,900	293,000	81,900	21.8

SOURCE: National Science Foundation, *Projections of Science and Engineering Doctorate Supply and Utilization, 1980 and 1985*, NSF 75-301 (Washington: NSF, 1975), p. 16.
NOTE: Details may not add to totals because of rounding.

shows a labor force of 375,000 doctoral scientists and engineers, with only 293,000 (78 percent) finding employment in science and engineering jobs. The BLS projections for these fields (Table 1) show a total labor force of 521,600, with jobs for 330,800, or 63.4 percent.

The totals for both current and projected supply and projected job openings differ between these two reports, resulting in differences in the numbers and proportion of projected oversupply. For example, in the physical sciences, NSF anticipates that 10.8 percent of the doctorate work force will not find positions in science and engineering in 1985, whereas the BLS finds an oversupply of 22.7 percent. In the social sciences, NSF finds 37 percent unable to be utilized in their fields while BLS projects 43.3 percent. The most radical difference occurs in the life sciences, where NSF sees only an 8 percent oversupply, and BLS shows a 47 percent excess.

The NSF "probable" model assigns double weight to the trends of the past five years, whereas the BLS model assumes a 3 percent per year increase in doctorate production to 1985 and a continuation of the Ph.D. pattern of use relative to other workers and to the proportion of persons obtaining doctoral degrees. These differences in assumption lead to a major difference in the numbers of new graduates projected; and there is also a large difference in the attrition rate assumed by the two reports (Table 3). But we should note that the BLS, which projects the higher supply, also projects higher demand in all science fields in 1985 than does the NSF. Thus, if the NSF estimates of demand prove to be more accurate than those of BLS, while the BLS supply figures are closer than those of NSF, then the oversupply would be greater than is projected by either of these reports.

TABLE 3: *Net Increase in Science and Engineering Doctorates, 1972–85, by Field*

Field	National Science Foundation			Bureau of Labor Statistics		
	New Ph.D's 1972–84	Migration, Attrition	Net Increase, 1972–85	New Entrants, 1972–84*	Migration, Attrition	Net Increase, 1972–85
Physical sciences	39,800	(19,900)	19,900	65,700	(5,400)	60,300
Engineering	40,300	(11,000)	29,300	51,500	(1,200)	50,300
Mathematics	13,300	(4,600)	8,700	24,200	(2,600)	21,600
Life science	62,400	(27,000)	35,400	101,200	(9,000)	92,200
Social sciences	83,900	(23,700)	60,200	113,700	(11,900)	101,800
Total	239,700	(86,200)	153,500	356,300	(30,100)	326,200

SOURCES: NSF 75-301, p. 16; BLS Bulletin 1860, pp. 13, 14.

* Only 70 percent of these entrants are assumed to have earned their Ph.D.'s in this time period.

Despite these differences in the numbers, however, these projections have in common one major finding: the number of persons trained to the doctorate level will exceed the number of job openings requiring such expertise, with the oversupply being of considerable magnitude. The persons represented by these numbers are a valuable national resource that should not be wasted. Further, if the doctoral training is not to be utilized, its cost should give pause to planners of such programs.

Oversupply for the Higher Education Market

Higher education produces the supply of new doctorates; it also is the traditional major employer of such persons. In 1972, 70.5 percent of the 335,000 employed doctorates were working in educational institutions; of the remainder, 14.6 percent were in business and industry, 8.2 percent in government, 3.8 percent in nonprofit organizations, and 2.9 percent in other employment. Of the doctorates employed in educational institutions, 50.4 percent were engaged principally in teaching, 32.8 percent in research and development, 8 percent in administration, 5.6 percent in professional services, and 3.2 percent in other positions. Only in the fields of engineering and chemistry were more doctorates employed in industry and business than in educational institutions. In some fields, such as arts and humanities, 95 percent of employed doctorates worked in educational institutions.[3]

The proportion of doctorates by field in 1972 was about the same as it had been ten years earlier: 48.3 percent in engineering and natural sciences, 19.1 percent in social science and psychology, 17.4 percent in education, 11.6 percent in arts and humanities, 1.6 percent in business and commerce, and 2.0 percent in other fields.[4] As yet, not much effort has gone into changing the proportions among the doctorate fields.

From the demographic trends projected for the next decade, it seems apparent that educational institutions will not afford expanding employment opportunities in the teaching of traditional-age students and that job opportunities must be sought in other employment sectors.

Universities, as both producers and major users of doctoral manpower, have some obvious problems to consider. They also have some potential choices to make. Or they can choose to do nothing to alter their tradi-

3. Ibid., pp. 1, 7, 12.
4. Ibid., p. 1.

tional patterns and await whatever may occur. To do nothing, however, is in itself a choice—with consequences. The alternatives to doing nothing are not completely clear and are certainly not obvious as choices; nor are they mutually exclusive.

First, colleges and universities can refuse admission to a significant proportion of all new students who seek higher education, particularly graduate education. This solution is advocated most often by older professional persons—in any area—who feel that their job safety can be guaranteed only by a shortage of persons trained in their specialty. Yet it includes several problems. It would doubtless mean a cut in college and university faculties, for there is little point in retaining teachers to teach students who are not admitted. It is blatant interference with the individual's right to choose the career area in which he or she wishes to compete and the level of training at which he or she does so. A third potential problem arises if the demand projections are wrong—as they often are. Indeed, data from different sources exhibit astonishing variance in both supply and demand figures even for doctorate personnel, and, at lower levels, the data are even less certain.

A second option is to continue to admit qualified applicants to a program of study. Under this choice, two paths may be taken. The first would continue traditional educational requirements. This path assumes that the student reaching the job market will simply compete with all the other people trained in that field, and may the best man or woman win. It removes the university from responsibility beyond that for the education itself.

ALTERNATIVE CAREERS FOR DOCTORATES

The second path is the more difficult one for universities and their faculties because it involves changes in traditions. It would require that students be kept informed of the best information then known about the job market not only in the field of their major but also in areas that might have peripheral interest. Persons who deal regularly with problems of supply and demand are continually astonished by mail from new graduates at all levels which indicates that their knowledge of the job market even in their own specialty is woefully inadequate. This second path may also call for changing course requirements for particular majors to allow and encourage students to pick up skills quite unrelated to their major field. And finally, and perhaps most important, it necessitates that faculty members change their attitudes in order to encourage not only the poorest but also the average and the best students to expect, and prepare for, the probability of nontraditional job opportunities.

The above discussion is simplistic in that it does not take into account that working professionals transfer from one field to another and from one type of activity to another. Field switching occurs when changing interests or better opportunities bring about a move or when lack of opportunity pushes people out of their chosen field and they enter other specialties where opportunities do exist. There are as yet no good measures of the incidence of field switching, the reasons for it, or its directions. A recent NSF report shows that women scientists are more likely than men to have switched fields after the doctorate.[5] Since the increased participation of women in the professional work force seems assured, studies of why and how successfully they have made field changes might produce useful information.

We can be sure, however, that if lack of opportunity in one field forces specialists to change, they will be happier if they do not have to deal excessively with unmet expectations. Thus it is important that students be directed in such a way that they will not see themselves as failures when their talents and education are not put to use in traditional or expected ways.

MAINTAINING THE ACADEMIC MARKET

Another option for colleges and universities is to modify their admission requirements to include persons who have not previously had easy access to formal higher education. The most obvious group is women who are older than traditional students. Although several programs are available to help women who have been out of the labor market for several years, the demand for such service has not been met, and opportunities for expansion exist almost everywhere. This option would increase the demand for teaching personnel, but also would increase the supply of trained people seeking suitable professional employment.

An option that would increase demand without materially increasing supply is the establishment of programs of educational enrichment for older persons who can afford and would like to continue a formal education interrupted many years earlier.

Another group, for whom special programs are needed, is persons in

5. National Science Foundation, *The 1972 Scientist and Engineering Population Redefined*, Vol. 1: *Demographic, Educational and Professional Characteristics*, NSF 75-313 (Washington: NSF, 1975), pp. 138–85.

the work force who wish to update their knowledge, improve their credentials, and be ready for better job opportunities. Again, this group does not expand the work force, but continuing education programs provide additional job opportunities for educators. In general, the major programs of this kind now being offered are those in the science and engineering areas which have been organized by professional societies rather than academic institutions.

These suggestions for programs to increase job opportunities in higher education are all being practiced in some places at some level. None, however, has been adopted widely enough to reach all the potential users.

For college graduates and advanced degree holders, the increase in numbers will require many of them to take jobs that have previously been filled by people with less education. This situation is bad only if it results in gross wastefulness of the investment in an education so specialized that employment outside the specialty means inability to work with satisfaction.

A majority of tomorrow's new doctorates will not find employment in teaching. Graduate students must no longer be led to believe that success is necessarily marked by following in the career of their thesis adviser. This dictum is easy to say and understand, but hard to put into practice. It may mean change in doctoral requirements. Most of all, it means a change in faculty attitudes, including increased concern for job opportunities for new graduates.

Students have begun to question the widening cost-benefit ratio of higher education, especially doctoral education. A study by Richard Freeman and J. Herbert Hollomon indicates that the rate of return on a college education has dropped from 11–12 percent in 1969 to 7–8 percent in 1974.[6] During this same period, the proportion of 18–19-year-old men enrolled in higher education fell from 44 percent to 33.4 percent, the proportion of women remained stable, and the proportion of black men students rose from 5 percent to 9 percent. If this declining trend continues, both the supply of new graduates and the demand for their services as teachers will be reduced.

If as much as two-thirds of our doctoral population in 1985 must find nontraditional jobs or be unemployed (I think this proportion is much too high), either the two-thirds must be rejected as doctoral students,

6. "The Declining Value of College Going," *Change*, September 1975, pp. 24–30.

with the attempt being made to reject the least able, or they must be prepared for alternative vocations. The third option is to continue as in the past, in the hope that those students whose unmet expectations make them angry do not band together and turn on the institutions that nurtured them, destroying the good with the bad.

Is it up to the university and its faculty to be concerned with the job market for its graduates? I believe it is. I believe it is also a responsibility of the university to expand educational opportunities to nontraditional student groups and to work with the private employment sector and professional societies to expand the job horizons for new graduates. Certainly it is a university responsibility to provide education that will allow its graduates to seek meaningful employment in peripheral and nontraditional fields.

The educational pipeline is a long one—particularly to the doctorate. Projections for ten years ahead should not be mistaken for forecasts. Further, they should not be an exclusive basis for encouraging or discouraging students in particular fields because too many unforeseen changes can occur. The very publication of a projection will to some degree change the outcome, thus making the projection turn out wrong. But projections are useful tools to warn us of potential problems.

The case is not hopeless, however. Universities, after all, house a concentration of capable, highly trained persons who must be asked to be as creative in finding new job opportunities for their students as they have been innovative in other ways.

Implications of the Changing Employment Patterns

DAVID STAGER

THE LIST OF ISSUES related to higher education and the changing labor market is extensive. In the past, the short-run changes have tended to dominate discussions and studies, that is, the apparent shortages or surpluses of professional and paraprofessional manpower as they occur during demographic cycles and economic development cycles. The quantitative effects of such cyclical patterns are clearly recognized; the qualitative effects on higher education are less clear. Even more uncertain are the implications—both qualitative and quantitative—for higher education that flow from the longer-run changes in the employment market: increasing labor force participation by married women, increasing emphasis on employment opportunities for minority groups, increasing demand for credentials in hiring practices, increasing geographical concentration of population and employment, increasing demands for periodic recertification of professionals, increasing summer unemployment for students, increasing use of early-retirement schemes, and, in some cases, increasing nationalism and demands for more restrictive immigration policies. And, some would add, a decreasing respect for the "work ethic." The list could be lengthened, and its implications could be compounded by taking into account the interactive effects among these several changes. Each has an influence on institutions of higher education, either as employers or as centers for learning.

THE MARKET FOR CONTINUING EDUCATION

Another element, the continuing education of employed persons, seems to me to represent one of the closest links between higher education and the employment market. It is, however, often omitted from discussions. Educational planners have not given high priority to continuing education, particularly to part-time degree study, possibly because the numbers of persons and the magnitudes of resources involved were small by comparison with enrollments and costs for full-time programs. The American record may be different, but in Canada until fairly recently part-time students were not included in the efforts to project university enrollments. The first published projections of part-time enrollment for Canadian universities appeared in 1967, when the technique applied was simply to estimate part-time enrollments as a percentage of projected full-time enrollments. This method continues in use despite significant discrepancies between the projections and the actual data. The more complex technique required would take into account factors influencing the educational participation rates of the 25–35-year-olds rather than the 18–24-year-olds. Unfortunately, some of the strongest influences may be the most difficult to forecast in the intermediate and longer term.

It could be argued, for example, that the same demographic factor that led to planning and financial difficulties in primary-secondary and then in postsecondary education—the postwar baby boom—should now be having its effect in continuing education. This group is now at age 25–30. The majority of persons involved in adult education, now and in the past, have been the 25–35-year-olds. Thus the demographic bulge alone could be expected to lead to larger adult enrollments. In addition, this immediate-postwar group, in comparison with its predecessors, has had more formal education and enjoys a higher level of real income, both of which are major determinants of participation in continuing education. With the increasing geographical dispersion of universities and community colleges, geographic proximity—another important determinant—would also have its effect.

If the emphasis on professional training and retraining increases and if the students' opportunity costs in foregone income rises significantly, the financial problems would be multiplied not only by the increasing enrollments but also by rising real costs per student. Demands for larger public subsidies for such programs could be expected to increase if only because the adult students of the future either enjoy or perceive a growing public support for full-time postsecondary education. Moreover, public regulations may require continuing education for professional practitioners such as doctors and dentists, who in turn can be expected to demand public support for their programs.

Statistical evidence on the growth of part-time undergraduate enrollments in Canada seems to support this kind of continuous growth model for future projections. During the 1960s, part-time undergraduate enrollment increased at an average annual rate of about 22 percent while full-time enrollment rose at annual rates of about 11 percent. In the early 1970s part-time enrollment has continued to increase at almost the same annual rate—about 18 percent—whereas full-time enrollment is increasing at only 2–3 percent annually.

Apart from a few isolated surveys in specific institutions, little has been known about the personal, occupational, and educational characteristics of part-time students from which future enrollments might be projected. As part of a study on university costs and financing, I surveyed a sample of part-time students in Ontario universities in the 1970–71 session. (Although the results cannot be taken as representative for Canada, part-time undergraduate enrollment in Ontario constituted 44 percent of the Canadian total.) The personal characteristics were roughly as expected: enrollments were equal between men and women; two-thirds were married, the average age was 30 years. It was more surprising, however, to find that 83 percent were in full-time employment. Of these, 54 percent were teachers, and, of the teachers, 75 percent were in elementary and junior high schools. The other 46 percent of the sample were widely distributed across the occupational classifications.

Furthermore, the teachers were much more job-oriented in their motivation for undertaking further study than were other persons. Over 70 percent of the teachers gave anticipated salary increase, promotion, or new job as their primary reason for studying, whereas these reasons were given by only about 27 percent of the persons in other occupations. The nonteachers tended to emphasize the satisfaction of studying and learning.

Elementary school teachers have always been the predominant group in part-time university enrollments in Ontario. Until 1973, a degree was not necessary for teacher certification, but it would bring additional salary and promotions. Since then, however, a bachelor's degree has been required for admission to the profession, and this requirement has had the once-for-all effect of pushing into part-time study the younger teachers who want to protect their long-term job prospects in teaching. When this group has completed the bachelor's degree requirements, future enrollments in part-time study will depend largely on persons outside the teaching profession; only 4 percent of the part-time students sampled were teachers who already had bachelor's degrees. Hence, the continuous growth model outlined earlier must be examined carefully in light of evidence that a substantial portion of part-time undergraduate enrollments are drawn from what might be a dwindling base.

I have focused on this example of a link between higher education and the labor market not because it is directly relevant to the American scene—it probably is not—but because it illustrates the need in educational planning to examine specific occupational labor markets and the events or forces that are influencing them.

CHANGING PATTERNS IN THE PH.D. MARKET

A somewhat similar problem can be illustrated by a quite different example, the market for Ph.D.'s. The notion of a "Ph.D. surplus" has attracted much attention in the popular press, but little attention has been paid to the employment distribution of new Ph.D. degree holders. It is widely recognized that there has been a decline in the percentage of new Ph.D.'s who enter university teaching and that this trend is expected to continue over at least the next decade because of the slower growth of enrollments and increasing financial difficulties in the universities. What is not so well known—at least in the Canadian case—is that even during the period of rapid university growth only one-half of the new Ph.D.'s were employed by the universities.

TABLE 1: *Immediate Postgraduation Employment of Canadian Ph.D.'s,
by Occupation*

Occupation, by Location	Percentage Distribution			
	Ontario, 1964–69	Canada, 1971–72 (N = 1,446)	Ontario, 1973–74 (N = 841)	Canada, 1973–74 (N = 1,757)
University teaching				
Canada	32	25	23	23
Elsewhere	16	13	11	10
Community college				
Canada	2	3	2	3
Elsewhere	0	0	2	1
Industry				
Canada	7	7	9	8
Elsewhere	5	2	1	2
Research fellowship				
Canada	7	18	15	16
Elsewhere	18	9	8	8
Private research institute				
Canada	1	3	4	5
Elsewhere	1	1	2	2
Government				
Canada	7	6	8	10
Elsewhere	2	2	1	2
Unemployed				
Canada	0	3	2	2
Elsewhere	0	1	3	1
Other				
Canada	0	6	7	6
Elsewhere	1	1	1	1

SOURCE: M. A. Preston, "Employment of New Ph.D. Graduates," mimeographed (Toronto: Council of Ontario Universities, 1975).

NOTE: Columns may not total 100, due to rounding.

Table 1 shows the employment distribution of new Ph.D.'s from Ontario universities during 1964 to 1969. Data for the total of Canadian universities are not available for this period, but a comparison of the percentage distribution for Ontario and Canada in 1973–74 suggests that the Ontario data for 1964–69 are at least rough proxies for Canada. It will also be noted that Ontario Ph.D.'s constitute about one-half the Canadian total.

Research or postdoctoral fellowships continue to account for about one-quarter of the Ph.D.'s; the majority of these are now held in Canada rather than elsewhere, as they were in the 1960s. There is also a slight increase in the employment of Ph.D.'s in Canadian government services. Unemployment has indeed become a regrettable reality for about 3 percent of the Ph.D.'s. This rate, however, is down from 5 percent in 1970–71, although the number of Ph.D.'s awarded over the following two years rose by about 20 percent. Thus, since the 1960s, the shift in

Ph.D. employment has been toward private research institutes within Canada, to that ubiquitous category "other" (which includes high schools), and to the community colleges.

The Ph.D.'s who have taken employment "elsewhere" tend to be those who were in Canada on visas and who represented about 11 percent of the total doctorates. Of the Canadian citizens, 84 percent were located in Canada after graduation, as were 65 percent of those with landed immigrant status, but only 23 percent of those on student visas remained in Canada after their Ph.D. degrees were awarded.

This brief look at adjustments in the market for Ph.D.-holders illustrates the need to examine in detail the market adjustments that have been taking place in the late 1960s and early 1970s before further aggregative educational planning decisions are taken. In the Canadian case, it appears that the government decision makers presumed that the sharp reduction in demand for new Ph.D.'s in the universities requires a reduction in resources allocated to Ph.D. programs. Although such a reduction may indeed prove to be true in the future, further attention must be given to the specific ways in which Ph.D.'s are used in the expanding areas of nonuniversity teaching and private research institutes.

Trends in Language and Cultural Studies

REMUNDA CADOUX

Over the past few years, the study of language and culture in American higher education has faced new challenges to which the response has been a wide range of innovations and adaptations. Traditional programs in foreign language and literature still predominate, but even the most traditional have been changed in response to the ferment of the 1960s and 1970s. Teachers of foreign languages have shown a willingness to supplement or even replace established programs with more practical courses which reflect the growing awareness that the world is now an interdependent community where the knowledge of foreign languages and cultures must play an important part.

The professional activity attendant upon such change has been tremendous, so great that it is possible here only to review briefly some general trends. Most of the data were obtained from articles in the *Bulletin of the Association of Departments of Foreign Languages* (ADFL) which furnishes a sampling of current thought and action. Obviously, for every innovative program that is reported, many others are being planned; for every revised curriculum that is cited, others have been implemented.

INTERNATIONAL ACTIVITIES, UP;

FOREIGN LANGUAGE ENROLLMENTS, DOWN

The vast number of changes in program offerings was sparked by the crisis in foreign language enrollments. As a result of surveys conducted in 1970, 1972, and 1975, the Modern Language Association of America (MLA) reported that, in a sample of 400 colleges, enrollments between 1970 and 1974 dropped: in French, by approximately 28 percent; in German, by 24 percent; in Russian, by 12 percent; and in Spanish (which seems to be becoming a secondary language in the United States), by 5 percent. Only enrollment in Italian courses increased—by 3 percent.[1]

The decline in the percentage of students studying foreign languages is astonishing in view of the growing American involvement in international activity during approximately the same period. In 1960 there were some 3.5 million students in colleges and universities, 17 percent of whom were studying foreign languages. In 1972, with almost 9.25 million students registered, only 10.5 percent were enrolled in foreign language courses. While the number of foreign language students increased appreciably, their percentage of the total college enrollment decreased by about 38 percent. On the other hand, a glance at just a few areas of American involvement in international activity reveals great percentage increases.

According to the Institute of International Education, between 1955 and 1972, the number of foreign students studying in the United States increased 244 percent, while the number of American students studying abroad increased 333 percent. According to the appropriate government agencies, between 1950 and 1972 the number of pieces of mail sent abroad increased by 120 percent; the number of overseas telephone calls, by 3,789 percent; the number of Americans traveling abroad, by 1,083 percent; the number of foreigners visiting the United States, by 1,219 percent; the amount of direct investments made by American firms abroad, by 629 percent; and the amount of foreign investments in the

---

1. "College Language Enrollments, Fall 1974," *Bulletin of the Association of Departments of Foreign Languages*, May 1975, p. 3. The MLA report shows the drop in enrollments for 1970–72 and 1973–74. The figures are composites of both periods.

United States, by 303 percent (with the investments made by the OPEC countries since 1973, this percentage will continue to increase).[2] The United States is the largest trading nation in the world, accounting for 15 percent of world trade. Some 3,200 American firms have branches or representatives abroad. More than 1,500 foreign firms have interests in the United States.[3]

The reason most often given for the general decline in the proportion of foreign language enrollments is that many colleges abolished the foreign language entrance and degree requirements. A preliminary survey report by the MLA revealed that in 1965–66, nearly 90 percent of B.A.-granting colleges had a functioning language requirement for the B.A. degree; in 1974 the proportion was only 54 percent. During the same period, the proportion of colleges that required a foreign language for entrance decreased from 33.6 percent to 18.6 percent. What of colleges having neither the entrance nor the degree requirements? In 1965–66, they represented only 9.1 percent of the institutions surveyed; in 1974–75, they represented 38.2 percent—an increase of more than 400 percent. One positive note might be added: "Of the 540 colleges reporting in 1974 that they have no all-college degree requirement, 286 (53 percent) indicated that one or more academic departments in their institutions require a language for the B.A. major."[4]

The dropping of foreign language requirements was not an isolated phenomenon in the social and cultural climate of the late 1960s and early 1970s, but simply one phase of the reaction against all formal requirements. The claims most often made in favor of abolishing language requirements were that language study is neither relevant nor useful and that it is tedious, time-consuming, and not worth the effort.

Another explanation given for the decline in foreign language enrollments is the changing character of the student population. American colleges no longer attract only the elite, but also draw a great number of students whose objective is to possess a salable skill at the conclusion of their studies. Community colleges, for example, of which there are about a thousand, claim a student population of at least 2.5 million.[5]

2. New York State Association of Foreign Language Teachers, "Public Relations Kit, 1974," p. 2.

3. Lucille J. Honig and Richard I. Brod, "Foreign Languages and Careers," *Modern Language Journal,* April 1974, p. 161.

4. "Language Requirement Survey," *Bulletin of ADFL,* March 1973, p. 3.

5. E. R. Mulvihill, "And What Next?" *Bulletin of ADFL,* March 1973, p. 13.

CAREER-ORIENTED TRAINING

The response of the foreign language profession to declining enrollments has been vigorous. Innovations have taken place in course offerings; articles have been written on both the humanistic and practical values of foreign language study; surveys have been conducted to establish the usefulness of foreign language skills in various occupations. The most striking trend at present is the emphasis on foreign languages for careers. Many American colleges and universities, especially those in urban areas, offer such courses as Commercial French; Commercial Spanish; Spanish for Health Care Workers, Social Workers, Police Officers. Many of the courses have become routine offerings. Lehigh University is offering German for Science, Business, and Industry; Russian for Science, Business, and Industry; and Practical and Business French. Howard University offers Scientific French and Spanish for Social Services. Many other examples could be cited.

In view of the growth of international business and industry, a number of surveys were undertaken to determine more precisely what occupational opportunities exist for personnel with a knowledge of foreign languages. In 1972 the MLA conducted a survey entitled "Survey of Foreign Language Skills in Business and Service Organizations," which revealed that "nearly 70% of the respondents said they do use, could use, or expect to use people with foreign language skills. For some positions, knowledge of at least one foreign language is a special requirement. For many others, it is an enormous help or tool that is used regularly. . . . A substantial number of employers stated that, given two job candidates with equal abilities in their area of specialization, they would hire the one who knows a foreign language."[6] Another survey of 100 business establishments showed that more than 8,539 positions existed for personnel with a knowledge of German; 1,136 of these positions were designated as being held by nonnative speakers of German.[7] Another survey showed that a large number of language-essential positions in the United States government are not being filled by linguistically qualified personnel.[8]

6. Honig and Brod, "Foreign Languages and Careers," pp. 159–60. This article is a comprehensive discussion on careers and the need for personnel with foreign language skills.

7. Rita Terras, "The 'Market' for German-Speaking Employees: A Survey of Business and Non-Academic Organizations," *Bulletin of ADFL*, March 1975, p. 26.

8. Giselle Huberman and Vadim Medish, "The Language Gap," *Bulletin of ADFL*, September 1973, p. 23.

Opportunities exist for people who can use a foreign language as an auxiliary skill in the fields of business, education, industry, commerce, law, library science, the media, science, the social sciences, services (such as health, social, religious, and missionary services), travel, tourism, and civil service.[9] For the use of foreign languages as a primary skill, the principal opportunities lie, of course, in teaching, interpreting, and translating. A number of points need to be emphasized. First, there is a need— sometimes termed "desperate"—for personnel with foreign language skills. Second, except for teaching, translating, and interpreting, knowledge of a foreign language is an auxiliary skill. In such fields as business administration, engineering, political science, marketing, chemistry, and the like, technical ability in the area of specialization is the primary consideration in hiring.

What can colleges and universities do to fill the needs of business, industry, research, and government for personnel with foreign language skills? Foreign-language professionals have been slow to recognize the potential usefulness of programs in which students can develop simultaneously a knowledge of language and culture and advanced training in another specialty. The language profession has thought too much about preparing language majors and not enough about providing substantial training for students with other majors.

Models for training students in language and culture as auxiliary skills are available in higher education in other nations. Professor Lucie Kirylak, bilingual publications editor, translator, and German teacher, combined the study of two foreign languages with an economics major at the University of Mainz in Germany. Professor Kirylak describes programs that seem arduous, but they are thorough and provide students with skills and knowledge that are marketable in our highly integrated world community. For example, after Britain joined the European Economic Community, several of its institutions initiated four-year degree courses combining the study of two modern languages with economics and political science.[10]

Will American colleges and universities institute such programs? Professor Cormier of Temple University reported that one of the areas of current exploration and activity in the Department of French and Italian at Temple is "a new sequence of courses in international business/legal/

9. Honig and Brod, "Foreign Languages and Careers," pp. 155–58.
10. "Foreign Language Career Preparation," *Bulletin of ADFL*, September 1973, pp. 42–47.

diplomatic French studies in cooperation with Temple's School of Business."[11] Will such cooperative programs become a combined major or a major in one area of specialization with a minor in language and culture?

With Ford Foundation support, the International Education Project was launched August 1, 1973, by the American Council on Education. The project is designed to identify and broaden the constituency and resources for international studies. The project's Task Force on Language has made many suggestions for improving the preparation of international specialists. The Task Force on Language also stated its belief that "specific projects should be launched immediately to explore new cooperative arrangements in specialist training."[12]

Another recent development in the area of international education may help open the door to cooperative arrangements. The International Education Project was awarded a $25,000 grant by the Exxon Education Foundation to set up a Task Force on Business and International Education. Among the suggested areas where improvements must be made is that of "nonbusiness course options in international, comparative, and area studies which can be utilized more effectively and/or adjusted to provide the student with broader global perspectives."[13] Language and area studies should be included among the nonbusiness course options. Certainly no other study can provide students with broader global perspectives or better facilitate international interaction than can studies in language and culture. Cultural knowledge needs no justification; regrettably, language study in the United States must constantly be defended. Learning a new language, however, is learning to live a new culture, to feel, see, and understand as a native feels, sees, and understands. Language is not a mere recoding of universal concepts: it is the medium that expresses the life of the culture of which it is an integral part.

In addition to the growing interest in preparing students to use language as an auxiliary skill, increased interest has been shown in training students for careers in translation, in which they will use the foreign language as a primary skill. In 1973, approximately twenty American

11. Raymond J. Cormier, "Areas of Current Exploration and Activity in the Department of French and Italian, Temple University," *Bulletin of ADFL*, September 1974, p. 26.

12. Rose L. Hayden, "In the National Interest: International Education and Language Policy," *Bulletin of ADFL*, March 1975, pp. 11–18.

13. "Business Task Force Funded by Exxon," *Bulletin of ADFL*, May 1975, p. 4.

colleges and universities offered varying amounts of training in translation. Yet many colleges and universities that wished to formulate programs in translator training turned for assistance to the Committee on Translator-Training of the American Translator Association. The committee prepared a series of guidelines for students who are majoring in foreign language but wish to minor in translation, especially in scientific-technical fields.[14] Indicative of the trend toward increased translator training is the Center for Translation and Intercultural Communication, established at the State University of New York at Binghamton and funded from September 1973 to October 1974 by the U.S. Office of Education. In addition to French, Spanish, German, and Latin which had already been included since 1971 in Binghamton's Translation Workshop, classical and modern Chinese, Russian, Polish, and Yiddish were planned.[15] At Carnegie-Mellon University, the Translation Center of the Department of Modern Languages received a grant from the Pittsburgh Foundation to develop still further its innovative programs in translation.[16] Professionals hope that the increased need for translators will give rise to additional programs. Materials and methods for translator training being used in other nations, such as those of the Ecole Supérieure d'Interprètes et de Traducteurs of the University of Paris, should be investigated.

New Curricula

Are there other new trends in language and cultural studies besides career–oriented programs? New course offerings are so diversified that it is difficult to distinguish any other single trend except that of an increased effort to meet a wide variety of student needs and interests. Area studies conducted in English continue to flourish. For example, at Eckerd College in Saint Petersburg, Florida, in addition to the usual language major, seven programs in area studies are offered: Afro-American, East Asian, French, German, Soviet, Spanish, and Latin American—the last two in alternate years. This wide range of programs, which consists of modular courses (two courses in a seven-week period), is offered to all students, and sophomores are required to take two of them.[17]

14. Royal L. Tonsley, Jr., "Guidelines for College and University Programs in Translator-Training," *Bulletin of ADFL*, May 1973, pp. 18–19, 15.
15. "Center for Translation and Intercultural Communication," *Bulletin of ADFL*, March 1974, p. 7.
16. "Translation Center at Carnegie-Mellon University," *Bulletin of ADFL*, March 1975, p. 4.
17. "Innovation at Eckerd College," *Bulletin of ADFL*, May 1973, p. 11.

The study of foreign literature in translation also continues to flourish. Here, too, increased effort is being made by some institutions to meet student needs and interests. Howard University is offering courses in Afro-French and Afro-Hispanic literature and civilization. One of these offerings may be taken to meet the two-year foreign language requirement. Class discussions are in English, and books are read either in the original language or in translation.[18] The Department of Slavic Languages and Literature of George Washington University offers a departmental major in Russian literature designed to meet the needs of students interested in the humanities and in comparative literature. Reading in Russian culture, literature, and literary theory may be done in translation, but students are required to have a reading knowledge of Russian.[19]

Offerings in language and cultural studies in the United States today, therefore, fall into three general categories: courses which are career-oriented; courses in foreign culture and literature conducted in English; and courses in literature, language, and culture conducted in the foreign language. The question remains, Are we serving our country's present and future needs adequately? The profession agrees that pragmatic solutions alone, such as those offered by career-oriented programs, cannot and will not be the only answer. Humanistic studies that deepen appreciation, develop insights, and release the latent creativity of students must continue to occupy an important place. Means, therefore, must be found to meet the dual objective of practicality and humanism for our highly diversified student body. In a world community that is becoming increasingly interdependent, the United States cannot and, we hope, will not continue in linguistic isolation.

Changes in Higher Education: Two Possible Futures

ALDO VISALBERGHI

IN RECENT YEARS, educational problems, principally at the higher education level, have been the subject of a huge number of articles and books in most of the advanced countries. The writings are, in part, the product of research projects, often international in character. The Carnegie Com-

18. Paula Gilbert Lewis, "Innovations in a Department of Romance Languages," *Bulletin of ADFL*, March 1975, p. 36.
19. "Russian Culture Major at GWU," *Bulletin of ADFL*, March 1973, p. 41.

mission on Higher Education and the International Council for Educational Development in the United States, the Council of Europe and the European Cultural Foundation on the Old Continent, the Organization for Economic Cooperation and Development and the United Nations Educational, Scientific and Cultural Organization for wider areas— these are among the organizations that have carried on research programs and sponsored the publication of several hundred volumes of preliminary studies and conclusions. Do their conclusions show common features? The answer is clearly yes.

Among these common conclusions, the most important are, in my opinion, the following:

1. *We are moving, or should move, toward forms of recurrent education, which will become, at the least, as important as sequential education at the postsecondary level.* The explosive expansion of postsecondary education, chiefly higher (college and university) education, even if now slowed slightly in several countries, remains impressive. Yet the spread of postsecondary education must not lead to a situation where everybody *must* attend a college or university after secondary school in order to avoid serious handicaps in the labor market, nor should highly selective practices, in effect, reserve higher education to the minority who are able to pass difficult entrance examinations. At least some forms of education should be preceded by a period of productive work. These themes, under different headings—"lifelong," "permanent," "continuous" education and recently more often "recurrent" education, which emphasizes the institutional aspect—are among the most widely discussed. Most Communist countries have *numerus clausus*, but encourage correspondence courses that may permit return to full-time higher education, and graduate studies are usually begun only after some years of productive work. Sweden, in its university admissions, now discriminates positively in favor of adult workers. Practices of "stop-out" or similar arrangements have been experimented with in the United States, Canada, and Japan.[1]

---

1. Henry Janne, "Permanent Education: An Agent of Change," *Permanent Education* (Strasbourg: Council of Europe, 1970); James A. Perkins, ed., *Higher Education: From Autonomy to Systems* (New York: International Council for Educational Development, 1972); Jarl Bengsston and Denis Kallen, *Recurrent Education: A Clarifying Report* (Paris: Organization for Economic Cooperation and Development, 1973); Selma J. Mushkin, ed., *Recurrent Education* (Washington: National Institute of Education, 1973); Carnegie Commission on Higher Education, *Toward a Learning Society: Alternative Channels to Life, Work, and Service* (New York: McGraw-Hill, 1973); Lewis B. Mayhew, *The Carnegie Commission on Higher Education* (San Francisco: Jossey-Bass, 1973); Dieter Berstecher et al., *A University of the Future* (The Hague: M. Nijhoff, 1974).

2. *Traditional university studies—that is, higher education—and other forms of postsecondary education are merging, or at least tend to become interrelated.* In some cases, as in Britain, a *dual system* has been implemented—university *and* polytechnic—in which the degrees conferred by two systems legally have equal value. But the Open University *is* a university, even though it serves principally working people. In Sweden, the university now tends to encompass every type of postsecondary education, and a similar goal is planned for the *Gesamthochschule* in West Germany. In the Soviet Union, specialized (including the *technicums*) and university education are unified under one ministry. In the United States, a great variety of institutions, but chiefly the public institutions, seem to be moving toward some kind of flexible integration in systems, where students can move more easily from one level to another and from one type of study or institution to a different kind.

3. *Short cycles of study are being developed and partly replacing the traditional continuous study that is interrupted only by normal recess periods.* Junior and community colleges in the United States, the French reform, and recommendations by several study committees give evidence of this trend.[2]

4. *Higher education institutions are moving from autonomy to systems,* usually regional systems, in which institutions, usually of various kinds and types, are drawn together and strong links established, chiefly for purposes of cultural, research, and planning services. This trend has been discussed by several studies, both American and European,[3] and examples such as Britain's polytechnics, the French universities created in the Paris area, the new Swedish local colleges, and advanced legislative projects like the German *Gesamthochschule* are concrete evidence of this trend.

5. *Cumulative records are to be adopted, summing scattered credits or "unités capitalisables" of any sort together.* Short cycles of study are not enough by themselves to facilitate and encourage recurrent education. French specialists talk of *unités capitalisables,* German experts of *Baukasten-Gesamthochschule,* and the Carnegie Commission recommends "shorter 'modules' of learning."[4] Although the size and characteristics of such blocks of curricula are not always conceived in the same

2. Organization for Economic Cooperation and Development, *L'enseignement supérieur court* (Paris: OECD, 1973).
3. See Perkins, *Higher Education,* and Berstecher, *A University of the Future.*
4. Bertrand Schwartz, *Permanent Education* (The Hague: M. Nijhoff, 1973).

way, and in spite of serious problems of sequential continuity of scattered units, the need to allow people to accumulate credits at different times and in different places and ways is strongly felt.

6. *Practical experience, production work, and civil or national services should be encouraged and evaluated in postsecondary education.* This trend is quite complex. On the one hand, it is related to the trend to broaden the subject offerings to make postsecondary education suitable for a much wider range of aptitudes and interests. On the other hand— and chiefly—this trend pursues a need to permit a growing proportion of youth to have experiences with real life. "Stop-out" practices and credit awarded for activities in various types of national and international organizations are already being accepted in the United States, as are also the so-called cooperative education programs, which are similar to British "sandwich education."[5] Sweden now has a university admissions policy that provides facilities for entrance after an adequate period of work. The requirements of work periods in most Communist countries has been noted above. This trend is also related to the labor unions' urging that workers have a right to periods of educational leave; at the moment, however, in countries where educational leave has gone into effect, its use has usually been limited to the lower educational levels.

In a broader framework, this tendency may ideally be connected with new forms of social planning aimed at vertical rotation of labor within industries. Most people would start at a low level and progress later through experience *and* study, so that "the difference between high-status and low-status jobs could thus, to an increased extent, become a matter of different stages in each individual's life rather than of early and definitive class distinctions."[6] Further, within society as a whole, it is felt some sort of work service can bring people closer to the social and moral rule according to which "all people ought to experience the disgust of a routine work," as we read in the new program of the Danish socialist party. In several countries civil labor service is advocated in some quarters either to substitute for, or be integrated with, compulsory military service, although its connection with formal education is scarcely considered.[7]

5. See Carnegie Commission on Higher Education, *Toward a Learning Society*, and Asa S. Knowles et al., *Handbook of Cooperative Education* (San Francisco: Jossey-Bass, 1972).
6. Gosta Rehn, "Toward Flexibility in Working Life," in Mushkin, *Recurrent Education.*
7. Segretariato Nazionale della Gioventù, *Servizio civile in Italia e all'estero* [Civil service in Italy and abroad] (Roma: 1972).

7. *Permanent drawing rights for education are advocated.* Chiefly in order to encourage postponement of postsecondary education, a system giving everybody the right to a certain amount of free postsecondary study, at any time convenient to the person, has been advocated both by European and American experts. The Carnegie Commission uses the expression "two years in the bank." A study sponsored by the European Cultural Foundation suggests an " 'educational fund' which is formed by the contributions of people at work."[8] Another study within the same framework, carried on by a group of experts coordinated by myself, considered "more radical solutions, where conventional university attendance (full-time attendance for some years closely following upon secondary studies) has to be 'pre-paid' in the sense that the period of compulsory work-service is somewhat longer for people aiming at such a formal attendance of university" in comparison with people aiming only at postponed recurrent education.[9] In any event, "educational bonds," in various forms, seem to be a rather widespread idea although as yet no country has actually experimented with a plan.

PROBLEMS AND HINDRANCES

All of the suggestions listed above are interrelated and seem to outline a picture of progressive, enlightened developments. But, if better analyzed, they show a more ambiguous nature.[10] In general terms, they can be easily reconciled with a regressive "scenario," in which supposed growth of postsecondary education would prove to be fictitious. Only some graduate studies, possibly in private institutions, would retain true higher education standards, in spite of a generalized but deceptive democratization. Each one of the tendencies described above might well work as a subtle form of social selection, even though giving people the illusion of moving toward a democratic "learning society." For such reasons, the concepts outlined are criticized not only by conservatives but also by some radical scholars[11] and by some labor organizations. In Italy, for instance, the new Federation of Labor Unions has worked out a "platform" for university reform, supporting the present system (which

8. Berstecher, *A University of the Future*, p. 121.

9. Aldo Visalberghi et al., *Education and Division of Labour* (The Hague: M. Nijhoff, 1974).

10. Aldo Visalberghi, "Lo sviluppo educativo nelle società avanzate e le sue contraddizioni" [Educational growth in advanced societies and its contradictions], *Scuola e Città*, January 1974.

11. André Gorz: "Le programme caché de l'éducation permanente," *Temps Modernes*, November 1974.

has been criticized by experts),[12] and rejecting short-cycle and postgraduate studies (because of the dangers of discriminating among students) and the elimination of short- and middle-length curricula.[13] But a careful analysis of the document reveals curious inconsistencies: for part-time study, it advocates the award of certificates similar to the rejected short-cycle diplomas; for prospective university teachers, it requests four years of postgraduate training similar to study for the doctor of philosophy degree. As another instance, there is mistrust of the secondary regional system, including decentralized institutions and services.

In my opinion, the above examples are indicative of the great difficulties that those interested in democratic reform of postsecondary education are experiencing when they face the above-described general tendencies. Apparently the new concepts are an outgrowth of scientific and technological progress rather than an issue of ideological choices.

PRESENT TRENDS AND THE "BIFURCATE FUTURE"

The reluctance to move toward such needed reforms may have its roots in some deeper motivation which is seldom made explicit. The trends outlined, although necessarily correlated with progress in general terms, are by no means neutral in leaving other things unchanged. They probably will work strongly, as they interact with other wider social and political developments, in one of two opposite directions.

As already noted, if the sociopolitical framework remains blurred, the concepts, if adopted, might promote new forms of meritocracy or, rather, of pseudomeritocracy related to a somewhat disguised hierarchical and authoritarian class structure. If, however, the general concepts interact with other kinds of sociopolitical changes, they might contribute strongly to a completely opposite scenario. Let me examine this "bifurcate future."

Alternative one: We know that in advanced countries the socio-occupational stratification tends to assume an egg shape that is radically different from the traditional pyramid.[14] Unskilled, repetitive, alienating labor becomes a minor and decreasing proportion of the total number of jobs needed in the economy—the bottom, pointed end of the egg shape. Conceivably within two decades this segment of work will occupy

12. Barbara Burn, "Il sistema emergente di educazione superiore in Italia" [The emergent system of higher education in Italy], in Bisogno et al., *Università, diagnosi e terapia* (Roma: Officina edizioni, 1974).

13. "Università: la piattaforma unitaria," *GGIL—Sindacato e scuola*, June 23, 1975.

14. Torsten Husén, "Lifelong Learning in the 'Educative Society,'" *International Review of Applied Psychology*, 1968, no. 2.

something between one-fifth and one-tenth of the work force or total worked time provided the "ratio of change" of work by advanced nations is not altered greatly. Yet it is easy to imagine that all the educational developments noted above, but principally the expansion of recurrent education, would have the effect of giving most people a second chance to move into the intermediate social strata (probably not to the top), leaving at the bottom only the fifth or tenth needed for the most unskilled, repetitive, and frustrating types of labor. Inasmuch as the lowest stratum is made up mostly of people who are suffering the consequences of early cultural deprivation, such a pseudomeritocracy will consolidate the class structure through giving it a fictitious rationality.

Further movement toward a hypothetical *perfect* meritocracy should be capable of neutralizing the social conditioning and eventually cause a downward social mobility equal to the upward movement. This development is highly improbable because the middle and upper classes would react strongly against the possibility of having any of their children placed in the lowest occupational strata. A more probable sequence is a further development in the international division of labor, like that which already prevails in many highly developed countries: Immigrant workers do the heaviest and less skilled jobs, and investments are made in the developing countries that, in effect, exempt the most advanced people from a part in such jobs. This latter sequence requires that migrant workers remain quiescent if they need to retain their jobs, as must the developing countries themselves if they need foreign investments and fear retaliations. The phenomena are familiar under such terms as racism, neoimperialism, and neocolonialism, which seem to connote the necessary framework.

Thus, one route of our "bifurcate future" seems to point toward a model of society where internal class tensions are *partially* discharged at the international level because the advanced (chiefly Western) countries enjoy a highly privileged economic situation. How long this state can last is another question. But the model is self-consistent in the middle period if not in the long run; and a new role of postsecondary education, developing all the concepts outlined above but expanding chiefly the "further education" and "recurrent education" sectors, fits in with it perfectly well.

The Radical Progressive Alternative

In direct contrast to alternative one is *alternative two,* which—surprisingly enough—would contain much the same ingredients in educational developments. The difference lies in the general sociopolitical framework and in a more structured and systematic, even if gradual, implementation of the single elements. One element would be of particular importance—the interconnection of work and study.

In such a model, education at the postsecondary level is a universal right in fact because it is *prepaid* by universal work service (for instance, one year for all young people and possibly a year and a half for people aiming at full-time sequential education). In such a model, much of the labor would become available for unskilled work needed chiefly in such fields as environmental protection, surface and sea communications, and so on. Additional labor for unskilled and menial work would be available through the practice of having work careers start at the bottom (assembly lines, cleaning, delivery services, repetitious office work), with everyone later moving up the occupational levels, assisted by a highly flexible system of recurrent education. This model would implement Gosta Rehn's idea noted above, "the difference between high-status and low-status jobs could thus, to an increased extent, become a matter of different stages in each individual's life rather than of early and definitive class distinctions." New agreements between employers and labor unions will be the main instruments for developments of this kind. (Some recent labor contracts in Italy tend to unify blue- and white-collar careers and also stipulate the right to paid educational leave.)

Compulsory work service and, in general, initial entry into the labor market at the humblest level—these two elements combine to form a job ladder, though individual life, that puts the burden only on the young but still does not exhaust all needed lower level work. But in a fairly advanced technological society, these two mechanisms will be conducive to a "quality jump" so that other forms of labor rotation fit naturally into the structural change, both in industry and other areas. A concept of people's leading many-faceted, active lives should be encouraged through much more flexible labor laws, even laws that would permit intermediate activities between free-time leisure and occupational calling.

THE LEARNING SOCIETY

This second scenario may be enriched at will and also may be diversified according to the prevailing degree of freedom or restraint, centralization or autonomy, equality or competition (at the middle and highest levels only), and so on. But the features described are those indispensable for structural consistency. The general condition would then be a society with a great *abundance of competences*, that is, universally widespread

knowledge and skills, to a degree never before achieved in any large society but fairly possible in the "educative" or "learning society" that is
forecast by many experts. Several Israeli *kibbuzim* have developed such
characteristics by structuring themselves as small, classless societies with
a considerable degree of vertical rotation in their work. This development has been possible because of the unique initial conditions for such
a social experiment. However, no large country has made a similar move
even when it is ideologically engaged in closing the gap between manual
and intellectual work, as in present-day China. The occupation structure
of China is a pyramid with a very large base that at present prevents
the universal practice of a vertical rotation of labor.

This second model may be labeled as utopian and unrealistic; nevertheless, in the most advanced countries, all the emerging tendencies concerned with the evolution of postsecondary education find in it a consistent and harmonious integration. As for its utopian character, it might
be objected that utopia is an imaginary state of affairs unconnected with
the actual situation. Yet several recent developments of radical and even
liberal thought seem to point toward models of this kind. One important aspect of the new left and of movements born in 1968 has been
the growing perception of the lasting class stratification even in allegedly
Marxist countries.

On the other side, utopia *is* realistic in the present dead end of our
civilization. *L'Utopie ou la mort* (either Utopia or death) is the title of
a recent book by the French agricultural expert René Dumont.[15] His
utopia includes work service and vertical rotation of labor. Some speak
about a "need of utopia" in contemporary society,[16] warning that ideal
solutions for advanced societies may be unsuitable for backward ones,
even within the same nation. But Dumont is advocating technologically
sophisticated solutions in advanced societies to enable them to aid the
less advanced societies in ways that are truly appropriate.

For present purposes, one particularly important characteristic of this
model is the link connecting educational development, chiefly postsecondary education, and the implementation of the new model. The learning society is a society in which the knowledge industry becomes the
leading one. Culture and education are no longer superstructural phenomena nor are they epiphenomena; their size and economic importance

15. Paris: Editions du Seuil, 1973.
16. Carlo Tullio-Altan, "Bisogno di Utopia" [The need of Utopia], *La Stampa*,
Aug. 26, 1975.

make them really structural in the Marxian sense. But there are acute contradictions to be solved. First is the overproduction of skills which, in traditional situations, produces intellectual "unemployment" and can be counteracted both by pseudomeritocracy and the exploitation of Third World nations, which leads back to our first model.

A more appealing solution, at least in a modern "learned" society, would be to make the sociopolitical relations correspond to the productive forces. Then superabundance of competences is a necessary condition of progress, not just a shortcoming; recurrent education is the key mechanism of society, not just a device for giving people limited second chances in a pseudomeritocratic system; work and study alternation and interrelation are a socially accepted imperative, not simply rhetorical indulgence to some idealistic request (or simply an efficient instrument for continuous training). And so on. In any event, the new model would not come about as a mechanical result of the objective situation. The core question will be that of hard cultural and political choices, concretely grounded in reality and not utopian in the derogatory meaning of the term.

Ends and Means

This second model is useful because it implies not only the development of new procedures and institutions but also new cultural content for education. It projects far-reaching ends to be faced in the light of the past and in the light of other ends and values. If we rightly conceive ends in terms of means, several things we are already striving for, vaguely defined as "progressive" ends, acquire new meaning as well as a more precise context. We become fully aware of the ambiguities we are involved in; we can adjust our sights; we can enrich our daily action with a precise consciousness of our stake in the future, which is not only educational but also and necessarily cultural and political.

In different countries different ways can be taken toward a common goal. A national service system might be developed on a voluntary basis in some places, but elsewhere it may be grafted onto an existing military service, retaining of course a compulsory character. In any case, the duty for everyone to perform his share of the humble, nongratifying work needed by the human society must be something like an article of faith or postulate of the new culture and, therefore, of the new education.

The word *progress* is rightly in crisis, as well as the word *growth* and many others, which until recently were themselves articles of faith. The word *progress* might be requalified quite simply if progress is conceived as everything which frees each man from the slavery of lifelong, stupid labor and gives each man the sense of duty for taking joyfully on himself his share of the burden. Such a transformation in human cultural tradition, centered until recently on the social division of labor, might well be considered as the historic challenge of our age by most people working in higher education, both those in teaching and in scientific research.

This postulation may not be a neutral vision, but it is at least a consistent and stimulating one.

• 7 •

Equalizing Educational Opportunity for Women

What Kind of Equality for Women?

RIVKA W. BAR-YOSEF

THE MATTER OF EQUALITY has been one of the most persistent issues in the intellectual and institutional history of human societies. As an abstract idea, it has been discussed from the perspectives of theology, philosophy, and ethics. As an empirical problem, it has been studied by political scientists, economists, and sociologists. As a practical dilemma of social policy, it is an integral part of all social structures. A society or social group, whatever its nature, needs to define the desired or accepted balance between equality and inequality, for even the most hierarchic societies are built on groups of equals and even the most egalitarian ones include some factual inequalities.

In spite of this duality, most sociological studies analyze the dynamics of inequality, and only a few try to understand the social structure from an egalitarian perspective. The emphasis on dynamics may have resulted from the view, widely held among students of the subject, that stratification—the institutionalized form of large-scale inequality—was a necessary and nearly ubiquitous feature of all societies. But whatever the perspective of the scholar, and whatever the differences between countries and time periods, it is generally agreed that some factors of social differentiation are universal. Some rewards are societal and can be achieved, whereas other factors are inherent characteristics which serve as bases for ascribed status. Biological and demographic characteristics such as age, sex, color, race, origin, and religion are often used for ranking people as criteria for selection.

143

According to Eisenstadt,

> In all societies, individuals are classified to some extent in terms of these attributes; but only rarely does one of these attributes function as the sole principle of stratification, decisively linking a differential evaluation with the allocation and use of social rewards. One seldom encounters a society in which most of the significant rewards are allocated according to age, or in which sexual differentiation gives rise to a distinct, wholly exclusive style of life, and the power of controlling access to all highly valued positions. In most societies, such a system of stratification is precluded by the nature of the family unit, which is usually the focus or model of a style of life that is shared by individuals of all ages and both sexes.[1]

This type of differentiation Eisenstadt calls "a partial stratification." I prefer the term "secondary stratification" to emphasize that, unlike other stratification criteria which create a vertical hierarchy of groups, age and sex are the differentiating characteristics within each of the ranked groups. Inequalities based on sex and age are present even in such highly egalitarian societies as the Israeli kibbutz and small holder cooperatives, and studies of stratification tend to emphasize the common aspects of age and sex as ascriptive, primordial bases of status differentiation.

RAMIFICATIONS OF SECONDARY STRATIFICATION

In matters of equality, a cardinal distinction is made between age and sex. Inherent in age-based inequality is a sequential equality throughout the life cycle, as each person goes through each age period. Holter sees sex differentiation as a separate distributive system that may or may not be correlated with class stratification, with sex ranking geared mainly to the "horizontal social structure," especially the relationship between the family and other spheres of activity such as the occupational, economic, educational, and political. "Gender differentiation may have different functions in each of these main institutions. . . . There tends to be a considerable spread of sex differentiation from one . . . [sphere] to another. In spite of many formal barriers between the sectors, the degree of sex differentiation in one of them typically affects the degree of sex differentiation in others. It is possible, for example, that equality between marital partners in the modern family contributes to a certain

1. S. N. Eisenstadt, *Social Differentiation and Stratification* (Chicago: Scott Foresman, 1971), pp. 65, 66.

measure of companionship between men and women in work life, and vice versa."[2]

One important point is that sex differentiation and the other distributive principles are interdependent. Thus the relationships of the sexes and the relative position of the women vary according to age, race, and class stratifications, at the same time that inequality between the sexes may reinforce or be in conflict with the existing hierarchies. This interdependence, often mentioned, is only scantily explained or documented.

Although theoretical and empirical literature on stratification is abundant, there is little systematic analysis that includes sex differentiation. Sociological theories of stratification have a primarily masculine perspective, based on three premises: "1. The family is the unit in the stratification system. . . . 2. The social position of the family is determined by the status of the male head of the household. . . . 3. Females live in families; therefore, their status is determined by that of the males to whom they are attached. . . ."[3] Consequently, much of the research on women deals with sex and family roles, and it is only in theories on the family that both sexes and their behavior are included, with the male usually considered as the prototype for universal human behavior.[4]

As a result, the functions and dysfunctions of sex differentiation have been studied mostly within the framework of family sociology, and sociological theories of stratification seldom apply to the problems of women in other than family roles. In addition, a large part of the research refers to white, middle-class American women and in many instances, both in and outside the United States, is dominated by the model of the American middle classes. Often when women are studied in other than family roles, the emphasis is on the conflict between "women's two roles," with their position in other institutional spheres neglected. There is no parallel tendency to analyze men's two or even three or four roles. "The relative neglect of men's roles by social scientists is probably, in part, a reflection of the fact that it is women, not men, who complain most about the bases of role differentiation. It is

2. Harriet Holter, "Sex Roles and Social Structure," *Universitets forlaget,* 1970, pp. 225–27, 223.

3. Joan Acker, "Women and Social Stratification: A Case of Intellectual Sexism," *American Journal of Sociology* 78 (1973):936–45.

4. For a criticism of male perspective in social science models see, for example, Cynthia Fuchs Epstein, "A Different Angle of Vision: Notes on the Selective Eye of Sociology," *Social Science Quarterly* 55 (1974): 645–56.

also probable that social scientists make the common assumption that men constitute the norm with which members of the deviant sex, women, should be compared."[5]

It is reasonable to predict that a change in attitude in the social sciences would lead to a reformulation of considerable parts of the sociological theory. Besides the scientific interest in such a reformulation, it is needed for practical purposes. If we want to achieve greater equality by planned intervention, it would be helpful to know the conditions under which inequalities can be reduced and to learn about alternative ways of action and the probable consequences of each type of intervention. For example, Gans tries to describe the changes that would occur in several institutional areas if distributive principles, among them sex differentiation, were more egalitarian.[6] I shall not here supplement Gans's "utopian scenario" with the missing chapter on sex equality in higher education. But even a much less utopian endeavor must try to answer such questions as, What is the desirable goal? What are the prerequisites for its implementation? and, What will happen in other parts of the society after it is implemented?

CHARACTERISTICS OF THE DISCRIMINATION

Assuming, as I have, that the issue of equality is present in all social structures, it follows that I also believe in the desirability of equality in general and of sex equality in particular. Belief in the rightness of equality should, in itself, be a satisfactory reason for wanting a more egalitarian situation at the academic level, and there are other reasons to reinforce belief in equality for women. (1) Assuming that intelligence is not sex determined and that higher education is an important stage for the development and utilization of intellectual resources, the intellectual resources of women should not be wasted. (2) Higher education is at present the prerequisite for full participation in high level activities in other areas, such as the professions and political and academic leadership. (3) In a society where knowledge and science are highly valued, universities are symbols of prestige. Equality at the universities symbolizes the sex-free bestowal of prestige. (4) The right to maximum development of one's capabilities, if desired, should not be hindered by one's sex.

Cross-culture data on the position of women in higher education

5. Holter, "Sex Roles and Social Structure," p. 17.
6. Herbert J. Gans, *More Equality* (New York: Pantheon, 1973).

shows some common trends in inequality. Although the amounts of inequality may differ, the similarities (at least in the industrialized societies) are overwhelming: Men students usually outnumber women students. The proportion of women decreases at each higher level, whether the system has two levels, as in the United States and some European countries, or three levels, as in the British, the Russian, and Israeli systems. The choices of the field of study reveal a high degree of sex segregation. Some fields are everywhere chosen by a high percentage of women students and thus are labeled "feminine" subjects, while others are "masculine." Nursing, social work, education, languages, and literature tend to attract more than 50 percent women students; sciences, technological studies, and economics and business administration tend to have men in the majority; social sciences, philosophy, and history show no consistent sex-based pattern of choice.

Some fields vary with the cultural setting. Thus, medicine and dentistry seem to be male strongholds in the United States, whereas they attract a high proportion of women in the Soviet Union and some other Communist countries. Chemistry and biology have low proportions of women students in the United States and Australia, about 33 percent in the Soviet Union, and 50–60 percent in Israel.

Women are underrepresented on all faculties, even compared with their proportion among Ph.D.'s, but the higher the level, the lower the proportion of women. The proportion of women faculty members does not depend on the proportion of women students; indeed, these two proportions are often inversely correlated. In coeducational colleges and universities, the proportion of women in the top administration, such as deans or presidents, is even lower than on the faculties. In any event, the cross-cultural uniformity of these findings is remarkable.

A considerable number of empirical and theoretical research studies are trying to clarify and interpret the phenomena of sex bias in higher education. In general, three types of analysis can be discerned: some studies focus on sex characteristics, genetic or learned; a second type looks at normatively defined sex roles; the third type seeks the explanation in the organizational structure of institutions of higher education.

The fundamental reasoning in the first type of research might go as follows: A prerequisite of academic performance is the possession of certain personal resources that may be randomly distributed between the sexes or may be sex determined. If there is a difference in resource distribution between the sexes, then the seeming inequality is caused by women having inadequate resources. These prerequisites may be intellectual capabilities, motivational energies, behavioral programming, or a combination thereof.

Capabilities. It is well documented that there are consistent differences between the sexes in the various dimensions of intellectual ability. Females show better verbal skills and language use; males have higher mathematical ability. It also appears that the cognitive style of women is less analytical than that of men. Men surpass women students in problem solving when the solution sought involves restructuring. There is no fully satisfactory explanation about the genesis of these differences but there is no doubt about the reinforcing effect of early socialization and the culturally defined and socially legitimized expectations about the differences.[7] Thus men's cognitive resources are more adequate for scientific performance than women's. But within each sex there are large variations and a high probability that, when other social status variables are matched, the underutilization of intellectual capabilities will be higher for women than for men.

Motivations, interests, and commitments. Women in general, including women students and scholars, have been found to score lower than men on measures of achievement orientation and ambition. Horner, in an often cited study, has identified in women a "motive to avoid success," which she sees as a "stable, enduring personality characteristic."[8] Success avoidance acts as an automatic brake that restrains the gifted women from attaining success—goals such as high achievement in the university or a prestigious career. However, a replication of Horner's study, which did not produce the same results, points toward social rather than psychological explanations, and its authors wonder whether the ready acceptance of Horner's theory is not a proof that the theory is consonant with the social expectations and sanctions toward female achievement.[9] A different approach presupposes that women may be as ambitious as men but that their goals and their styles of achieving goals are different. Compared with men, women are less competitive and more altruistic, and are more interested in the quality of performance and in intrinsic rewards. They are less interested in prestige and mobility. These findings bear out research data on the occupational and aca-

7. Eleanor Maccoby, ed., *The Development of Sex Differences* (Stanford, Calif.: Stanford University Press, 1966).

8. Matina S. Horner, "Toward an Understanding of Achievement: Related Conflicts in Women," *Journal of Social Issues* 28 (1972): 157–75.

9. Adeline Levine and Janice Crumrine, "Women and the Fear of Success: A Problem of Replication," *American Journal of Sociology* 80 (1975): 964–74.

demic interests of women. Women, more than men, seek education, culture, and self-development at the university. In their occupations they are more person-oriented, more concerned with the integrative needs of the organization, and want to help others.[10] In a competitive academic system, these orientations are dysfunctional for academic success—especially if they are in harmony with a traditional feminine image—and for a distinct definition of the role of women students and scholars.

Role orientations and role behavior. The basic model for this type of study is drawn from the sociological and sociopsychological theories of role. Role theories see normatively defined roles as the main determinants of stable social behavior. Through identification with role images and role models and under a system of rewards and sanctions, the role incumbent learns the role and is socialized into accepting its norms. The actual role behavior is the outcome of interaction between role in the context of the given role and the conflicts, compromises, or integration with the other roles of the incumbent.

In theory, in a modern society such roles as student and scholar are supposed to be neutral, not differentiated by class, race, or sex. Nevertheless, it has been found that the role of women students and academic scholars is perceived differently from that of the men.[11] Women students are considered as being less committed to, and less competent in, their studies and as having weaker career orientation than their male peers. It is often suspected that their main aim is, not to study, but to find a husband. Although the proportion of men and women students who marry is about the same, no such stereotype exists for men. Women students have less derogatory but similar ideas about their own role. They are more ready than the men to study "just for culture"; many of them expect to work outside their field of study; and they underestimate their ability and performance.

Women scholars take more time to achieve their Ph.D.'s; they are also more involved in teaching and are producing fewer papers and books than their colleagues. They are often perfectionists and are more critical of their own work than are men. A partial explanation of the

10. Ralph Turner, "Some Aspects of Women's Ambition," *American Journal of Sociology* 70 (1964):271–85; Michael P. Fogarty, Rhona Rapoport, and Robert N. Rapoport, *Sex, Career and Family* (Beverly Hills, Calif.: Sage Publications, 1971), pp. 391–425.

11. Cynthia Fuchs Epstein, *Woman's Place* (Berkeley and Los Angeles: University of California Press, 1971); Harriet Zuckerman and Jonathan R. Cole, "Women in American Science," *Minerva* 13 (1975): 82–102.

role differentiation between sexes can be seen in the respective quality and quantity of personal resources of each. An alternative or possibly complementary proposition is the "self-fulfilling prophecy."[12] Women behave as they are expected to by their role partners, and they also develop the appropriate complementary personal attributes.

ROLE CONFLICT

The role conflict theory provides another argument, which says that even in modern society women's primary allegiance should be to their family. The family role is supposed to be a "greedy" role that molds the behavior of women in general and claims a large part of such scarce resources as time, energy, and interest. Nonfamily roles, such as those discussed here, presuppose a high level of commitment, use up resources heavily, and thus unavoidably conflict with the priority of the family.[13] The conflict theory appears as a logical explanation of the phenomena and is one of the most popular and popularized propositions. Its wide acceptance in itself raises some suspicion: the theory fits the current stereotypes too well and contains a not-so-hidden hint about solving the conflict by eliminating the second role, which is always the nonfamily role.

Other arguments also point to the possibility that the conflict exists in its present form because it is socially defined as such. The need for ranking priorities is a feature of social life, and men are not exempted from it. In many societies marriage and parenthood are as important for men as for women. Nevertheless it is expected that men will manage to integrate several competing, probably conflicting roles, whereas women are expected to suffer a stress of conflict if they try to combine scholarship or profession with their role in the family.[14] There are also some theoretical doubts about whether multiple roles inevitably produce stress. Sieber shows that role accumulation can produce substantial benefits when all the roles are recognized by the social environment.[15]

Role analysis thus reveals the social mechanisms of the inequalities in educational success. It shows a measure of incompatibility between the prevalent definition of women's role and the role images of the

12. Epstein, *Woman's Place*, pp. 22–24.
13. Saul D. Feldman, "Impediment or Stimulant? Marital Status and Graduate Education," *American Journal of Sociology* 78 (1973): 982–94.
14. Rose Laub Coser and Gerald Rokoff, "Women in the Occupational World: Social Disruption and Conflict," *Social Problems* 18 (1971): 535–53.
15. Sam D. Sieber, "Toward a Theory of Role Accumulation," *American Sociological Review* 39 (1974): 567–78.

student and the scholar. Because of this contradiction, the fulfilling of both roles is expected to create conflict and stress. Social pressure is then exerted, which ensures that the conflict is felt. The conflict in turn diminishes the chances for the women to develop the appropriate role behavior.

INSTITUTIONAL STRUCTURE AND SYSTEMATIC DISCRIMINATION

The organizational setting of higher education is shown by some studies to be unfavorable or outright discriminatory for women. The adverse conditions are at the least attributable to an institutional structure in which it is assumed that only the masculine definition of the student-scholar role is institutionally relevant. Although these role definitions are unrealistic even for men, as Komarovsky proves, they are nevertheless tenaciously maintained by the academic organization. The obsolescence of these assumptions is especially evident in Israel, where few male students are able or willing to be exclusively committed to their studies and career, but regardless of these findings higher education continues to operate unchanged.[16]

This hidden male ideal finds its overt expression in the actual composition of the academic elite. The faculty, the high level administration, and even the heads of the student organizations are predominantly men. Thus the power structure, the prestige structure, and the role models for successful performance are men. It is not proposed here that men cannot serve as educators, teachers, or role models for women, or women for men. But for the women students who are discouraged and doubtful about the legitimacy, desirability, and workability of a successful career, the visibility of female role models is important. The exceptional cases of one outstanding woman among many men do not prove that the position is generally attainable. Neither do they provide life style models that can be adopted by the average woman student and scholar.[17]

The inadequate representation of women in the upper levels of the academic power and prestige hierarchy strengthens the existing system in its traditional form and helps to perpetuate the marginal position

16. Mirra Komarovsky, "Cultural Contradictions and Sex-Roles: The Masculine Case," *American Journal of Sociology* 78 (1973):873–84; Rina Shapeera, "Halevi Etzioni Hava" [Who are you, Israeli student?] (Tel-Aviv: Am-Oved, 1973).
17. Elizabeth M. Almquist and Shirley S. Argrist, "Role Model Influences on College Women's Career Aspirations," in *The Professional Woman*, ed. Athena Theodore (Cambridge, Mass.: Schenkman, 1971), pp. 301–23; Epstein, *Woman's Place*, pp. 53–71.

of the women in the academic world. As a byproduct it also excludes a large proportion of academic women from access to the important formal and informal sources of information. Thus the women have few opportunities to learn about efficient tactics that are no less necessary (or at least helpful) in the academic marketplace than in any other large organization.

Overt discrimination is the most obvious obstacle confronting women. Its presence and nature are as universal as the other problems discussed here. There are discriminatory entrance norms, especially to the departments that train for such male-dominated occupations as medicine and engineering. Men are often preferred candidates for scholarship and travel grants, the preference being justified by the unpredictability of women who "marry and become pregnant." Women have less chance of being hired and promoted for faculty or administrative positions, and their incomes are lower than those men. A considerable increase in the number or proportion of women in a departmental faculty is deemed detrimental to its prestige, and hiring and promotion decisions thus might be influenced by such a consideration.

The forms of discrimination described above are all rooted in the same fundamental, preconceived ideas about women and their roles. The analysis here attempts to point up their interdependence and to confirm that there is indeed a system based on the principle of sex differentiation. This system includes theories about the biological and psychological attributes of women, views of their personality, norms of role behavior, and organizational patterns defining their position. All these elements are mutually reinforcing, and their cumulative effect is a loosely cohesive, resilient system that can tolerate occasional changes without essential transformation of the system itself. A minimal aim of equalization might be limited to partial changes, but if a substantial increase in equality is to be achieved, the system itself will have to undergo changes.

EQUALITY: WHAT KIND AND HOW MUCH?

I am not in a position to estimate the feasibility of such far-reaching, initiated social changes, and certainly the possibility would require further research and systematic thought. Any change, whether partial or comprehensive, will need some preliminary definition of "desired equality." The considerable multidisciplinary literature on inequality and equality includes discussions of alternatives within egalitarianism.

Gans defines equality as "equality of resources, equality of treatment and equality of outcome."[18] I have tried here to analyze each of these aspects of inequality, implying that they are related and should be so treated and that in an integrated system of inequality, the chances of maintaining equal opportunities are negligible.

Inherent to the concept of equality, or even the less pretentious "more equality," is a comparison. In our case, women are compared to men. Equalization means changing the relationship between the sexes, but such a change could take several forms. Rossi outlines three models of equality: the *pluralist* model—the equal but different label—which is in essence the traditional pattern; the *assimilation* model, in which women have to be like men and acquire equal positions in the existing structure; and the *hybrid* model, which aims at changes in both groups and in the structure.[19] Rossi advocates the hybrid model and thinks that it would benefit men as well as women. "From this point of view, the values many young men and women subscribe to today are congenial to the hybrid model of equality: the desire for a more meaningful sense of community and a greater depth to personal relations across class, sex and racial lines; a stress on human fellowship and individual scope for creativity rather than merely rationality and efficiency in our bureaucracies; heightened interest in the humanities and the social sciences from an articulated value base; and a social responsibility commitment to medicine and law rather than a thirst for status and high income."[20]

A program for change in the academic world could be judged by its comprehensiveness and the difficulty of the obstacles. The first step should be to eliminate all formal discrimination in such matters as scholarships, entrance opportunities, hiring, and employment conditions. Even so obvious a change needs the active and continuous support of the women involved.

A more elaborate program should facilitate the academic activities of women without, however, making major changes in the socialization practices, family roles, and the social position of women. The university should sponsor services for families with or without children. It should provide learning sequences that allow for periods away from the uni-

18. *More Equality*, pp. 62–73.
19. Alice S. Rossi, "Equality between the Sexes: An Immodest Proposal," *Daedalus* 93 (1964): 638–46.
20. Alice S. Rossi, "Sex Equality: The Beginnings of Ideology," cited in Lynda Lytle Holmstrom, *The Two-Career Family* (Cambridge, Mass.: Schenkman, 1972), p. 162.

versity and reentry. In Israel there are two patterns, but both are mainly for men. One is for the younger men who have reserve duties in the army and are called up each year for twenty to forty or even sixty days. A set of norms has been developed to cope with the problem, the principle being that reserve duty should not jeopardize the academic development of the student or the career of a faculty member. The second pattern is open mostly to men around age forty who are starting a second career and are either retired career army officers or members of a kibbutz. Similar programs should be developed for women. Several Israeli universities maintain preacademic courses to assist immigrant and underprivileged students and prepare them for entrance examinations. Preparatory courses of this kind could increase the number of women in such fields as medicine and engineering.

More comprehensive programs aimed at basic changes toward a hybrid model in the universities, in education in general, and in the larger society are proposed by Rossi, Graham, and Fogarty and Rapoport.[21] The effects of a comprehensive equalization on the principle of sex distribution would be revolutionary and difficult to predict. Some of the costs of such a change should be considered. No doubt the life style of men would be changed. Says Rossi: "No amount of entreaty will yield an equitable distribution of women and men in the top strata of business and professional occupations, for the simple reason that the life men have led in these strata has been possible only because their own wives were leading traditional lives as homemakers, doing double parent and household duty, and carrying out the major burden of civic responsibilities. If it were not for the wives in the background, successful men in American society would have to be single or childless."[22]

The validity of Rossi's statement is not limited to the United States or to business and the professions. Certainly it is valid for the academic world. Changes in the criteria for academic achievement are challenging the established status of the academic elite, which attained its position through the traditional criteria. Academic productivity, as measured at present, is a special kind of productivity which stems from a rather narrow definition of the functions of higher education. Incidentally, it is also contrary to the abilities of the women and a not negligible number of

21. Alice S. Rossi, "Women in Science: Why So Few?" *Science* 148 (1965): 1196–1202; Patricia Albjerg Graham, "Women in Academe," in *The Professional Woman*, ed. Theodore; Forgarty et al., *Sex, Career and Family*, pp. 473–511.

22. "Sex Equality: The Beginnings of Ideology," cited in Holmstrom, *Two-Career Family*, p. 163.

the men. Will a change in these criteria lead to a slowdown in scientific developments? Will it lower the quality of research, teaching, and the academic community? These are weighty questions, and the answers do not depend solely on our sociological skill to analyze and predict future developments.

Like any large-scale social change, sex equality will involve social and human costs. It depends on one's values whether the outcome will be deemed worthwhile.

Beyond Title IX: Nondiscrimination Is Not Equality

ROBERT M. O'NEIL

WHAT MORE, one may well ask, can be said about title IX? With all that has been written on the subject recently, the question is quite proper. At some risk of redundancy, I offer yet one more view on this topic, with a slightly different perspective. I suggest, in brief course, that title IX is (*a*) necessary; (*b*) diversionary; and (*c*) minimal. By title IX, I mean not only the underlying 1972 Higher Education Act amendments but also the recent regulations and memoranda from the Office for Civil Rights of the Department of Health, Education, and Welfare.

Title IX is necessary. It is, in fact, long overdue, for the barriers and inequities at which it is aimed have tainted higher education for many decades. Data about the exclusion of women from some fields and their acute underrepresentation in others are well known. Yet, quite simply, the academic community did little to reform its own practices—somewhat less, it may be noted, to remove discrimination against women than comparable bias against racial and ethnic minorities. The insensitivity of academic leadership in the 1960s—the decade of expansion when almost anything was theoretically possible but little actually done—made external intervention inevitable in the 1970s. The perpetuation of double standards and sex quotas in admissions could no longer be tolerated by legislators and other public officials who were feeling pressure from a newly aroused female constituency. Recruitment, hiring, and evaluation systems, which were premised on an informal, male-dominated network, not only kept *women* out of the higher academic ranks, but also effectively barred nontraditional *male* groups. The homogeneity of the professoriate, even today, is a striking fact of academic life and one that is bound to generate pressures for change from without inasmuch as internal catalysts have been largely ineffective.

If title ix was necessary in the early 1970s, it has become even more vital in mid-decade. The recent contraction of new academic openings would almost certainly have decreased the proportion of women in the professoriate (unless, of course, salaries declined to the point where, as in the Great Depression, many men could no longer afford to teach and women would gain by default). The recent data from the Lipset-Ladd survey of the academic profession show that, even with federal affirmative action requirements, the gains of academic women in recent years have been slight.[1] Whether or not title ix will be *effective*, there should be little doubt about the necessity for some such form of government regulation.

What is true for faculty and professional staff is also true for students. The focus is not only on admissions, where title ix is breaking down some ancient walls, but also on financial aid, which rising inflation has made an increasingly vital component of educational opportunity for middle as well as lower income students. Because the allocation of fellowships, scholarships, and the like has tended in the past to favor male students, some formal guarantee of nondiscrimination in this area has been essential.

Title ix *has been diversionary.* The statute and particularly the implementing regulations have generated controversies peripheral to the main issue and have diverted attention from the primary problem. The best example is the highly publicized attack of the National Collegiate Athletic Association and other sports groups on particular provisions of title ix. Although sports are a relatively minor part of the package, the average television viewer or newspaper reader would naturally assume that they were the prime, if not the sole, focus of new federal equality laws. This distortion of the real meaning of title ix—and the invitation to locker-room humor on the sports pages—is unfortunate by itself. The deeper meaning of a major new law and the need for it may have gone largely unappreciated by the public and even by many in the academic community.

My greater concern is, however, with another kind of diversion. Over the past year or more, spokesmen for some of our most distinguished

1. Everett Carll Ladd, Jr., and Seymour Martin Lipset, *The Divided Academy: Professors and Politics,* Sponsored by the Carnegie Commission on Higher Education (New York: McGraw-Hill, 1975), pp. 171, 172.

universities have challenged the whole concept of federal affirmative action regulation. Title IX seems to have been the final straw or at least it has been the lightning rod.

Yale University President Kingman Brewster, for example, has become a forceful critic of affirmative action programs and policies. In a spring 1975 speech to the fellows of the American Bar Foundation, Brewster charged, with specific reference to affirmative action, that the federal government was using public funds to achieve goals that were highly questionable both legally and as public policy. One excerpt will illustrate: "[I]f we are to receive support for physics, let's say, we must conform to federal policies in the admission of women to the Art School, in women's athletic facilities and in the recruitment of women and minorities—not just in the federally supported field, but throughout the University. This is constitutionally objectionable, even in the name of a good cause such as 'Affirmative Action.'"

This analysis is misleading for two reasons that go to the very heart of federal regulation of higher education. First, it is misleading because it suggests that federal funds would be denied to one program because a university practiced sex discrimination in another unit; in fact, title IX expressly limits the *sanction* to the offending area. Second, this position posits an unrealistic model of the university. An institution may indeed receive federal support for physics, but not for art. That distinction does not, however, confine the scope of federal law to directly assisted departments. Surely the art school benefits indirectly from the substantial overhead the institution receives on its federal grants and contracts. External support of one program releases general funds for others and thus benefits even those areas for which government subvention is unlikely or remote. Moreover, a university cannot be compartmentalized in the way the Brewster model implies; art students take physics courses— and vice versa—and may change majors; faculty members hold joint appointments in federally aided and nonaided departments; subsidized and nonsubsidized units may share buildings, and so on.

Finally, it is misleading to suggest that government may not require some action as a condition of receiving federal aid which it cannot compel outright. It is true that an individual (or presumably an institution) cannot be forced to surrender a constitutional right as a condition of eligibility for public funds. But that is not the case with any current legislation to which Brewster and others have referred. Such a problem might have arisen if, for example, the title IX regulations had banned "sexist" teaching or textbooks and required the dismissal of male faculty members who made chauvinistic remarks in class. Academic freedom clearly protects the right to hold and express sexist views. But nothing in title IX or the regulations compels colleges or universities to violate the rights of faculty members or, for that matter, abridges the rights of recipient institutions themselves. Yet the public debate on these issues has probably left many people with the impression that rights and liberties have been jeopardized by the new forms of regulation.

One point of clarification is important. Because a particular form of regulation may be constitutionally valid, it is not necessarily sound or wise on public policy grounds. The limits of federal regulation of higher education critically need to be reassessed as acts of Congress and administrative rules encroach ever further into the administrative and even the academic domain. (No administrator of an Ohio public university could be insensitive to this issue after being forced to create a Department of Family Practice out of whole cloth in ninety days or forfeit all future subsidy for medical education.) Indeed, the raising of hypothetical or unreal legal claims only *diverts* attention from the vital public policy issues on which the counsel of the academic community is urgently needed. It is this diversion, an unintended but probably inevitable effect of title IX and the regulations, which is most worrisome.

If *title* IX is both necessary and diversionary, as I have suggested, it *is also minimal*. At most, it ensures nondiscrimination in certain aspects of higher education. It does not promise, and probably could not promise, equality of opportunity for academic women. Some of the most critical steps needed to achieve equality lie well beyond the reach of federal law. Statutes and regulations such as title IX can do little more than prohibit discriminatory practices; they can only begin, in this way, to promote equality.

The achievement of equality of opportunity depends on institutional and individual responsibility that is effectively beyond the reach of laws. The academic environment, for example, is critical to the success and confidence of both women and minority students. Attitudes of faculty members and administrators, as expressed in class and outside, are absolutely crucial, but clearly cannot be controlled by legislation or administrative regulation. The content of textbooks and other teaching and curricular materials can have a vital effect on women and minority students, yet the drafters of the title IX regulations quite properly stopped short of this sensitive area of academic life. Options for part-time study in formerly and traditionally full-time fields are important to mature women and those with family responsibilities; yet here again federal law does not reach and is not likely to reach. Academic programs in women's studies and the infusion of greater concern about women in traditional courses can also make a major contribution, though it seems unlikely that government will even subsidize, much less require, such curricular reforms. Child care programs, special counseling services, women's social and study centers—all these and many other options contribute to equalization of opportunity for women in higher education. Such programs as these are, and probably should be, beyond the purview of federal law. It is in this respect that title ix must be regarded as a starting point, a threshold form of regulation.

The critical concern, with which I conclude, is whether even this limited degree of formal regulation may deter institutional progress toward equality. There is unquestionably a backlash in higher education, directed not only against racial and ethnic minorities, but against women as well. In part, the counterpressure is aimed at sometimes heavy-handed or insensitive government edicts in a new and complex area of regulation. But the backlash is also aimed at the substance of federal antidiscrimination laws and their impact (real or imagined) on higher education. There is no simple solution, for the laws in question are as essential as they are controversial. Better understanding and a willingness to suspend judgment will surely help. But the road to equality will not be an easy one, even if paved with the best intentions.

· 8 ·

Autonomy and Accountability

Autonomy and Accountability in Latin America

LUIS GARIBAY G.

DESPITE FREQUENT USE OF the words *autonomy* and *accountability*, neither conveys the same idea universally, and both concepts are characterized by ambiguity and vagueness. Ernest L. Boyer has pointed out that accountability is a "very fuzzy notion, connoting different things to different people." Even more indefinite is the concept of autonomy in higher education. John W. Nason, for example, thinks that complete autonomy would be absurd, whereas Luis Alberto Sánchez is of the opinion that "autonomy . . . exists or it doesn't. Half-tones are not possible."[1]

Recently, when I asked the distinguished German educator Dietrich Goldschmidt to explain briefly his idea of university autonomy, he began by pointing out that "autonomy of a university should be understood within the singularity of each national system." But, of course, even within each nation, there are marked differences among the educational institutions.

In the Continental European systems, according to Goldschmidt, state authorities provide budgets, are responsible for general planning, make the final decisions in designating at least the senior faculty members, and establish the requirements for state examinations. "Autonomy" of the

1. Boyer, "Some Reservations about Accountability," in *The University's Response to Societal Demands,* ed. James A. Perkins and Philip Altbach (New York: International Council for Economic Development, 1975), p. 141. Nason, *The Role and Responsibilities of College and University Boards* (Washington: Association of Governing Boards of Universities and Colleges, 1974), p. 6. Sánchez, *La Universidad Actual y la Rebelión Juvenil* (Buenos Aires: Losada, 1959), pp. 260–61.

universities consists then only of the right to make appointments, hold academic examinations for the doctorate and for teaching or job qualifications (particularly for government employment), and decide on research projects to the extent that funds requested of and provided by the state will permit. The balance of autonomy shifts when the views of state authorities and university representatives differ. The state then turns from merely formal control to actual control of appointments, examinations, and so on. At that point academic freedom becomes a real issue.

The English universities have a strong tradition of autonomy. Although they were financed, first, by treasury grants and, later, by increasingly larger state subsidies, the support was channeled through the Universities Grants Commission (UGC). In this way, the traditional English universities were not exposed to the state control exerted on Continental universities or to other pressures. Nevertheless, the traditional autonomy in England—or, rather, the balance of autonomy—seems to change when the state and the market exert influence. As one example there appear to be progressive differences between the universities and the present Labor government.

In the United States of America, formal autonomy of state and private universities is considerably greater than in Continental Europe. There is practically no state control over curricula, examinations, or appointments, but there is considerable intervention by the state and the public through market forces. Special admission policies, funds for special projects for minorities, reaction to the labor market and to interests favored by agencies, foundations, and private philanthropy, all these, without a doubt, have affected the freedom of institutions of higher education. In this age, the extreme politization of the universities is not only directly affecting their autonomy but also provoking resistance and reaction from those who finance the educational operation.

In Latin America, the issue of autonomy assumes particular patterns, which I shall describe and evaluate. First, however, I must clear up a supposition that causes many misunderstandings. The misconception is that Latin America is homogeneous in its anthropological, social, economic, cultural, and educational aspects. Such a supposition, as Mayz Vallenilla justly put it, encompasses "the most explosive of contents."[2]

---

2. Ernesto Mayz Vallenilla, *De la Universidad y Su Teoría* (Caracas: Universidad Central de Venezuela, 1967), pp. 223–25.

In reality, this presumption is a half-truth from which it is not possible to deduce that the Latin American university is, should, or can be a generally uniform institution, or that its mission is the same throughout the different countries, regions, and population groups which constitute Latin America, or that a concept such as autonomy is interpreted uniformly or applied with uniform intent and in the same degree. With that comment, I shall try to explain the issue of autonomy as viewed in most of the Latin American countries.

EVALUATION OF AUTONOMY IN LATIN AMERICA

From a historical standpoint, the idea of autonomy is thought to have been born in the Middle Ages along with the universities. The institutions were founded by authority of a high, remote power—a pope or a king—who protected them from the lesser authorities and granted them numerous legal and economic privileges. Thus the concept appears in the "rules" of Federico Barbarroja referring to the University of Bologna, in the "regulations" of the University of Paris granted by Pope Celestino III, and in the "Partidas" of Alfonso El Sabio under which the University of Salamanca originated. In the last, Law V provided for the isolated and tranquil physical environment; Law VII, for student privileges; Law VIII, for exemption from taxes for the institution and scholars; and Law IV, for self-government.[3]

In the constitutions of the first Latin American universities, Salamancan influence predominated. The university, under the dual sponsorship of the pope and the king, was part of the state but at the same time was autonomous, with its own democratic laws and with student participation in its government.[4] From these beginnings, the situation evolved toward greater submission to, first, ecclesiastical authorities and, later, to political authorities. The change came slowly, but university autonomy sank with the change. At the end of the last century, the universities that had not been closed (almost all the Mexican institutions were closed) became completely subject to government authority.

It was then that concern for autonomy was reborn. In Mexico, Minister of Education Justo Sierra thought in 1881 that "the time has come to

---

3. Jorge Siegrist Clamont, *En Defensa de la Autonomía Universitaria: Trayectoria Histórico-Jurídica de la Universidad* (Mexico: Editorial Jus, 1954), pp. 23, 34–44.
4. Sánchez, *La Universidad Actual*, p. 47.

create autonomy of public teaching,"[5] and he proposed the founding of the National University of Mexico as an independent corporation. But his idea of autonomy was restricted inasmuch as he would not allow the university to function in conflict with the public administration, and thus the government had the right of *patria potestas* regarding higher instruction, even to instruction essentially concerned with science.[6] Intervention, which consisted of a veto of reforms decreed by the university body, gave the executive power the right to decide regarding appointments of professors and inspection of total activities of the institution.

The German education system of the nineteenth century inspired Sierra's idea of university autonomy. When Wilhelm von Humboldt participated in the founding of the University of Berlin, he contributed a new conception which, according to Eric Ashby, can be summarized in two words: solitude and freedom. Humboldt believed that the free pursuit of knowledge should not be contaminated by outside obligation and that the society of teachers and students should be capable of living according to its internal logic, striving for intellectual solitude and with freedom to achieve it.[7] His associates in this daring venture agreed with him. Johann Gottlieb Fichte supposed that the modern university should have the freedom to formulate ideas or concepts as an essential element.[8] And Friedrich Schleiermacher established that the state should not interfere in the administration of the universities.[9]

In France, Renan sought autonomy in 1875, reacting against the statism of Napoleon I; and Jules Terry, in the following decade, insisted that the universities exercise self-determination in order to escape provincialistic regionalism.[10] In Peru, the rector of the University of San Marcos Juan Antonio Ribeyro, wrote in his memoirs of 1873: "Inde-

5. Sierra, "La Universidad Nacional: Proyecto de Creación," *El Centinela Español* (Mexico), Febrero 10, 1881.

6. Sierra, "El Gobierno y la Universidad Nacional," *La Libertad* (Mexico), Mayo 25, 1881.

7. Ashby, "The Case for Ivory Towers," in *Higher Education in Tomorrow's World*, ed. Algo D. Henderson (Ann Arbor: University of Michigan, 1968), p. 7.

8. Teofilo Fichte Juan, "Plan Razonado Para Erigir un Establecimiento de Enseñanza Superior Que Esté en Conexión Adecuada con una Academia de Ciencias," *La Idea de la Universidad en Alemania* (Editorial Sudamericana), p. 28.

9. Schleiermacher, "Pensamientos Ocasionales Sobre Universidades en Sentido Alemán," *La Idea de la Universidad en Alemania*, p. 121; Agustín Basave Fernández del Valle, *Ser y Quehacer de la Universidad* (Monterrey: Universidad Autónoma de Nuevo León, 1971), pp. 125–38.

10. Sánchez, *La Universidad Actual*, pp. 220–21.

pendence of the University is more than a measure of public convenience; it is a social necessity."[11] Testimony of this kind abounds in other Latin American countries, advancing ideas that finally provoked the so-called Latin American university reform, which had as a point of departure the manifesto published by students of the Argentine University of Córdoba in June 1918.

This reform movement was directed toward radical change in the universities in all aspects—governance, instruction, and social and political doctrine. Its central element was a sweeping demand for university autonomy. It is impossible to cover here the many causes that gave rise to the movement, its fundamental ideas, its meaning and the favorable or unfavorable consequences it had, first, on higher education in Latin America and, later, on contemporary education. I shall, however, comment on some of the main points.

The reform arose from discontent with an inadequate, insensible, and tyrannic educational system, as well as from disagreement with local and international ideologies and politics. The reformist trend asked not only for greatly improving educational institutions and activities, but also for self-determination of peoples, union of Latin American countries, and liberation from political and economic oppression. It was, in addition, an expression of youth revolt—the first revolt of any importance to occur in this century and in this continent.

From Córdoba, the reformist unrest spread to other Argentine universities, such as the Universidad de Buenos Aires, the Universidad de La Plata, and the Universidad del Litoral. And from Argentina, the movement extended to Peru in 1919, to Chile in 1920, to Colombia and Guatemala in 1922, to Cuba in 1923, to Mexico in 1929, and in different ways spread later to Paraguay, Bolivia, Ecuador, Puerto Rico, Costa Rica, Brazil, Venezuela, El Salvador, Panama, Nicaragua, and Honduras. This does not say that in all these countries the same idea and attitude toward autonomy exist or that autonomy is in force in all these countries.

In fact, in a majority of Latin American countries at this time, universities either do not enjoy autonomy or have only limited autonomy. But in all these countries the reform movement provided an important experience that, besides having an influence on higher education, was reflected in many aspects of the sociopolitical history of this geographic region. On the other hand, the promoters of university autonomy have

11. Luis Alberto Sánchez, *La Universidad No Es Una Isla* . . . (Lima: Ediciones Perú, 1961), p. 51.

come to be the most important leaders in democratic movements in their respective countries.

RIGHTFUL COMPONENTS OF AUTONOMY

Although Luis Alberto Sánchez notes that autonomy does not consist of "nominal definitions, but of effective conduct,"[12] in order to speak of autonomy—there being so many different interpretations of the term—a definition is needed or at least an idea of the diverse meanings that have been given the term. Pinto Mazal wrote that often "the term 'autonomy' has been confused with the principle of freedom of teaching and research as if they were the same thing."[13] Of course, the principles are closely related, but they are not identical. Freedom of teaching and research makes up a part of the idea of autonomy but can exist within a university that does not have autonomy. In the beginning, the concept of autonomy referred to relations of the university with the state; today it refers more and more to relations of the university with its economic, political, and social environment.

Autonomy is that prerogative which a university should have duly recognized by the state and by society in order to choose the standards that shall govern its organization and its internal affairs and in order to make, without external pressures, its own decisions and direct its own operations. According to Goldschmidt, "it announces a careful balance between the power of the state and other public agencies and private organizations" which will permit responsible institutional self-determination. It is a capacity for self-determination with reference to social values that are based, principally, on the university recognizing its missions and striving to fulfill them, but recognizing also that the university itself knows best what should be decided in particular matters of its performance. This prerogative can be divided into three principal sections: academic, governance, and financial.

To the academic prerogatives belong freedom of expression, teaching, and research; capacity to appoint, promote, or remove academic personnel, and to select students, design programs of study and research; and to issue diplomas and certify studies.

To the governance division belongs freedom to choose its standards of organization and administration, to have its own moral and ethical

12. Sánchez, *La Universidad Actual*, p. 21.
13. Jorge Pinto Mazal, *La Autonomía Universitaria* (Mexico: Universidad Nacional Autónoma de México, 1974), p. 7.

character, to appoint and discharge university authorities and officials, to establish their functions, to determine procedures and regulations, and to have at its disposal a site where university authority governs but without violating the laws which protect and obligate the inhabitants of a nation.

Finally, the finance division implies that the university uses both moneys provided to it and its own income and distributes them as it considers best according to its objectives and constraints. Thus it can fix salaries and prepare, apply, and control its budget through the machinery and mechanisms determined by the university itself, but will also present a meticulous accounting to the bodies that are responsible for fiscal control.[14]

PERVERTED USES OF AUTONOMY

There have been other less appropriate or definitely mistaken demands made in the name of autonomy which, instead of strengthening the concept of autonomy, weaken and undermine it. One of these is immunity which exaggerates and corrupts the notion of a "free site" because it goes beyond the most demanding of legitimate immunities and always ends in a flagrant violation of university autonomy by persons who, moved by extrauniversity interests, act outside the law.

At this point, I emphasize another important aspect of university autonomy: Autonomy of what? As noted above, in the beginning it was considered that the freedom of the university was being threatened only by the state. Today, detrimental action by other pressure groups—groups of political action, active and electoral parties—is felt more and more. Sánchez warned against those actions inside the university "which taught [students] to reject everything that did not agree with the prejudices and adhesions" of certain teachers and students who convert "education into a [sectarianism] and the pupil into a sectarian, into a culturally and politically prefabricated being," creating negative attitudes among the young people of the institution.[15]

On one occasion, I listened to a similar warning made by the then-president of Colombia, Carlos Lleras Restrepo: "But it is that the concept of university autonomy has become deformed in many nations of

14. Luis Garibay Gutiérrez, *Reforma Universitaria* (Folia Universitaria Guadalajara, 1972), pp. 41–42; Siegrist, *En Defensa*, pp. 230, 314–15, 349, 369–70, 410, 424–34, 456; Pinto, *La Autonomía Universitaria*, pp. 7–8; Sánchez, *La Universidad Actual*, pp. 21–24.
15. Sánchez, ibid., p. 115.

Latin America by political inspiration; wanting to make the university something totally independent of the government, not for the purpose of protecting or defending the freedom to study, ideological and doctrinaire freedom, but rather to convert it into a small fort for determined political movements," "and that has been carried to such extremes that precisely contradict the essence of that which was sought through university autonomy." Autonomy carries meaning only in the values that it guarantees. When the free discussion of ideas is impeded rather than promoted, its raison d'être is lost.[16]

If in fact the university is inherently autonomous, then the mistaken conception of autonomy and a perverted exercise of autonomy can seriously harm the university. According to Alfonso Borrero, the university can go into a decline for reasons that fall into two categories: abdication of essential responsibilities; and the mistaken exercise of those responsibilities.[17] The best way to avoid both risks is to achieve internal cohesion of the institution and to foster its sense of responsibility. Both conditions are also requisites for autonomy.

COMPATIBLE CONCEPTS

Because I reason in this way, I am surprised by the view that there is incompatibility between autonomy and accountability.[18] In my opinion, autonomy and accountability complement and foster each other when, and only when, as James A. Perkins has noted, each obtains in its rightful dimensions.

Ernest L. Boyer has commented acutely on accountability.[19] I should like to add a comment provoked by a semantic matter that makes me reflect philosophically. In the Spanish language, one word *responsibility* expresses what in English is expressed by two words: *accountability and responsibility*. The first word, *accountability*, emphasizes the rendering of accounts in measurable, quantitative form to an external authority. This sense of the word seems to me fitting and should be fully supported. But it should be remembered that *responsibility* includes, besides, a transcendent moral meaning: the idea that responsibility is a necessary

16. Lleras, "Palabras de Saludo en la Segunda Reunión de GULERPE," *Memorias de la Segunda Reunión* (Cali, Colombia: Universidad del Valle, 1966), pp. 13–14.

17. Alfonso Borrero Cabal, "Autonomía: Concepciones, Patología," *Mundo Universitario* (Asociación Colombiana de Universidades), Separata del No. 1, Octubre, Noviembre y Diciembre, 1972, p. 17.

18. Perkins and Altbach, *The University's Response to Societal Demands*, p. 5.

19. Boyer, "Some Reservations about Accountability," pp. 141–50.

consequence of freedom of will and of attributability founded thereon. In virtue thereof, each moral person—whether the university itself or any person affiliated with the university—should answer to his conscience and to the ethical world around him as regards a decisive cause of his constructive or detrimental actions. This kind of responsibility is compatible with autonomy and in no way excludes accountability.

Something similar could be said about the supposed incompatibility between autonomy and planning or coordination. Every responsible autonomous university must accept, without distrust, a democratic, rational, carefully thought-out planning program which brings coordination and freedom into harmony but which does not sacrifice the autonomy of the institution to the authority of absorbing and rigid systems. Creative coordination is necessary. The difficulty in establishing such coordination stems, not from the application of a wholesome concept of autonomy, but rather from other inadequacies of human resources and materials; lack of adequate organization, structures, and procedures; and the constant violation of autonomy itself by both external and internal forces.

In short, the university which has attained a high capacity in determining for itself the standards that shall govern its organization and its internal life without undue external interventions will also be the most responsible, and the most willing to collaborate in an intelligent, systematic, and prudent planning program.

The Japanese System of Indirect Support
to Private Institutions

TSUNESABURO TOKOYAMA

EDUCATION, BY ITS NATURE, is not, of course, productive in the same way as business and industry. Inasmuch as education, and especially higher education, has been getting steadily costlier, the private institutions cannot be maintained without public support such as governmental aid or philanthropic contributions. Such support, however, always carries with

This presentation reflects the author's opinions and does not necessarily represent the views of private higher education in Japan.

it the question of how a private institution of education can keep its diversity, freedom, and independence, free from the influence of government and donors.

In July 1975, the Japanese Diet passed a law providing national support for private schools. Under its terms, governmental aid will not be granted or loaned directly to individual institutions, but instead will be channeled through the Japan Private School Promotion Foundation, which has already been incorporated as a semigovernmental foundation. This system was developed mainly in light of the characteristics of Japanese private institutions, which have played a significant role in modern Japanese history. Let me describe how the Japanese educational system has developed, why a new law had to be established, and how the policy will be implemented through the foundation.

JAPANESE EDUCATION BEFORE MODERNIZATION

The first Japanese school was private, established in a temple about 1,150 years ago by the great Buddhist priest and scholar Kobo-Daishi (774–835). Temple schools became widespread, with instruction being given not only to prospective priests but also to children of samurai and common people. Later, the temple schools became so popular that many were operated outside temples (though still called temple schools) for children of the common people. The number of such schools at the end of the Tokugawa period (1867) is estimated at more than 15,500.

During the Tokugawa period, the shogunate founded a government institution of higher education, which adopted the doctrine of Chu-tsu (a school of Confucianism) and excluded all other teachings. The Chu-tsu doctrine was considered to serve the government more faithfully, and schools and education were treated as means to support the Tokugawa government.

During the same period, scholars and intellectuals started private schools that not only contributed to raising the intellectual standards and to educating talented youths, but also provided a place to study doctrines that were banned by the Tokugawa shogunate. For example, Western culture, science, and technology and Japanese classical literature were studied only in these private schools. This historical perspective reveals a prototype of the modern Japanese school.

First, private schools were started more than one thousand years ago and survived through history by developing a spontaneous response to the needs of the Japanese people. The large number of temple schools for common people discloses that the private schools made education popular, and they provided the foundation for the modern school that was established during the Meiji period (1867–1912).

Second, the institution created by the Tokugawa government turned out to be the prototype for the modern government university: it was founded and operated by the central government and adopted only one doctrine, which was utilized as the servant of the government. The concept of education to serve the needs of the Tokugawa government remains in the depth of Japanese minds as *okami-ishiki* (a sense of respect for the ruler). In the Meiji period this tradition was perpetuated in the system of government-sponsored higher education that dominated Japanese higher education and whose purpose it was to serve national concern.

The third prototype is seen in the private schools where scholars and intellectuals unrelated to the government studied the banned doctrines. These institutions show that among the Japanese people there has been a strong will to study and to learn. During and after the Meiji period, this tradition was transmitted to diversified, liberal private institutions of higher learning that were developed as a countermove to public higher education.

Continuing Influence of the Meiji Period

Many government and private institutions of higher education were founded around the time of the Meiji restoration (1868). As noted above, both types were patterned on their predecessors of the Tokugawa period.

The first modern government institution was founded by the Meiji government as a privileged Imperial University to serve the national needs. Its nature was clearly stated in an 1886 ordinance, which stipulates, "The Imperial University aims to teach and search for essentials of arts and sciences that serve national needs." To achieve this purpose, the government fully supported the finances of the university. In other words, from the start there was a strong tie between the Imperial University and the government. Such close attachment caused criticism within the university itself, whereas during the Tokugawa period questions were raised only outside the government school. Within three years after the Imperial University was founded, some faculty members were criticizing its status and saying that it should be independent; others insisted that it should be incorporated so that the government could not interfere with it. Later, the matter of autonomy was recurrently questioned, but the nature of the Imperial University as prescribed by the ordinance was never changed.

In the meantime, private institutions of higher learning, from their beginning, declared their independence. Keio University, founded in 1858, adopted "Independence and Self-respect" as its motto. Waseda University was founded in 1882 with "Independence of Learning" as its guiding principle. It is interesting to contrast the statement of purpose of Waseda University with that of the Imperial University. According to its Declaration of Aims, "Waseda University aims to uphold the independence of learning, to promote the practical utilization of knowledge, and to create good citizenship." Apparently, for Waseda University, its most important purpose was independence of learning that would enable scholars and students to pursue their diverse studies freely. Its founding spirit is revealed in more detail in the last half of the declaration.

> To uphold the independence of learning, the University shall strive to emphasize freedom of research and investigation, and to encourage original and creative studies, thereby contributing to the advancement of knowledge.
>
> To promote the practical utilization of knowledge, the University shall endeavor to foster ways and means of utilizing knowledge side by side with the carrying on of academic research and learning, thereby contributing to the progress of civilization.
>
> To create good citizenship, the University shall stress the building up of character which enables one to respect individuality, to enlighten himself and his family, to promote the welfare of state and society, and to extend his influence and activity to the world at large.

The private institutions of higher education were financially independent. Because they received no government subsidies, they always had financial difficulties and were barely able to balance expenditures with the income from tuitions, contributions from alumni, and donations of benefactors. The government sometimes interfered with private colleges and universities, but the institutions tried to withstand such interventions. Their passion for freedom and independence led the private institutions to develop gradually, put their roots down in Japanese society, and increase in number. Today, the private colleges and universities of the Meiji period are the leading private institutions of higher learning.

Postwar Democratization of Institutions

As a result of the enforcement of the new constitution in 1946, the Japanese educational system was reformed in 1947. National institutions as well as private institutions were standardized under the 1947 School Education Act. The new purpose of postwar higher education was determined as being independence and freedom of learning and the training of leaders in a democratic society. These purposes are in a sense a rephrase of the aims of Waseda University—independence of learning and creation of good citizenship. In other words, the former Imperial University and other public colleges and universities now had to adopt the aims of the private universities. Eventually the era of state domination of public colleges and universities ended. Yet a problem remained. Although the public institutions were released from the service of teaching and research for national needs, their expenditures were still supported by government funds. The private institutions, despite their having the same purpose as the public institutions, recevied no government funds. The government simply carried over the prewar policy that the founder of a private school should be responsible for its financing. This problem of unbalanced treatment has remained until recently.

Financial Aid to Private Schools

The first adjustment in the unbalanced funding between public and private institutions was made in 1952 by establishing a semigovernmental corporation, the Private School Promotion Association, through which national funds were loaned at low interest rates to private schools. The remedial measures, however, were insufficient to better the financial problem of private institutions, and as their fiscal situations worsened, the quality of education deteriorated. The private institutions of higher education were left to solve their financial problem by themselves. When the situation continued to deteriorate, action was finally taken in 1969 to resolve the problem. A policy was initiated under which the national government would begin in 1970 to fund private institutions of higher education up to a maximum of 50 percent of their total current expenses, including expenditures for personnel. To implement this policy, a semigovernmental foundation, the Japan Private School Promotion Foundation, was inaugurated in 1970 by legislative action to operate as the new vehicle to manage distribution of government funds to all private institutions of higher education. The new foundation also took over the Private School Promotion Association and its business.

The reasons why the national government has started funding private schools are several.

Because private institutions have responded to the needs of society, the national government has recognized the significance of private institutions of higher education. In the United States, since World War II, public higher education has grown to accommodate the increased enrollments. However, in Japan, it has been the private higher education sector that grew and accepted almost all of the expanded enrollment. The national government has made insufficient effort to expand the public colleges and universities.

In order to maintain a high quality of education, private institutions of higher education should spend the same amount of money per student as do public institutions. However, without governmental funds, the private institutions could not afford such expenses and consequently the education and teaching had deteriorated and badly needed to be upgraded.

Private institutions have played a highly significant role in teaching and training a great majority of the students who became Japan's manpower in the postwar period. The institutions are expected to continue in this role and to contribute to the Japanese society.

The gap in tuition fees between private and public institutions needs to be narrowed.

There are several reasons for the government to entrust to the Japan Private School Promotion Foundation the distribution and lending of national funds and other related business: (1) To meet the need for a professional agency that commands expertise and knowledge of private schools. The agent is charged with handling a large enterprise that affects all private schools in Japan. (2) To guarantee the academic freedom of private institutions. Funding is indirect and not restricted in use. (3) To mediate between the national government and private institutions. It can reflect the policy of the government while respecting the independence and diversity of the private institutions as it distributes and lends funds.

The significant element in this system of funding is that private institutions can use the funds for any suitable purposes without intervention from the government, with no strings attached. Each institution is, of course, accountable for the subsidies and is required to submit a financial report to the proper authorities.

With respect to the foundation's management, the Japan Private School Promotion Foundation law provided that administrative staff members are to be drawn from the private sector, as follows: the president, one out of four vice-presidents or executive directors, three out of four members of the Board of Directors, and six out of ten members of the Council advisory to the president. The remainder of the high-level administrators are to be businessmen and men of knowledge and experience. The present chairman of the Council, for example, is the former president of the Bank of Japan.

The foundation has a Committee of Examination of Contributions which investigates contributions from benefactors to private schools and colleges. According to the present policy, if a contribution passes the examination of the committee, the contribution from a corporation is tax exempt, whereas a contribution by an individual is tax exempt only beyond the first ten thousand yen.

LEGISLATION FOR INDIRECT PUBLIC FINANCIAL SUPPORT

As previously described, throughout Japanese history, private schools have responded to the social needs for education, which were rooted in the voluntary demands of the people. Especially in the postwar period, private colleges and universities have played a leading role in expanding the availability of higher education. As a result, private colleges and universities have dominated in both enrollments and the number of institutions of higher education (see Table 1). Of the institutions, 75 percent are in the private sector, as opposed to 25 percent operated by the

TABLE 1: *Enrollments in Japanese Institutions of Higher Education, by Type and Control, May 1, 1974*

	Control		
Institutional	Private	National	Municipal
Four-year colleges and universities			
Number of institutions	299	78	33
Enrollment	1,267,117	342,296	49,925
Two-year colleges			
Number of institutions	432	26	47
Enrollment	300,882	11,883	17,595
Technical colleges			
Number of institutions	7	52	4
Enrollment	7,117	37,342	3,932

national and municipal governments. With respect to the number of students, the private sector accounts for 77.3 percent of the enrollment. Therefore, raising the standard of education and research in private institutions of higher education should contribute significantly to Japanese higher education. In this context, promotion of private schools has been one of the greatest concerns in the recent national program of Japanese education.

Finally, in 1975, a bill for the national subsidy was submitted to the Seventy-fifth Diet. It provides for national nonrestrictive funding up to a maximum of 50 percent of the current expenses of private schools. The bill was passed, and the law concerning support for private school promotion is to become effective in April 1976. The Japan Private School Promotion Foundation (the vehicle for the funding) having already been established by legislative action, the appropriations for national subsidies had been eagerly awaited. Because the national funds were not prescribed by substantive law, they were budgeted by administrative resolution. Enactment of the 1975 law is, then, significant for establishing the legal foundation for national financial aid to private schools.

Another significance of the law is that it provides for national aid not only to higher education but also to all other levels of private schools, from kindergartens to high schools.

As a representative of the Japan Private School Promotion Foundation and as an economist trained in a leading private university in Japan, I have been greatly pleased by the passage of this law, and all those who are in charge of the administration of private educational institutions are looking forward to its enforcement. Although the problem of unbalanced national funding between public and private schools has not been completely solved, the new law provides us with a brighter prospect for the future of private school education.

Autonomy and Accountability in a Shrinking Enterprise

MELVIN A. EGGERS

SURELY, ALL COLLEGE and university administrators are deeply aware of the sorry fiscal condition of higher education. I sometimes feel that a time bomb is ticking away and that our actions are so constrained as to make us its helpless victims. We cannot even call attention to the ticking because we fear we will either cause panic or be subject to ridicule. Nonetheless, present trends in the financing of higher education and in the age distribution of the population bluntly warn of portentous adaptation problems.

The higher education establishment cannot be totally an instrument of the state or the instrument of any of its other constituencies and still be society's major instrument for the transfer of knowledge and the search for truth. For the same reasons, each higher education institution must be, to some extent, an island. Yet there must also be accountability. The essence of accountability is the specification of what an institution or complex of institutions must do or may not do in relationships with constituencies, along with a scheme to appraise compliance and to impose sanctions.

The constituencies to which institutions of higher education are accountable include faculty, trustees, donors, government units, students and parents, accrediting agencies, and others. The accountability scheme is highly complicated. What appears to be common to all categories to which an institution is held accountable is that all are parties at interest seeking to bend the institution to the goals they favor. If there is dissatisfaction with the performance of the higher education complex, or a part of it, pressure is often exerted to change the accountability structure and thereby, in the pressure generator's view, make the complex operate more responsibly. Faculty unionization is one illustration. The introduction of another accrediting agency into institutional functioning and the revision of accrediting standards are other examples.

Changes in the pattern of accountability are not necessarily the result of motivation to improve the *quality* of education. For example, in recent years higher education institutions have been brought to increased account to government units for their employment practices in order to improve employment opportunities for women and minorities. The effect on the *quality* of higher education is a by-product.

When the higher education complex was expanding and enjoying favor in the society, there seemed to be something for everyone and at least a measure of tolerance, if not satisfaction, with the outcome. Making the complex more responsive to one group did not necessarily make it less responsive to another. It was a nonzero sum game.

A Central Assumption

Society does not now provide the higher education establishment with the income necessary to maintain the resources (faculty, support services, physical plant) allocated to it, nor is it likely to do so in the future. Resources must be *released* to make income adequate to maintain the resources that remain. One might argue that income—the total financial support—should be adjusted to permit maintaining all the resources currently allocated to higher education or, better still, to support the enlarged resources it should have. Perhaps so. Although either course might make a good argument, neither is a good planning assumption.

The situation of higher education presents a dilemma. Resources must be separated because there is too little income to maintain them. The separation of resources leads to charges of higher education's not being adequately accountable. Demands for increased accountability then make separation of resources more difficult and may even reduce income still further.

How, then, can the higher education complex divest itself of some of its resources and yet avoid severe and perhaps irreparable damage? It is predictable that, as the higher education establishment shrinks, discussions about accountability will be concerned with defining what is to constitute responsible performance. The worrisome thing about the accountability arrangement is the little concern being exhibited for what is happening to the higher education complex or to the welfare of the individual institutions of which it is composed.

My thesis here is that *the accountability arrangements as they now operate appear to be unsuited to the emerging condition in higher education,* specifically to the condition that the complex needs to divest itself of resources. As suggested above, when the answer to the question "Shall we do this or that?" could be "Both," certain constraints may be tolerable. When the answer is "Neither," the same constraints may be intolerable. The danger faced by any declining industry (one whose income is insufficient to hold the resources allocated to it) is that the process by which resources are separated tends to debilitate the entire industry. In the higher education complex, the accountability system must permit an institution to divest itself of some of its resources without being destroyed or seriously damaged in the process. There should also be arrangements through which the termination of whole institutions may occur with little or no damage to those which remain.

Those within the higher education establishment, including those who are now responsible for its accountability arrangements, cannot by their own resolve forestall the process of debilitation that accompanies divestment of resources. It is difficult enough for a *managed* institution to handle adversity without damage to its quality; for a *nonmanaged* complex, adversity converts the complex into a jungle.

A NATIONAL COMMISSION ON HIGHER EDUCATION

What appears to be lacking at this stage is reliable, objective judgment on how the higher education complex can adjust to new conditions with minimum damage. The judgments needed are those made by people who are astute but who are not directly involved in the outcome. I suggest the time is right for the President of the United States to appoint a National Commission on Higher Education, this one to concentrate on shrinking rather than developing the higher education complex. The commission should be composed of people other than educators and education regulators. Those who served on the Commission to Investigate the CIA represent the caliber of persons who should be called to this task.

The commission would not be another body to coordinate, integrate, or regulate higher education or one to promote and finance studies by men and women who have a stake in the enterprise. Rather, it should delve into governing considerations in the guiding and constraining of the higher education complex and its institutions; it would bring to bear the judgments of those who have the capacity to see the complex whole and to understand what is happening to it but have no opportunity for direct gain from what it recommends.

Now, surely, higher education should, for the most part, be guided by the judgments of educators and those to whom they are accountable. Yet there is also need to ensure that the views of the educators and their regulators, especially during times of adversity, have been informed in a systematic way by judgments about the educational complex made from a perspective different from that of persons involved by their own or their institutions' welfare. People in higher education offer judgments on societal issues, and society is presumably the better for them because educators approach the issue objectively. The proposal made here reverses the line of evaluation.

This proposal for outside judgments has the ring of heresy. How can one understand the education establishment without being in it? How can a nonprofessor say how the professoriate should adapt to the changed circumstances in higher education? Shouldn't those whose welfare is at stake be the ones to resolve a problem? Not always. Neither the railroad brotherhoods nor the bondholders' protective committees nor the Interstate Commerce Commission nor the cities served by the railroads, separately or together, did much to effect the orderly divesting of resources by the railroads to keep the industry healthy as it shrank. There must be a better way to shrink an industry, and there must be times when those whose welfare is at stake are not the best judges.

MATTERS FOR IMPARTIAL JUDGMENT

Among the broad issues on which the higher education establishment could gain much from the judgments of some of the best minds outside the education fraternity are the following:

1. By how much should the higher education complex shrink? The amount of resource divestment needed to restore health to the complex is probably not great. Without a reliable judgment on the amount of the excess resources (and a program to make the removal relatively painless), there is serious danger that the process initiated to squeeze out the relatively small excess may so weaken the system that additional "excess" would appear. The squeezing process leads to dissatisfaction with higher education, which then leads to disillusionment about its value and, as a consequence, to further withdrawal of support. And so on. The loss of resources is not so damaging as are the by-products of the divestment process. A national commission's judgment that only a relatively small proportion of resources need be separated may break the vicious circle. Without such assurance, fear of "what might happen" leads to various kinds of counterproductive behavior.

2. If the higher education establishment is to shrink, where should the shrinkage occur? Which services have the *lowest* priority? Society's needs for education are defined almost entirely by educators and the educators' regulators. Because different needs are met by different kinds of institutions and different people, educators are unlikely to settle the priorities by consensus sought through discussion and persuasion. Without guidelines, resolution is likely to come about as a painful and destructive process of attrition. Perhaps a national commission could help reduce the pain and destruction by offering judgments about the lowest priorities. When higher education needed to *expand*, the *highest priorities* were important —a much easier ranking than when the need is to contract.

3. A third issue is the mix of public and independent institutions. As

income in higher education declines, the détente between the public and independent sectors will almost surely dissolve. For the independent sector, the predictions are especially unattractive. But what is fair judgment on the relative efficiency and effectiveness of the two sectors? What does a healthy independent sector contribute to quality in the higher education enterprise, and what portion should it be in order to make its optimum contribution? Should most of the shrinkage come from the independent sector?

The two sectors will not agree, and assertions on both sides will be considered self-serving. The associations either are dominated by one sector or cannot touch the issue (sectoral issues are kept off the agenda). Yet society has a right to a higher education complex in which interinstitutional struggles do not adversely affect the quality of the complex. For credible judgments we must turn to noninvolved persons such as those appropriate to serve on a national commission.

The public—not long ago—supported the higher education establishment in order to increase its capacity to meet the rapidly growing demands: funds were provided to develop an increased resource base, and income was provided to maintain that base. These developments were guided to a significant extent, first, by President Truman's Commission on Higher Education in 1946 and, then, by President Eisenhower's Committee on Education Beyond the High School in 1956. Their task was relatively easy because it concerned development and expansion. Society was generous and helpful. And there was something in it for everyone.

Implications for a Reduced Establishment

While the complex was expanding and the economy was relatively stable, there was little resistance to accepting tenure as a life contract, to expanding a resource base dependent on soft money, and to financing programs with endowment income. Now that the complex must contract and the economy has experienced both recession and inflation, practices that seemed reasonable then are almost strangling.

It is clearly time for a new commission. The problem now is shrinkage. If it was right for society to facilitate the development of the higher education complex by extraordinary means, is it not reasonable to consider how society might facilitate its shrinkage, perhaps also by extraordinary means?

If the idea of naming a Presidential Commission on Higher Education seems old-hat or trivial, consider the extraordinary makeup and mission of the proposed group. It would include no educators; and it would be charged with guiding higher education in reducing its resource base. Moreover, all proposals must provide that higher education will continue to perform responsibly toward the constituencies to which it is accountable and that its programs will not diminish in quality.

A new presidential commission will have to consider some extraordinary measures, just as did the earlier groups. One such measure comes to mind. A central problem for institutions facing adversity is that they cannot separate resources as rapidly as their incomes can decline. Why not, then, provide a public facility to which academic resources, when deemed excess because of reduced income, could be assigned for maintenance at public expense? The important point is that the surplus resources must be taken out of use without cost to the respective institutions. In this way the trauma and deterioration which often follow straightforward staff dismissals would be minimized. Also held to a minimum would be the frustration that inevitably results from attempts to find, through interinstitution competition, new uses for surplus resources when the income level for higher education is fixed. The proposed government facility could serve as a reservoir and halfway house: some resources would probably be returned to academia, and others would find new uses in other areas. During the period the government facility has the resources, it, and not the institutions which declared them surplus, would maintain them. Call the facility an "academic resource bank." The similarity between this suggestion and certain agriculture programs is probably obvious. That industry, which was assisted in adjusting its resource base to the income society was willing to provide, is now the wonder of the world. The railroad industry, which was largely left to fend for itself with its accountabilities intact, suffered a less noble fate.

The overriding concern in higher education should be about the accountability of the entire complex to society, including accountability for maintaining its integrity and quality as it adjusts to changing conditions. Help from outside the higher education establishment will be required to bring about (1) a clearer understanding of what society should expect from higher education, and (2) innovations to facilitate the separation of resources. Both a statement of what society should expect from the higher education complex and a statement of acceptable ways to separate resources need to be validated by noneducators. A presidential commission might be useful as society's validating agent.

Higher education will be permitted the autonomy it needs only if it is viewed as concurring in the mission that those outside education set for it, and as maintaining its quality and integrity while it adjusts to changing conditions. The erosion of autonomy comes from lack of agreement on mission or from deterioration in performance relative to an agreed-upon mission.

The time to assure the future autonomy of higher education institutions is now. The way to do it is to find the way to contract with style and dignity.

· 9 ·

The International Intellectual Community

The Role of the International Intellectual Community

ASA BRIGGS

In 1798, President John Adams recommended that a party of French scientists should not be admitted into the United States. "I really begin to think," he explained, "or rather to suspect, that learned academies, not under the immediate inspection and control of government, have disorganized the world, and are incompatible with social order."

Neither the thought nor the suspicion was a private preserve of President Adams or of his generation. Even in less revolutionary times, academies—and academics—not "under the immediate inspection and control of government" have been considered subversive. They have been so considered not simply because of an antipathy to independent, intermediate institutions and to the people directing them but because the concerns and aspirations of the academies—and academics—have been or are thought to have been dangerous to the status quo. Moreover, at least some of the academics have taken pride in the fact that their teaching and research know no frontiers. This attitude was true of most of the eighteenth-century academicians who were, in President Adams's mind, the family of *philosophes* who felt, as Diderot told Hume, that they "belonged to all nations" and were "citizens of the world." Whatever their place of birth, their concerns were common concerns and their aspirations were universal. It had been true even earlier—as it has been many times later—of migrant scholars moving from one city or one country to another. Even before the word *international* came into currency or passports were invented, science provided its own distinctive set of credentials.

President Adams referred to the "social order" and not to the political order, although he saw government as the guardian of the social order. He was writing at a time, of course, when the machinery at the disposal of government for "immediate inspection and control" was far less expensive and sophisticated than it is now, and at a time long before the learned academies were associated with an expensive and sophisticated system of higher education organized in a huge nexus of institutions. Yet his words would undoubtedly be intelligible at once to ministers and politicians in most countries today, whether or not they would be prepared to agree with them.

As government has become stronger in its instruments and more comprehensive in its scope, it has certainly not lost its sense of vulnerability on this particular front: indeed, there has been at least as much talk of a crisis of authority during the last ten years—on both sides of the Atlantic —as there was during the period of intellectual ferment preceding the French Revolution. A striking difference, of course, lies in the pattern of the communication media, the history of which must always be studied in relation to the history of education as well as of government, but one of the biggest differences between then and now is the presence of "big" education. Because the financial stake of government in the higher education sector has increased so greatly during the last ten years, government in, probably, most countries has recently been drawn into a more detailed inspection of "learned academies" and universities than had been customary earlier in this century and has been tempted—if not activated— into more deliberate and more planned control.

The current situation, then, is increased concern of government with higher education, with some of the key decisions being reached behind the scenes and not argued out fully before the electorate. During the next ten years there may be even more difficult transactions. Economic factors alone—and in practice they are meshed with social and political factors —will limit expansion in many national systems of higher education and may in certain circumstances lead to contraction. Almost inevitably, therefore, discussions within the scattered international intellectual community will be concerned with urgent practical questions, often to the exclusion of more fundamental questions about the distinctive set of academic credentials necessary throughout the world in this century and the next. The argument will tend to be nationalized, and each institution and each institutional system will tend to have its own agenda. There will be an inevitable tendency for detailed argument—whether within universities, between universities, between universities and other institutions of higher education, or between universities and government—to focus on what seems to matter most. There will be numbers games with projections of enrollments (the main basis of finance) and calculations based on different student-faculty ratios; juggling with capital and equipment resources; the search for cheaper alternatives to universities; unionization within academic faculties; the rationalizing and coordinating both of teaching and research, and so on. The list is not exhaustive, but even if similar items are added to it, the list will still represent shrinking horizons. The argument will undoubtedly be redeemed intermittently when international or interregional comparisons are drawn as part of the game though not necessarily as part of decision making.

Management problems in the higher education sector are so complicated that it becomes easy to forget that the rest of the world exists. Yet there is a contrast here. In retrospect, the 1960s, which began with such optimism about expansion of numbers and ended so stormily in debates about the content and role of university education, were years when international argument and both ideas and discontents crossed frontiers with a speed that no head of state could have checked. The costs have often been calculated in terms of personal and institutional accounting. But the gains were real: an interest in innovation for more than the sake of novelty; a willingness to consider structures as well as processes; a debate that was not solely concerned with management; genuine interest in the diverse responses of other countries; a sense of, and often a commitment to, there being a Third World in education as in everything else. Behind the contrast between then and now—or between then and the 1980s—there has been a dialectic. It is not only governments that have reacted (in very different economic conditions) against what happened then and since. The reaction can be measured in many countries by numbers of people wishing to go to a university or by what they wish to study there.

Given the set of limited national and regional preoccupations that are likely to dominate in the next period of higher education, can the scattered international intellectual community identify a new agenda? And what will be the relationship between that agenda and the social order of the future? Three points out of many are picked out here.

INTERNATIONAL NETWORKS

Discussion on an international basis will have to include some practical preoccupations, which will be all too easy to limit to consideration in only limited local settings (given the right mix of participants), and out of the practical discussion other points will naturally emerge. There is scope for at least four kinds of exchange of experience and opinions: (1) within geographically linked groupings of countries where common or related policies could be evolved; (2) within historically linked groupings of countries, where common traditions have influenced the course of the history of higher education; (3) within geographically scattered and historically diverse groupings of countries which sense that current problems and aspirations have much in common; and (4) within a global network of countries with very different kinds of past and present experience.

Each of these four kinds of exchange demands its own exploration, and for each there are already examples. It would be possible to explore the first from the angle of Africa, divided though that continent is by both borrowed and indigenous languages. The European Economic Community (the example I know best) is worth brief consideration here. An EEC commissioner in Brussels has responsibility for education, although the Community has no educational policy as such. So far, discussions on higher education carried out under the aegis of the Community have concentrated on the dullest as well as the most difficult of subjects—equalization or at least harmonization of professional qualifications. An effort has been made to formulate codes rather than to analyze criteria. Yet there has also been one interesting and provocative report by Henri Janne, a former Belgian minister, on the kind of educational objectives that mght be shared by the EEC countries—objectives that would direct a positive policy to make Europeans more knowledgeable about a united Europe and its place in the world of the future. The report, which was commissioned by the Community, has been read, if not widely, but not acted on, and no single government is committed to it. Meanwhile the arguments about higher education in the Europe of the Nine continue in their national settings.

It is already clear from incomplete experience that the educational matters being discussed at or through Brussels either under Janne's headings or under the kind of headings ordering current national discussions cannot be left to governments alone or to ministries of education. They require the fullest possible participation of the European intellectual community. And the discussions must relate—if they are to be taken seriously—to the practical preoccupations which ministries of education and universities share in their own countries. Sometimes there can be an alarming schizophrenia. The British government, for example, is beginning to worry about the cost of providing subsidized postgraduate education for non-British subjects just when European universities are feeling the need to encourage movement of postgraduate students between countries. The French government gives little support to its own postgraduates who wish to study in other countries, but encourages the maximum number of postgraduates from abroad to study in France. Things do not add up. And in all countries—not simply those within the European Community—planning procedures pay little attention to the role of universities as international centers. Local factors determine conceptions of resources, size, and mix. Far more attention is being paid—and much of it may be overdue—to the local community role of the university, and far too little thought is given to the necessary relationship between local and international alignments and responsibilities.

Because there are inconsistencies and inadequacies in national policies along with common problems—the nature of which is often misunderstood—it is useful to have nongovernmental centers where issues can be studied comparatively, that is, across national boundaries. For this reason, in Europe, a regional institute has recently been established in Paris—with support from the European Cultural Foundation, the European Economic Community, and the International Council for Educational Development—where people from the international intellectual community in European (and non-European) countries can work on common programs. It will be important that some of them be on secondment, inasmuch as in all such institutes there should be a process of withdrawal and return.

The ICED's interest shows that sensitivity to the common and the comparative is not confined to regional groupings. To be outward-looking involves transcending not only the local and the national but also the regional. Within historically linked groupings of countries, there are already well-established associations such as the British Association of Commonwealth Universities, which increasingly exchanges information and holds meetings. And there has always been a trans-Atlantic traffic in people and ideas which includes a substantial noninstitutionalized element. Institutionally, the lines are strong; for example, in recent years communication has been as great between representatives of the United States and British universities as between representatives of German and British universities.

The third and fourth forms of international discussion contrast with each other. The third form is characterized by shared depth of involvement, whereas the fourth form exhibits deliberate variety. Third World countries whose current problems and aspirations have much in common have thus far engaged in relatively little interchange of persons, and, as in the case of media traffic, the movement tends to be from metropolitan centers. But whatever the governmental patterns, communication between Third World ministers of education differs from communication between Third World members of the international intellectual community. It may well be that the most effective way of securing such communication will be through the creation of an international network—once again, the term is borrowed from the media—of the kind that the United Nations University is envisaging.

Rightly, the U.N. University has not conceived its task simply or mainly as that of bringing into existence yet another university institution—the nth since 1960—but of concentrating and focusing the activity of a number of members of the international intellectual community on problems of a global character. The existence of the network will be just as important as the existence of the base. If the problems are properly defined, the network could be something like the letter-writing network of the scattered group of eighteenth-century *philosophes* who pondered general problems of the future of mankind. Their speculations certainly did not suffer from their not all being gathered under one institutional roof.

COMMUNITY MEMBERS

In the formulation or implementation of any agenda, the term "international intellectual community" should be interpreted to mean something much broader than the institutional managers who inevitably will bear the immediate anxieties of the years ahead, just as they bore the immediate strains of the late 1960s. This conclusion follows from the last point. The United Nations network, if it is to work, will depend on people, not on representatives of institutions. But to be effective, it will also need institutional backing—backing that cannot be taken for granted. Far from being citizens of the world, many members of the international intellectual community become—have to become—branch managers (although some of them, perhaps, are not sure of the name of their parent company).

Of course, the majority of the members do not "manage" at all; they stay put within their own system. Others look outside. Alongside the international institutional complexes that relate universities around the world to each other, there are the international associations of academics concerned with a particular subject or field, peer groups who devote most of their international meetings to research and (to a lesser extent) to curricula. It was members of these groups who were responsible in large measure for many of the innovations of the 1960s; it was within subjects or through interdisciplinary interaction as much as through institutions that the challenge was made to the status quo. We go back to President Adams's fears. Before the great university expansion began in most parts of the world, Lipset noted how what happened inside subjects or in interdisciplinary reaction had wider repercussions: "In spite of the powerful conservatizing forces [within the intellectual community], the inherent tendency to oppose the *status quo* will still remain. . . . Any *status quo* embodies rigidities and dogmatisms which it is the inalienable right of intellectuals to attack, whether from the standpoint of moving back to traditional values or forward toward the achievement of the equalitarian dream."[1]

Lipset was wise to leave the option open—option as general description, not as prescription—for it is unclear how the spectrum of segmented international intellectual communities (a phenomenon unknown to the eighteenth century but fostered during the late nineteenth and twentieth centuries) will react to the kind of pressures and counterpressures of a period when, in many countries, the higher education sector will not be expanding. Some segments will doubtless become preoccupied with the battle for priorities within their own institutions. Others will turn to their unions. Some will try to stake special separatist claims for governmental support. (Note the heterogeneity.) Whatever the attitude of the international intellectual community toward the status quo may become, many of its members have always conceived of themselves as servants rather than as critics. Willingness to accept inspection, if not control, has informed their actions; there have been jobs to be done, and they have done them. Much of the teaching by the academic community has been essentially preservative. It was not in late nineteenth-century Japan alone that a distinction was drawn between teaching (which could be relied upon to support the status quo) and research (which had to be separated from teaching because it depended on academically necessary but socially dangerous "free thought"). The distinction may at first appear as absurd as the eighteenth-century distinction between the teaching of reading

---

1. Seymour Martin Lipset, *Political Man: The Social Bases of Politics* (Garden City, N.Y.: Anchor Books, Doubleday, 1963), p. 371.

and the teaching of writing to young children, but it has influenced educational policy for far longer.

There is need to continue to draw upon the entire international intellectual community, however divided—not simply its managers—if we are to establish convincingly what I term "the distinctive set of credentials" necessary for mapping higher education during the rest of this century. In establishing those credentials, account must be taken of how the international intellectual community (with all its specialties and divisions of outlook) can cooperate in urgent interdisciplinary problem solving. The kinds of problems to be dealt with are outlined in the prospectus of the United Nations University and in other public and private documents: environment and human relations, human needs and social indicators, the new economic order (however interpreted), and the organization of international relations on a global level. Account will also have to be taken of the continuing need for the international intellectual community to criticize as well as to solve, to argue as well as to inform, to probe as well as to implement. The advancement of knowledge will always disturb, for research goes beyond the elementary examination of the background of a problem just as teaching goes beyond the transmission of knowledge.

Relations with Government and the Communication Media

During the next period, much more is likely to be heard about the relationship between the higher education sector and government and also about the relationship between education as a whole and the communications sector. Both sectors have been under attack—and have attacked each other—and in the Third World countries both are often related in strategies for development. It is well known that in the advanced countries television watching occupies more time than formal schooling, but little is yet known about the long-term consequences of the development of television and other media on higher education. As long ago as 1922, Walter Lippmann, writing at the end of a period in media history, which now seems almost as remote as 1798, pointed out—and like Adams's comment, it is still pertinent, however great the changes—that "the press is no substitute for institutions. It is like the beam of a searchlight that moves restlessly about, bringing one episode and then another out of the darkness into vision. Men cannot do the work of the world by this light alone. They cannot govern society by episodes, incidents, and eruptions. It is only when they work by a steady light of their own, that the press, when it is turned upon them, reveals a situation intelligible enough for a popular decision."[2] Looking ahead, Lippmann hoped for better informed management backed by research institutions, a kind of running audit which would ensure that the state of the human account would always be known.

Since 1922 research institutions have proliferated as the technological basis of the media has changed. The international intellectual community is far larger than ever before, and is backed by knowledge industries and supporting private and semipublic agencies as well as by government. Yet the old questions remain alongside the new. It may be that this bigger international intellectual community is more influenced by the media than it influences them (an interesting question), that it is so fragmented that it can act only intermittently or through particular groups (like the Pugwash scientists), that in the likely circumstances of the future it may prefer to cultivate its own gardens. But it must not go on the defensive vis-à-vis government or any other sector. Lippmann's image suggests—and the image goes back to the eighteenth-century Enlightenment—that the world (not just a nation or a region) cannot do without the international intellectual community. Indeed, the more the world becomes in many respects one world—however slowly that change is recognized—the more, not less, the intellectual community must become international in its outlook.

Barriers to Internationalism

STEPHEN R. GRAUBARD

I AM FAIRLY CONFIDENT that higher education exists; I am less certain that the same can be said for the international intellectual community. In fact, I wonder whether the latter is not a fictitious construct, invented principally for those who find it useful to talk about interdependence, discovering it in the intellectual as well as in the economic sphere. In my view, there is no international intellectual community; nor do I believe that there is any prospect of there being one, at least not in our lifetimes. Some will find that idea heretical; others will think it mistaken, but not very dangerous. It certainly contradicts the commonly accepted view.

2. *Public Opinion* (Copyright by Walter Lippmann 1922; Copyright renewed by Walter Lippmann 1949. New York: Free Press, 1922), p. 229.

I do not question the importance of the continuous international travel of scholars today, or of the publications, general and technical, that cross national frontiers freely and that unite men and women who would otherwise have scant knowledge of what others were thinking and doing. What I do question—quite seriously—is whether an "educated class" exists throughout the world today or even in great parts of it, and whether those who are educated have any intimate knowledge of what others, with different linguistic, ideological, and professional attachments, are thinking. The concept of international intellectual community implies some sort of dialogue. I wonder whether that dialogue exists today and whether it liberates many of us from our national and linguistic prisons.

CHARACTERISTICS OF THE DISCIPLINES

All professions are supposed to be international; some in fact are; many others are not. The same may be said for individual academic disciplines. Mathematics, for example, is certainly an international discipline; to the extent that it exists everywhere, it is everywhere the same. In many of the sciences, a comparable international bias exists, with no major differences between what is held true in these matters in one part of the world with what is thought to be true elsewhere. If particle physics is pursued at all, it will be pursued in precisely the same way in New Delhi as it is in New York.

That same international tendency is far less evident in a discipline like economics. It is not simply that the economics of the socialist world differs from that prevalent in capitalist countries, but between capitalist countries, different schools and interests predominate. While the Anglo-American school, with its Scandinavian and Low Country extensions, may think almost nothing of what passes for "economics" in France, that sentiment is more than amply reciprocated. Each camp studiously neglects the other; there is no continuing discussion between them, though the gulf is not created simply by ideological differences. The same, I think, may be said of disciplines as disparate as philosophy, sociology, psychology, and history.

The Oxford school of philosophy has enjoyed considerable influence in the United States; it has not had great resonance in France, India, China, or Brazil. Philosophy, for these countries, has a quite different character, and its agenda of concerns is a very different one. Something of the same situation prevails in sociology. Who would today accept the preeminence of certain American "schools" of sociology? Who cares to dispute what certain prominent scholars in the field are saying? Their influence, all too often, is limited to specific countries. Psychology, with all its method-ological differences, remains similarly provincial; ideology is only one of the forces that causes this isolation and mutual neglect.

In my own discipline, history, such divisions are also evident. To an extraordinary extent, history, particularly modern history, is the creation of the nationals of the country or society being studied. United States history is largely the creation of a company of U.S. scholars engaged in the study of certain kinds of questions, making use of certain kinds of data. Of course, a British or French scholar may also engage in serious historical researches that touch on the United States, but such inquiry is relatively uncommon and almost never influences the main course of this country's historical scholarship. Americans, as intellectual imperialists, often engage in serious scholarly inquiry into another country's recent his-tory. Their work sometimes enjoys a considerable reputation in the United States; it rarely enjoys a comparable reputation abroad. When one con-siders the thousands of U.S. scholars who have studied modern Europe and asks whether many of them have influenced scholarship abroad in significant ways, the answer, almost always, is no. U.S. historians, studying Europe, write mostly for a local market, a U.S. market.

There is, in short, a substantial difference between disciplines and professions that have an international bias (and membership) and those that are nationally or linguistically confined. There are equally important differences created by ideological factors, which influence what is done and how it is done.

What, some will ask, has any of this to do with an international intel-lectual community? Why should I discuss at such length individual aca-demic disciplines when my subject permitted me (indeed, required me) to examine a much larger canvas? The answer can be simply given. There is *no* larger canvas. There are few intellectuals in New York today who have any great familiarity with the issues that preoccupy intellectuals in Rome, Prague, Leningrad, Jakarta, Tokyo, or Peking. Only on the most superficial level—generally in respect to certain contemporary world events—do intellectuals in these various places address the same issues. There is little dialogue between East and West, not very much more between North and South.

CULTURAL MEDIA

Despite the plethora of translations (at least of certain best-sellers), what is read in Athens today is not what is read in Cambridge, Massa-chusetts. To an extent that is not always acknowledged or recognized, most intellectuals today live largely or exclusively in their own national societies. Few of them move with any ease into other societies with which they have, at best, only occasional or haphazard relations. Whether it be in the area of politics, literature, philosophy, history, art, or music, what is held in common today is often the remnant of an eighteenth-, nineteenth-, or early twentieth-century culture, which was once the common possession of certain educated and leisured European and American classes.

Youth today may have its own culture (especially in music and litera-ture), but a good deal of this culture is also nationally based. Some, I know, would deny this view, but a glance at the phonograph records sold in Paris to the young will suggest that they are not the ones sold in New York, though the company that produces them may be the same and the techniques of salesmanship may be similar. In publishing, trans-national ownership is rare; publishing houses are generally national insti-tutions; they have an occasional interest in making some foreign works known to their publics through translation.

In politics, Marx is the one nearly universal intellectual figure of our century. The number who actually read and know his works is consider-ably smaller than the number who pretend to do so, but this is of no great import. After Marx, there is no true rival; Mao, by comparison, is a minor figure. So is Rousseau; as for Jefferson, he scarcely exists for an international intellectual community.

Nor should it be imagined that the film or video culture of today is the universal culture. To an extent that is not always appreciated, tele-vision remains largely national. The Canadian viewer may see what is principally intended for the American, but neither has the vaguest notion of what is being shown in Tokyo, Moscow, or Paris. As for films, while they do circulate internationally, even this is done more selectively than is sometimes realized. The Japanese film remains an exotic experience; when shown abroad, it is largely intended for an urban American audi-ence; these films are not being seen in Prague, Peking, or Istanbul.

We live, in short, within fairly narrow national and linguistically de-fined intellectual and cultural enclaves. We claim to be international-minded; we imagine that five-minute news summaries acquaint us with the political, economic, and social preoccupations of others. We delude ourselves. The mass media, with their vast technological potential, have only barely begun to liberate us from our national and linguistic prisons.

Indeed, even foreign travel, with its superficial admission to the culture of others, rids us principally only of the more common of our prejudices.

INNATE PAROCHIALISM

What significance does all this have for higher education? Those who agree with my view may feel that it proves nothing except that there is a great deal to learn, that life is short and hard, that time is a precious commodity, and that the individual cannot expect to know more than a little about most things. That is true, but there is a larger truth which also bears telling. Whatever the deficiencies of early twentieth-century European and American bourgeois or capitalist culture—and there were many—in great parts of the world, it helped produce a notion of the "educated individual." This was a meaningful concept to those who went to school or university, and it meant something also to those who made teaching their profession. There was a fundamental agreement then about the value and importance of certain kinds of knowledge. That knowledge existed principally for those who wanted to be educated; some of it was undeniably parochial; some of it had a more universal cast. The educated person belonged to a national society, but he or she also aspired to a familiarity with a good deal that was not purely national. Those who became "educated" were never numerous, but they took pride in their accomplishments and recognized their peers everywhere. That kind of general culture is less common today. What has replaced it, in my view, is a more amorphous set of special interests, some of which resonate across national and ideological frontiers.

In these circumstances, it is mostly work that brings people together today; and, as has been suggested, only certain types of work involve meaningful international association and discourse. Most universities prepare their students essentially for activity at home; they are primarily national institutions. They do not, except in isolated instances, seek to serve a world constituency. As for providing a general culture, without reference to the nation in which they are located, few institutions can even conceive this possibility. With all the opportunities for foreign study and travel, most young people live as prisoners of their national cultures. While some may enroll in courses in "The Modern German Novel" and "The Risorgimento," studying also "Japanese Grammar" and "Developmental Problems in Indonesia," few appear comfortable in the outside world except when they experience it as tourists. Few have any opportunity to know it in other ways.

Learning remains largely instrumental; universities are principally degree-granting institutions, preparing the young for specific professional tasks. There is no international intellectual community that is being created; there is no ideology in the West that sees an urgent necessity to create one or that has a strategy for doing so. Thirty-five years after the United States began its newest imperial expansion, and after tens of millions of Americans have lived or traveled abroad, the United States intelligentsia is still overwhelmingly provincial, with relatively few having any intimate or continuing association with colleagues abroad. Very few have any keen sense of what is being thought or said abroad.

As for what others know about the United States, that situation is even more disquieting. The most simplistic notions circulate in intellectual circles about the United States; these are endlessly repeated by the mass media. There is not a single work in any foreign language that does for the United States today what Tocqueville managed to do early in the nineteenth century. The explanation is not that American society has become more complex; the real cause, in my view, is that the interest in such large, synthetic work, based on firsthand experience, is today considerably diminished. Specialization and ideology impede the kinds of general studies that were once valued and that once made it possible for men and women to know societies quite different from their own but not, therefore, necessarily inferior.

"Interdependence" is a fashionable term today. Perhaps it expresses an unrealized ambition, for we do live in relative isolation, on too many levels. We exaggerate wildly what the mass media are able to tell us about others. We desperately need new ways of communicating—something more than the dissemination of information. We need agencies to foster dialogue, not because talk is a good in itself, but because it would suggest that more of those who are intellectuals have some concern with what others are thinking and saying. An international intellectual community presumes a willingness to argue across national, linguistic, and ideological barriers on matters of consequence. That is still, regrettably, an all too uncommon habit.

The Community: Its Nature and Responsibilities

IN MY PERSONAL LIBRARY I am fortunate to have a copy of the 1662 edition of Amos Comenius's *Janua Linguarum Reserata,* a language textbook with parallel texts throughout the book in Latin, German, and French. On the inside of the sheepskin cover, the contemporary owner of the book has written "Simon Segerdahl—légitime possesseur de ce livre, Paris le 21 Avrile l'an 1675." Segerdahl was one of the Swedish students who spent a few years at the University of Paris, a continental center of excellence to which Scandinavian students, among others, were attracted. In the *gymnasium* of his home province and most likely during a stay as an undergraduate at the University of Uppsala, he had become somewhat proficient in the lingua franca of the international community of scholars of that time, Latin. Thus, he had most likely bought Comenius's book in order to learn French which, like other modern languages such as German and English, was not taught in the European pre-university schools until well into the first decades of the nineteenth century. Comenius himself was a true international and pan-European scholar, who was born and grew up in Moravia but expelled during the wave of religious persecutions that swept central Europe. He then spent most of his active life in such countries as the Netherlands, Sweden, and Poland, incessantly working for international understanding on the basis of his pansophical ideas about the improvement of the spiritual and material conditions of mankind.

The decreasing use of Latin as a means of communication between scholars and professionals meant, at least for some time, an increased provincialism in intellectual affairs. A language is, however, not simply an instrument of communication. It also provides a common frame of reference for historical traditions, cultural referents, and ideas—something which also to a large extent was lost when Latin disappeared from the secondary school curriculum.

Whether English is to become the new langua franca among intellectuals and contribute to cementing international cohesiveness among them is, I assume, still an open question. I am quite confident that my French friends, for example, would not endorse this proposition. English as an instrument of communication plays an overwhelming role in southeast Asia. French, however, has a strong position in Africa because in some countries, such as Senegal and Zaire, it is the only language that is understood by everybody with some basic education, and in a way it defines a nationality among a cluster of tribes that by colonial coincidence were brought together into a geographical entity. In Africa one gets a strong impression of the role played by the two dominant European languages in articulating the intellectual profiles of the new elites.

When, in the following, I refer to "intellectuals," I shall have in mind primarily the "achieved" academics—teachers and researchers at the universities. But the mounting influence of intellectuals in the modern society evidently also operates from extramural bases, such as the mass media and the growing government bureaucracy which largely depend for staff on products from the universities.

ACADEMIC ETHOS IMPLIES UNIVERSALISM

The very idea of the university is linked to the crossing of national boundaries in order to achieve understanding of the national and cultural patterns of other lands. At the core of the academic ethos lies the hope of achieving the universalism and objectivity which is fundamental to scientific research. Nationalism and political bias are inimical to such endeavors. It is for this reason that academic freedom violated in one country is fervently defended by scholars and students in most other countries. James A. Perkins in 1966 eloquently expressed the thrust toward internationalism: "To join this community [of intellectuals] is to become part of a world that knows no boundaries, whose arena is the total knowledge acquired by all mankind, whose curiosity is never satisfied, whose standards and values are set not by tradition or belief but by the intractable nature of truth."[1] There is, indeed, something that Perkins refers to as an international creed among the university-based intellectuals which determines scholarly behavior, such as the unceasing, unbiased search for truth; the scrutiny of subject matter that seemingly has been settled; the rejection of prejudice; and the willingness to contribute to the international body of knowledge.

The international intellectual community is not invested with political power. Its influence derives from society's dependence on it to provide trained manpower, research, and services. Indeed, the community is a

1. "The International Dimension of the University" (Address delivered to the Women's Planning Committee of the Japan International Christian University Foundation, New York City, Oct. 21, 1966).

frail network of communication and cooperation that is in few respects institutionalized. Its cohesiveness depends on the strength of the academic ethos, which has itself in recent years suffered quite a few shocks.

There is a corollary to the above. Inasmuch as the institutional base for the community of intellectuals is a university in the home country of the individual scholar, radical changes in the university system in a country affect not only its intellectuals but also their role and contributions to the international community. This corollary applies with special force if the changes are entirely initiated and enforced by political bodies. Bonds that have taken generations of scholars to develop can thereby easily be destroyed.

INTERNATIONAL SOLIDARITY AND ACADEMIC FREEDOM

An important aspect of the international solidarity among scholars, and an indispensable part of the academic ethos, is the mutual support that intellectuals are ready to give when freedom of teaching and inquiry is attacked from outside or from within the university. Such attacks are usually thought of as resulting from state political oppression. But infringements of academic freedom can also come from within the university, when organized disruptions of teaching take place or facilities are occupied by students. Obvious outcomes of such upheavals are illustrated by the damage suffered by many European universities during the latter 1960s. Germany, for instance, is seeing a phenomenon that some fifteen or twenty years ago would have been unthinkable: an exodus of professors from the universities to independent research institutions. This, by the way, also reflects the loss of prestige that the European professor has suffered as a result of events of recent years.

During periods of acute political crises, academic freedom can suffer setbacks even in countries that like to think of themselves as being unsinkable democracies. I only need mention McCarthyism in the United States during the peak of the cold war and the loyalty oath controversy at the University of California during the hot days of the cold war. In the wake of the political crisis in France in connection with the de Gaulle take-over, some radical professors at the University of Paris were suspended. I submit that in present-day Europe the differences in intellectual freedom and in academic autonomy between countries with a parliamentary democracy and those ruled by governmental decrees are a matter of degree. There is a growing accumulation of power in all central governments that have at their disposal an ever-growing bureaucracy. And the growing power makes life incessantly more difficult for the universities, which are institutions where "success associated with intellectual achievement is actually linked to a propensity for social criticism."[2] Universities have become the only agents of independent criticism and are—to their mounting dismay—regarded as sanctuaries for "irresponsible" critics.

Thus, the international solidarity among scholars plays an important role in alerting public opinion to encroachments on freedom of thought and expression. This role applies particularly to the intellectuals who have universities as their institutional base of operation. The international community in this respect works both ways. It promotes a supranational allegiance to ideals of truth seeking and of free exchange of ideas and outcomes of research endeavors. It also operates as a network of guardians of freedom. Not least during the last ten years, when universities all over the world have been attacked both from outside and within, the international mutual support has been of immense value in protecting basic rights.

EFFECTS OF THE MOUNTING NATIONALISM

During the last couple of decades, there has been an observable mounting nationalism in higher education. In newly established or emerging countries there is a natural striving for national identity. Because the university represents the pinnacle of cultural and intellectual endeavors in a country, the establishment of a national university becomes an important symbol of identity. This patriotic role implies emphasis on supportive symbols, such as the national language (if any pervasive one exists), national history, and traditions. As long as proximity to a particular culture and to national tradition is a prerequisite for the transmission of particular competencies and for conducting research pertaining to problems in the national domain, such an orientation is no doubt beneficial to both major functions of higher education. But a proper balance has to be struck between parochialism and professional universalism.

In an increasingly interdependent world, internationalism is an inherent feature of the intellectual sphere. At the root of scholarly pursuits lies the endeavor to establish universally valid principles and facts. There is no particular British, Swedish, Iranian, or Chilean mathematics or

2. Everett Carll Ladd, Jr., and Seymour Martin Lipset, *The Divided Academy* (New York: McGraw-Hill, 1975), p. 313.

science. In the humanities the situation is less clear-cut. The social sciences are taking an intermediate position.

In most areas of scholarly pursuit, one could easily identify centers of excellence, places or institutions where—often after a long period of development, including personnel resources—the contributions to knowledge have been remarkable. These centers attract not only outstanding professors but also promising apprentices from other lands who join the ongoing pioneering intellectual ventures and then return home with new insights that will enrich their fields of higher education there. For instance, in the latter nineteenth century, young American graduate students went to German universities and returned from Berlin, Leipzig, and other places ready to pioneer advanced programs of study back home. A similar relationship has maintained between the universities of Oxford, Cambridge, and London and the former British colonies. Since World War II, the United States has been at the forefront in many fields of research and scholarship. No wonder, then, that students from all over the world—in recent years, more than a hundred thousand, many of them graduate students—have flocked to centers of excellence such as Chicago, Harvard, Columbia, Berkeley, and Stanford.

Some years ago I had the pleasure, as chairman of the Governing Board of the International Institute for Educational Planning, to work with a Soviet colleague who was also on the board. His professional field was aeronautics, in which during the 1930s he had taken a doctorate at the Massachusetts Institute of Technology. During the war he was an important link between the United States and the U.S.S.R. in operating the lend-lease program. On our board, he was not simply a highly competent technician. His education and experiences in two large countries had given him a perspective, not least on problems of higher education, which was of great value in an international organization. I remember well the fervor with which he defended the professional autonomy of the institute against attempts by the international bureaucracy for the sake of political expediency to infringe upon its freedom of research.

COMMUNICATION NETWORK AMONG INTELLECTUALS

During recent decades, communication among intellectuals and scholars worldwide has increased tremendously, and international congresses and conferences have proliferated. Many meetings are now so heavily attended that they become almost unmanageable and counterproductive to their purposes of promoting exchange of ideas, research findings, and professional experiences through paper presentations and small-group discussions. However, regardless of size of attendance, the most important yield is usually the interaction achieved by informal contacts and discourses with colleagues.

The international exchange of students and scholars has also increased enormously since 1945. By 1970, universities in Europe and the United States had enrolled more than a quarter million foreign students, to a large extent from the Third World. Although recessions have slowed the increase, it has been forecast that by 1980 the figure will approach a million students. A similar increase has occurred in the exchange of university-based intellectuals, professors, and researchers. Worthy of mention is the Fulbright exchange program which has been of immense value in promoting intellectual contacts and scholarly exchange between the United States and Europe.

Contributing to the network of communication among intellectuals are publications of various kinds. Books and learned monographs aside, there are three types, of which the first two mainly serve the intellectual generalist and the third caters to the specialist. In the languages that serve as linguae francae in the world today, some newspapers are more or less indispensable for the intellectual who wants to know what is happening on the international scene in domains such as literature, science and technology, education, and the arts. Illustrations are the *London Times* and its supplements, the *New York Times, Le Monde*, and *Frankfurter Allgemeine Zeitung*. Second, some magazines provide comprehensive coverage of cultural and intellectual events; among them are the *Economist*, the *Saturday Review, Le Figaro Littéraire*, and *die Zeit*. Such publications reflect the world intellectual culture and provide their readers with notions of the direction in which *der Zeitgeist* is moving.

The third category, the scholarly journals, present the outcomes of research endeavors in increasingly specialized disciplines.

INTERNATIONAL AND REGIONAL COOPERATION

During the last quarter century various international bodies have been created to promote exchange of information in various fields of culture, research, and education. The best known is, of course, UNESCO. In addition there are other specialized U.N. agencies that provide networks for professionals in particular fields.

The extranational networks of communication, exchange, and cooperation among scholars and intellectuals are to a large extent regional. Such cooperative endeavors are often based on shared political and economic interests of a group of countries. The Council of Europe and the Organization of American States are regional cooperatives that are promoting far-reaching cooperation in matters related to education and culture. Another example is offered by the Scandinavian countries. I have long been involved in the educational activities of the Nordic Cultural Commission, an organ of the Nordic Council, the political agency appointed by the parliaments. The close cooperation in intellectual matters between the four Nordic countries has, of course, been facilitated by the high degree of affinity among the languages of the Scandinavian countries, the existence of a common labor market, and a tradition of cooperation. The European Economic Community has recently entered upon cooperative programs that pertain to education and research.

It is beyond the scope of this paper to spell out the role of intergovernmental organizations in promoting an international community of intellectuals. I shall only point out that the very fact that an organization is intergovernmental can create problems of academic freedom and professional integrity. For example, one such agency has attempted to influence the content and the mode of publication of research reports which certain member countries had perceived to be unfavorable to them and therefore tried to use political leverage to stop publication of certain findings. Needless to say, if reports from cooperative endeavors have to be cleared by national governments before they can be published, international research runs the risk of becoming invalid and thus meaningless. Such working conditions can easily make it impossible to attract scholars to research institutes that operate under the aegis of intergovernmental organizations.

Over the past fifteen years I have gained some experience in building up and operating the International Association for the Evaluation of Educational Achievement (IEA), a cooperative machinery for multinational research in education. An incorporated private organization, originally created under the auspices of UNESCO, it is an association of competent educational research institutes in some twenty countries. Thus far, it has conducted surveys in seven subject areas for the purpose of identifying social, economic, and pedagogical factors that account for differences in scholastic achievements between countries, schools, and students. Some of the study outcomes have had important implications for education policy in the participating countries.

This type of multinational research illustrates that even in education, a field molded by national patterns, it is possible to agree on a uniform research design and to carry it through with the same methodology and timetable in countries with widely different socioeconomic structures, such as the United States, Hungary, Australia, Chile, and India. Despite varying styles in adhering to timetables and responding to letters (and with some fifteen languages involved), it proved possible to bring such an ambitious research endeavor to a successful conclusion. A series of reports—at present, ten volumes—bears witness.

THE NEED FOR GENERALISTS

Explosive specialization has affected intellectual life inside and outside the universities. The fragmentation of scholarly pursuits has increasingly impeded pursuit of general education goals within the university. The ideal of the educated man that still prevailed at the beginning of this century has succumbed. The common frame of reference that in earlier days pervaded the thinking and the values of the educated elite is gone.

Within the university, it has become almost impossible for the scholar who has an ambition to preserve an overview of a broad field of inquiry or who takes interdisciplinary approaches to keep up with the torrent of publications. In many disciplines, during the last few decades the number of reports published in scholarly journals has doubled every six to eight years, and in some scientific fields the number has increased by some 1,000 percent per year since 1945. In addition, most departments in graduate institutions distribute interim report series in order to speed up communication with their sister institutions.

The proliferation of literature has a consequence. The university intellectual generalist, who needs and has the capacity for synopsis, tends to be replaced by the specialist in a narrow field who has achieved, through what somebody has termed "a short-sighted scrutiny of documents," something that technically qualifies him for a professorship. Generalists, particularly in the social sciences, are needed in a society of increasing interdependence that calls for "systems solutions" to its problems. The specialized, fragmented approach to problems has been one reason why so much of our social and educational policy has failed.

What I have in mind here is not the polyhistor found in the seventeenth- and eighteenth-century European universities, the scholar who had, so to speak, read most of the books in many disciplines and had himself produced books in several of them. Rather, I am thinking of the philosopher of that era who, not too many decades ago, could still be found at our universities, a man who in the original sense of the word was an adorer of wisdom and knowledge that cut across all intellectual areas. Cartesius was an outstanding example of the all-embracing approach with a unity of knowledge about both nature and human affairs and no gap between the "two cultures."

Such remarks about the generalist-philosopher may appear nostalgic and out of place. But they have a particular relevance in an international context. It was no coincidence that universalistic minds, represented by Erasmus, Comenius, and Déscartes, were primarily internationally oriented. Their home countries—if they were allowed to reside in them— were regarded as anchoring places, and Europe was their field of operation. Their all-embracing intellectual curiosity was hindered neither by disciplinary boundaries nor by national borders. The universal approach in intellectual matters is, indeed, incompatible with a provincial or narrowly nationalistic orientation.

Too little attention has been paid to disciplinary fragmentation and the collapse of general education as major causes of the inner tension, fragmentation, and disintegration in the university today. A community of scholars with broad orientation makes sense, but a community of specialists is a *contradictio in adjecto*. To restore the cohesiveness and to countervail the institutional anarchy that characterizes the university of today, it will be essential to reconsider the goal of general education so as to reestablish a common frame of reference among senior and junior members of academia.

The world is a place of increasing interdependence to the extent that international cooperation and mutual assistance have become matters of life and death for persons as well as for nations. Intellectuals face the particular tasks of being in the forefront in building a spirit of cooperation and of mobilizing the massive technical competence needed to manage the concrete problems of interdependence—the global problems of production and distribution of food, fair distribution and utilization of natural resources and energy, the limitation of population growth, and the attainment of universal literacy. A large work force of technicians trained to deal piecemeal with these problems within a nation will not suffice to cope with them on an international scale. For instance, the technicians' contribution to technical assistance is easily crippled unless they have acquired a mind set to see their work in a wider context. The world needs what I (for lack of a better expression) call an international peace corps of intellectuals who, apart from their technical competence, see their overriding task as representing the world's conscience and who will devote their first loyalty to humanity.

· 10 ·

The International Dimension
in Higher Education

JAMES A. PERKINS

THE UNITED STATES IS UNDERGOING a transition in its foreign policy—a transition from a period of confrontation to one of détente, from a quarter-century of carrying the Western man's burden to one of partnership, from a time of leadership to one of collaboration. And as is usually the case, such glacial shifts in the public environment have their impact on the international dimension of higher education. Just eleven years ago the late Frank Bowles completed his trailblazing international study of access to higher education. He spoke at the American Council's annual meeting about the commitments of the higher education community to international education—the exchange of students, an internationally oriented curriculum, and area research centers in our graduate schools.[1] But even he was apparently not fully aware that his study, carried out under an international commission of experts selected by UNESCO and the International Association of Universities (IUA), on a subject of almost universal concern, was a piece of the future. Why is this so? Let me begin by stating five propositions that condition my analysis.

First, while technology has shrunk the world by its conquest of space and time, it has enormously enlarged the world for individual man. He must follow events in places whose names he cannot even pronounce. His frame of reference has become global, and he may flounder for understanding. Second, even though we in the higher education community must increasingly think in universal terms, we must act through national governments, domestic systems of higher education, and individual, somewhat autonomous institutions. Someday the process may be reversed—but not now. So we must, at this stage, blend our international dimension into our national programs. Third, higher education

---

1. "American Responsibilities in International Education," *Educational Record,* Winter 1964, pp. 19–26, and *Access to Higher Education* (Paris: Unesco and International Association of Universities, 1963), vol. I.

will be slow to change because, as Eric Ashby has said, the university is a social institution constructed on the principle of anarchy. As the custodian of much of our culture, it is also conservative. Change will take a very long time. Fourth, the teaching and research functions are, almost by definition, universal in their essential values. The academy will continue to press against the restraints of national prejudice and purely local interest. Fifth, the future is on the side of a growing international dimension to higher education. The drive toward larger scale in our thinking cannot be reversed, and thus surely the international dimension will be an increasingly significant feature of our concerns.

EVOLUTION OF INTERNATIONAL CONCERNS

Until the end of World War II, higher education was essentially domestically oriented—not isolated, but largely unaware that it lacked an international dimension. Although classical and humanistic scholarship had always embraced the ancient civilizations and the cultural heritage of western Europe, a concern for economic, social, and educational problems had hardly surfaced. And the exotic worlds were the province of specialists who returned with strange tales of strange people.

This nation contented itself with the notion that we had plugged the leaks in our isolationist dikes. World War I was considered an unfortunate aberration—never to be repeated. The munitions makers and the international bankers were clearly the devils who, for their own venal purposes, had dragged our country into the war, to no good end. To demonstrate our displeasure, we strangled the League of Nations and put up a fence of neutrality laws. Then something unprecedented occurred. Bombs were dropped on Hawaii—on United States soil. International affairs were now serious business. Attacking our European friends was bad enough, but to attack the United States itself!

With the dramatic and unprecedented *volte-face* that took place between 1938, with the last of our neutrality legislation, and 1945, this country both accepted and assumed the leadership of the Western world in order to make the world safe for the United States. And with the reversal came the all-out effort of the foundations, universities, and government to prepare this country with both experts and expertise. But the point to remember is that the university commitment to world affairs was for the development of a U.S. competence, created by internal effort, for U.S. purposes—however generously conceived. In foreign programs of economic and social development, U.S. democracy and U.S.

economic growth were the standards against which both purpose and progress were to be measured.

Although higher education did not realize it at the time, the dramatic expansion of our academic international interests had two built-in fragilities. The partnership with foundations assumed the continuation of foundation support, and the partnership with government assumed that public policies would be compatible with campus mores and public attitudes. In any event, these assumptions proved optimistic. The foundations have substantially withdrawn their former support of university-based research and instruction in international affairs. Much was accomplished, some activities were absorbed into university budgets, but the impetus was gone. The withdrawal of interest has been as serious as the reduction in funds. No program flourishes in an atmosphere of lowered priority. Partnership with government changed from government as friend to government as problem. The partnership became an abrasive relationship that seemed to corrupt the early public purpose to rebuild the world. Support of government policies to restore Europe and the developing world had received almost unanimous campus approval. But support of government cold war policies and the war in Vietnam was a different matter. The universities were split on the proper attitude toward the government partnership.

It is not clear that foundation sympathies were entirely on the side of the universities. The foundations may have shared some of the government view, that the campus experts they had supported were bitterly criticizing the very institutions that funded them. The traffic of personnel between the foundations and government may have created mutual sympathies and concerns. But it remains that by the 1960s the universities contained a substantial competence of professors and research staffs not prepared to accept the government policy that only those with access to the cables have the right to be heard or the right to speak. The ground had been well prepared for the strained relationship, which ultimately was seriously disrupted by the Vietnam war.

Détente and the military withdrawal from southeast Asia have changed the atmosphere. As the differences disappear, we find ourselves moving toward reestablishing a constructive partnership. Leadership in the American Council on Education and in the State Department are determined that the road back will lead to a more solid relationship.

While the estrangement was in progress, equally potent influences were at work that also forced a review of the premises and purposes of this country's postwar posture and programs. The outside world became less and less willing to accept the United States as the *primus inter pares* of Western civilization or as the guiding genius of economic and social development for the developing countries of the Southern Hemisphere. Europe and Japan had recovered from World War II; Russia and China had split. And the former colonies were in the agonizing period of deciding who they were and who they wanted to be. Whatever doubts they may have had, it was becoming clear that the United States and the other industrialized states were not, and possibly could not be, the models. Western-style universities were submitted to the torque of domestic priorities. The former colonies wanted our help but not necessarily our ideas about how to use it. Surely a reasonable stance, but one that undercut appropriations built on the notion of U.S. leadership.

Resistance abroad and doubts at home signaled the end of the euphoric period of U.S. commitment to international education. Interest and commitment will surely continue but without the heady feeling that this work receives first priority attention. The end of that period also signals the emergence of a new style based on the idea of cooperation and participation.

The Special Case of Higher Education

Higher education itself comes late to the international arena, although professionals concerned with economic and political problems have already become deeply engaged. We are only now becoming aware that educational matters as such are legitimate and important matters for international examination. There are two reasons.

First, higher education as an academically legitimate field of study is only a little more than two decades old. The literature on the subject was exceedingly limited. Now more books on higher education are published in one week than formerly there were in a year. The Carnegie Commission on Higher Education and the Carnegie Council on Policy Studies in Higher Education alone account for a great shelf of books on the subject. The student, teacher, and administrator are under the academic microscope; their institutions are examined with increasing rigor; their governance—the subject of critical comment—and their most deeply guarded processes are exposed, from entrance and tests to credit and degrees. If public interest is a sign of maturity, then higher education is aging rapidly.

Another complicating problem in our domestic development of higher education is the relation between university and federal government. The private academy has problems relating to government at any level, but necessity has triumphed over principle to produce, as such circumstances usually do, an uneasy, unstable relationship. The public institution has, over the years, come to terms with state governments. But the institutions, both public and private, are unsure of what would constitute wise posture toward the federal government: there is clamor for better government coordination, but also an equal concern expressed about the dangers of centralization. This kind of conflict calls on the resources of such intermediaries as the American Council on Education.

The domestic restraints make it unsurprising that international connections concerned with problems of higher education have not come easily. But they are coming. For domestic reasons also, they are at their stickiest when collaboration is attempted through public agencies. Dragoljub Najman of UNESCO is accurate in saying that criticism of international public agencies for delayed action on educational problems must be muted by the tacit inference that national societies do not really want their action in the first place. Nations demand leadership, but do they want to be led?

While UNESCO reports through foreign offices (not always noted for their sophistication in university matters), there are semiautonomous international or regional agencies that are relatively independent of our foreign policy makers—the Organization for Economic Cooperation and Development in Paris, the Organization of American States in this hemisphere, and, of course, newest of all, the United Nations University. And further removed from governmental and semigovernmental organizations are such organizations as the International Association of Universities and less formal associations like the Council on Higher Education in the American Republics. The International Council for Educational Development (ICED), with which I am associated, does not represent either governments or institutions but only the professional interests of its members.

At the traditional level, scholars are studying foreign educational problems, institutions, and systems for a variety of motives and purposes arising from their own professional interests. Thus, Burton Clark of Yale is producing a major book on the Italian university, Herbert Passin has written knowingly about Japan, and Lord Ashby, Joseph Ben-David, Alain Touraine, Dietrich Goldschmidt, and Michio Nagai have written about higher education in the United States. Increasingly, foreign appraisals are appearing in our journals and on bookshelves. And reports of university affairs and problems of higher education on an international scale appear regularly in the *Chronicle of Higher Education,* as well as the *Higher Education Supplement* to the *London Times,* the education supplement to *Le Monde, Minerva,* and the new journal *Higher Education,* with its international board of editors.

From the discrete national studies, by Americans and others, has come the relatively new idea of the joint study of similar problems. Germany and Sweden have finished a major joint examination of the impact of student participation on university standards. Under ICED sponsorship, Germany and the United States are currently examining the role of testing in the admissions process of federal education systems. Canada and Japan have just started a bilateral inquiry on several problems of national concern. And other studies are in progress.

Beyond these single scholar and bilateral studies are an increasing number of multination studies seeking enlightenment through a search for new solutions to old problems. Italian higher education was subjected to this kind of study and widely reported by the Italian members. The ICED has organized international seminars in Copenhagen, Bruges, Madrid, Stockholm, Williamsburg, and Japan in an effort to promote an international perspective on problems facing higher education.

Then, of course, there are the multinational studies and reports put out by international agencies such as UNESCO, OECD, the World Bank, and others. These studies are international in varying degree. As noted earlier, UNESCO and the IAU sponsored the first truly international study, on access to higher education, chaired by Frank Bowles, who years ago pleaded for an expanding commitment to higher education. His study still stands as the classic example of universal lessons carefully drawn from national facts. Some believe that French paving blocks would still be in place if French officials had paid more attention to Bowles's predictions of the forthcoming pressures on the French universities.

The patterns and networks of international studies are rapidly generating an international community of scholars, publicists, and public officials who are gaining an increasing awareness of higher education in other countries and a fresh perspective on their own policies and arrangements. If non-Americans get nourishment from our system of objective tests and community colleges, we in the United States learn from the University Grants Committee in Great Britain about how to plan and coordinate; from France we learn about how to run high-level professional schools;

and from Sweden we profit from their experience on how to handle the thorny problem of credit for work experience; from Germany we enlarge our view of how to relate institutes of basic research to traditional universities.

The networks and the international academic community of which we are inextricably a part will require some changes in American academics' attitudes and knowledge. The international process can be difficult. But we must adjust to this process because we shall all in some way be caught up in the new international dimension.

A FEW GUIDELINES

If we in the U.S. educational enterprise are to be increasingly involved in the rewarding ferment of international studies internationally managed, we must keep in mind certain requirements for the discourse. Some observations distilled from my more than a decade of experience in various forms of international education may be useful.

Communication across cultural and linguistic barriers is full of hazards. The same word means different things in different languages and areas. And the same thing is described by different words. One must listen carefully before he moves. If an overseas friend says he insists that you do something, he is probably not being *de rigiste* but simply using the nearest word he knows.

Styles of argument and analysis are different. The Anglo-Saxon derives his principles (almost always) from his facts. Those with a Roman law background do not know what facts they need until they have settled on their principles. Since the two processes are linked, it is stimulating to participate in the Hegelian resolution of these differences. International dialogue is the occasion for this mind-shaking process.

Roles of governments in higher education are not the same. Some believe that innovations should be initiated in government ministries. Others believe that deference to ministry process is stifling and that the innovation must be pressed on government, not by government. The first course surely leads to heavy government loads on its officials.

Styles of meetings vary. A Continental recoils at the idea of a meeting without papers. We in the United States believe progress requires free and spontaneous dialogue; others believe in the carefully prepared set speech—"interventions" they are called. To some, the interventions seem tedious. To others, they are necessary to escape frivolity. It is quite an experience to watch a dialogue devotee try to break into or reply to a set intervention or, conversely, to watch the pained patience of the set speech maker trying to bring order out of a rapid exchange. Perhaps the difference all goes back to the lecture versus the Socratic method of instruction.

Now let me draw some behavioral guidelines from these observations.

What is different is not, therefore, inferior. This failing is most readily noticeable in Anglo-Saxons and perhaps the French. The rest of the world is more charitable with difference.

A language barrier cannot be bridged by raising your voice. Your listeners are probably not deaf. They just do not understand you. Instead, speak slowly and listen for your own unconscious argot and local references. Not everyone knows what "sock it to 'em" means.

Some people do not reply to letters. They are not necessarily impolite. It may be that they do not know what to say. Or perhaps they do not have secretarial assistance and dictating machines. Some think the need to answer will disappear with time. They are frequently right.

Professional connections overseas generally improve with personal acquaintance. And if families are involved, the bridges are even more valid. In my experience, in meetings where spouses have been involved, an understanding has emerged that surmounted many cultural and ideological differences.

Finally, patience and the determination to understand are primary virtues. Without them, we had better stay at home. The never-ending tasks are to seek for common ground without forgetting important differences; to concentrate on the problem but not the problem maker; to work for the future from an understood base in the present; to bring the best of our civilization to the international discourse. If we can do these things, we may have opened the door to a more solid prospect for international intellectual collaboration.

· 11 ·

Education and the Future of the Republic

DAVID MATHEWS

IN VIEW OF THE RECENCY of my arrival at the Department of Health, Education, and Welfare, I will not attempt to discuss any of the details of the work at HEW. Rather I will try to lay out for you some of my more deeply held convictions about our common enterprise in education.

First, it is my opinion that there needs to be more attention to, and perspective on, the domestic, social, and human policy issues facing this country. We are, I believe, in a kind of valley, a place that is good for rethinking. Either we shall dedicate ourselves to shaping an architectural era or we will wallow around in our own misery, disquiet, and dismay. The obligation to develop some new perspective on social policies is an obligation that falls especially heavily on the higher education enterprise because of its mandate and because (despite what we like to think) broad public policy shapes the course of education—not the reverse.

I applaud the attention that the higher education community has given to revising federal regulations on education, redesigning the financial aid package, and attending to other immediate matters, for they do deserve your attention. But if you think you are reshaping the course of American education, I am afraid you are mistaken. My reading of the history of this country and the history of American education is that higher education is a plastic institution, shaped by the great forces of this society.

As a historian, I am particularly suspicious of people who continually claim that we are on the verge of some great new era. Despite rhetoric to the contrary, in the whole history of this country, there probably have been no more than three or four major new eras. If one were to convert the history of America into a wavelength, it would be a long line, slowly rising and falling, its turns and rises almost imperceptible. In the initial period of this country, there was an age that may be termed an Age of Religion. From the colonial period up to almost 1800, the events and activities can be characterized as efforts by the people to shape a government to the ideals of reformed Christianity. The architects were the American descendants of John Calvin and the Mathers and eccentrics like Roger Williams. They worked in different ways, but in nearly everything they did they were trying to make some kind of heaven out of the new earth they were privileged to inhabit.

When that age ended or when the next began is not specific, but it is obvious that by the 1800s, by the time of Thomas Jefferson, certainly by the time of Andrew Jackson, the people of this nation were doing something else—in a period usually called an Age of Democracy, because of its association with President Jackson. The people were not so much shaping the moral foundation of our political system as they were shaping the institutions. That was the period when the presidency and the Supreme Court took on their respective forms. We invented such things as political parties, and we were dedicated to the proposition that all our institutions had to be responsive to a wider audience and that we had to democratize not only our political institutions but also those of art and culture and education.

And so it was, until sometime in the last half of the nineteenth century. By then we were off in still another direction, and the great names were not Cotton Mather or Thomas Jefferson or Andrew Jackson. They were Andrew Carnegie, J. P. Morgan, and John D. Rockefeller and they led us into what we would later characterize as the Era of Capitalism. In it we laid the foundations for our economic and financial system.

That era ended; again we are not really sure when. The bench mark, in my mind, is a book written in the nation's capital by a government employee, sitting in some office a few blocks from here, whom nobody heard of then and few have heard much of since. But there should be a monument to him, for everything we do and think and believe in America about government results from the book he wrote in that office. Published in 1883, it was titled *Dynamic Sociology*, and the author's name was Lester Ward. Frankly, Ward's work had little effect until his ideas fell into the hands of masterful politicians like Woodrow Wilson and Franklin Roosevelt. They used his ideas to usher in the next new age, an Age of Government, if you will.

Until Ward's time, we had believed that government was, at best, a necessary evil. And it never occurred to any of us that we ought to use government to change anything. Not Thoreau or the wildest of the social reformers of the 1850s would ever have thought about using government policy as their instrument for change. Their instrument was the conversion in the hearts of the people.

But Lester Ward, sitting amongst what later became the great bureaucracies of government, saw in those scurrying clerks, in those masses of paper, and in the potential power of the federal government, a source for great social change. He said that government, rather than just being there, ought to become a positive force in the useful reconstruction of society. In his view, the problem of this country was not too much but, rather, too little government.

But that age, too, shows some sign of having run its course. Certainly no one would say that the real problem in America today is too little government. As for a name for the present age, perhaps a good candidate might be "The Age When Things Really Didn't Work Out as We Thought They Would." The more important question, though, is, What is next? If we are at the end of one of those long curves and are about to turn somewhere else, then where?

I think there are three possible answers.

A colleague named Richard Dorson, a folk historian who in the latter 1960s wrote *America in Legend*,[1] offers much the same argument for patterns in American history that I have rehearsed, and his phrasing reflects the time of his writing: "There is a nascent new national stance pitting Humane Man and The Movement against The System. Inevitably, throughout, it is Man (and men) against institutions which would restrict the individual and his humane instincts." He suggests that what is next is an Age of Neohumanism.

Another candidate, I think, is in the wings. But I do not have a good name for it. Rather than Humanism, it may be Individualism or Particularism. What is happening in the country now indicates a great shift away from mass anything to particular everything. It is evidenced in the renewed interest in ethnic origins and in the movement back to state and local governments. It is evidenced almost everywhere as we seek our identity in things that are more particular and more individual.

My own guess about what is next is that we are in for a new era of what may be called Naturalistic Humanism.

Changes in ideas are markers for shifts from one age to another and social historians look for those ideas that mark the dividing points. Certainly by the eighteenth century, the division was based largely on

1. New York: Pantheon Books, 1973.

attitudes about people. Those who saw people as being basically good were joined with Thomas Jefferson and Henry Thoreau, were interested in reform, and participated in the recasting of society. Those who were unsure about people were probably in the cast of Alexander Hamilton and were interested in building up structures that would place limits on unrestrained freedom of action.

But that easy distinction is no longer possible. And I have been searching my mind to decide what the new distinction might be. Recently, I was rereading Lester Ward and noticed how hostile he was to nature. Nature, he said, was an obstacle to overcome and the laws of nature were really the laws that brutalized people. They were laws of competition and strife. And, he said, human progress comes when the people overcome those laws of nature. The natural order was not a friend.

But today if one considers the dynamic movements—whether in Euell Gibbons' disciples or the let's-take-care-of-ourselves school of medicine or the environmentalists—and looks for the common thread in their argument, the feeling about nature is highly positive. Nature is good and we need to get in league with her. So attitudes toward nature appear to have become a dividing line. Certainly a sense of the virtues of nature seems to be a rallying point.

But nature itself may be too limited a guide. And that is why I have used it always in conjunction with Humanism—as in Naturalistic Humanism—because I think what is next will be a part of the progressive impulse.

I hope we will not use our reverence for nature to convince ourselves that we ought to stand still. Somehow, it seems to me, we must develop a social philosophy that allows our people to live with a great deal of complexity but in a productive way. Robert Frost has said that the real purpose of education is to allow us to live with complexity without losing either our tempers or our self-confidence. Surveys about the mood of the American people report that we are impatient and suffer great frustration from the things that we cannot fix immediately. I have certainly observed that mood in talking to people about the Department of Health, Education, and Welfare. But anyone who has spent any time with a large department like HEW knows that domestic problems do not yield to immediate solution.

Unless we find some way to live productively with the kinds of complexity and frustration that inhere in our economic, physical, and human environments, we will be in for a bad time. Albert Schweitzer, in a comment much like Einstein's on relating energy and matter, said that hope and energy were, in his judgment, interchangeable and that hope was the energizing force for our social action. If Schweitzer's equation be true, our hopelessness could both rob us of our capacity for positive social action and leave us victim to the backwashes of negative reactions.

What, then, does all of that have to do with this assembly of the American Council on Education and with the community of higher education?

I believe that the concerns about where the nation will go next and what it will do with its dilemmas are very much the business of education. And you, the leaders of the higher education community, need to use assemblies such as this one to address the broad social and intellectual issues of our day. You need to bring to this platform those who have studied and thought deeply about this country. Too often, we only massage each other with stories of either victory or defeat by one victorious or recently vanquished colleague.

I would like to see the day when the American Council on Education devotes itself to its own version of "career and adult education" by bringing before this convocation the scholars and thoughtful people who have thought and suffered over the broad issues before the nation so that we can be busy about discovering their educational imperatives.

It seems to me that we desperately need a broader focus. The dilemma of our age is to be addressed, not in the science of optics, but rather in the spirit of vision. Education that does not plan to be a part of the future cannot hope to be much of a part of the present.